Effective
Vulnerability
Management

Effective Vulnerability Management

Managing Risk in the Vulnerable Digital Ecosystem

Chris Hughes, M.S., MBA
Nikki Robinson, DSc, PhD

WILEY

This book is dedicated to my wife Kathleen and our children Carolina, Calvin, Callie, and Clayton, whose unwavering support enabled me to continue to grow professionally and who continue to be my primary purpose for always striving forward.

—Chris Hughes

I dedicate this book to my husband, Brian, and my daughters, Keira and Teagan. Without your constant support and encouragement, I would never be able to pursue the things I love. You all are my world. I also dedicate this book to my Grandma Osbourn—one of the strongest women I know. I'm lucky to have had such an independent and fearless female to look up to.

—Dr. Nikki Robinson

Contents at a Glance

Contents

Contents

Foreword

When I helped found Tenable Network Security, in many ways I was trying to get ahead of all the ways that we'd seen bad actors break into networks with our Dragon Network Intrusion Detection System. With Dragon, we saw all sorts of hostile state-of-the-art nation-state attacks and exploitations of unpatched systems as well as ankle-biter hackers. In starting Tenable, my cofounders and I wanted to make cybersecurity an obtainable and defendable goal. Continuous monitoring did not exist as a concept in the early 2000s. Annual penetration tests and even quarterly vulnerability scans were the norm. We wanted to make understanding cybersecurity risks easy for individuals and organizations.

As use of the Internet and dependency on it grew, so did nation-state threat actors. Our industry responded with IT regulations and frameworks. By 2020, we had the Payment Card Industry requirement, which was a wide variety of government standards that culminated in the National Institute of Standards and Technology (NIST) Cybersecurity Framework as well as the MITRE ATT&CK framework. During that same time frame, we saw the SANS organization publish their list of the Top 20 Vulnerabilities. This quickly became hard to manage and was replaced by the SANS Top 20 Controls, which was subsumed by the Center for Internet Security (CIS). We also saw hacking move from denial-of-service attacks on websites in the early 2000s, to crippling nation-state attacks that shut down hospitals, shipyards, and grocery stores.

As awareness of the risks of IT grew, new types of tech seemed to grow faster. From 2000 to 2020, we saw the introduction of Wi-Fi networks, mobile devices, virtualization, containers, software-as-a-service (SaaS) services, elastic cloud infrastructure, and embedded devices, and now we are grappling with implementing artificial intelligence (AI).

In the last decade, we have seen an increased role of government in IT. The Trump administration banned network technologies like drones, security cameras, and network devices from China, and introduced the "defend forward" concept that is still in use by the National Security Agency (NSA). The Biden administration recently added the Office of the National Cyber Director, which quarterbacks much of the

U.S. government's cyber strategy. It's very likely there will be more regulation to come that will impact how we defend and use the Internet.

However, as of late 2023, we don't have a consistent recipe or set of rules for securing data. If you are new to vulnerability management, this may seem surprising to you. How you perform vulnerability management is extremely subjective, based on the technology, the sensitivity of the data stored within it, the sophistication of the threat actors you are protecting against, your available budget, your people, and a wide variety of political, regulatory, and legal requirements. What works for a financial institution protecting trillions of dollars of transactions per day simply won't work for protecting the U.S. President's email. Protecting a video game service with millions of users is very different than keeping ransomware actors from stealing credit cards at your favorite coffee shop. Even though we all use the Internet, we all use it differently, with different technologies and tolerances for reliability and potential data loss.

It's because of this that I am very happy to have been asked by Nikki and Chris to write this book's Foreword. No matter what type of network security background you have, this book does an excellent job of covering the various aspects of vulnerability management. It presents several different advantages and limitations of technology for measuring vulnerabilities and remediating them across a wide breadth of technologies. It also covers the different types of frameworks that can be used to make sense of assets, their vulnerability, and compliance data, which can be extremely overwhelming. Whether you are learning vulnerability management concepts for the first time or looking to run an enterprise team focused on securing the network of a major bank, this book has the proper topics covered.

—*Ron Gula, President, Gula Tech Adventures and*
Co-Founder, Tenable Network Security

Introduction

We live in a world that is enabled in countless ways by software. Over a decade ago, Marc Andreessen quipped, "Software is eating the world," and it indeed is. From our personal leisure activities to critical infrastructure and national security, nearly everything uses software. It powers our medical devices, telecommunications networks, water treatment facilities, educational institutions, and countless other examples. This means that software is pervasive, but as software use and integration into every facet of society has grown, so have the vulnerabilities associated with our digital systems. This has manifested in tremendous levels of systemic risk that can, has, and will continue to impact our daily lives.

The World Economic Forum (WEF) stated that at the end of 2022, a total of 60 percent of global gross domestic product (GDP) was dependent on digital technologies. That said, the WEF also conducted a survey in 2023 with respondents projecting a "catastrophic" cyber incident within the next two years. The threats of vulnerability exploitation are growing each year, in combination with the ease of use of malicious tools for creating and distributing ransomware and malware.

Since the earliest days of computer systems, researchers and practitioners have been trying to address vulnerabilities in digital systems by practicing what is referred to as "vulnerability management." As defined by the National Institute of Standards and Technology (NIST), a vulnerability is "a weakness in an information system, system security procedures, internal controls, or implementation that could be exploited or triggered by a threat source."

Digital system vulnerabilities and the ability for them to be exploited were documented as early as the 1970s, with a report titled "Security Controls for Computer Systems," also known as the "Ware Report" because a RAND employee named Willis Ware chaired the committee producing it for the U.S. Department of Defense (DoD). In addition to the report touching on vulnerabilities in systems, it discusses the need to design systems with security in mind throughout the software and system development life cycle. In 2023, the U.S. Cybersecurity and Infrastructure Security Agency (CISA) issued guidance titled, "Shifting the Balance of Cybersecurity Risk: Security-by-Design and Default

Principles," which called for technology manufacturers to shift to creating products that are secure-by-design.

Despite the calls for secure-by-design systems and the awareness for over 50 years of the vulnerabilities of digital systems and the ability to exploit them, as an industry we continue to struggle with remediating vulnerabilities in digital systems as well as ensuring that security is a core part of system design and development. As modern digital environments have only gotten more complex and software more pervasive, organizations struggle to keep up with addressing vulnerabilities, now leading to unforeseen levels of systemic risk in our digital ecosystems.

Tremendous growth has occurred in publicly disclosed and tracked vulnerabilities, with notable sources such as the NIST National Vulnerability Database (NVD) seeing Common Vulnerabilities and Exposures (CVEs) grow from merely a few hundred in the 1990s to over 190,000 in 2022. These vulnerabilities are seen across a sprawl of software, hardware, libraries, and tools (in both open source and off-the-shelf solutions). With the complexity of software and applications across organizations, the sheer volume of vulnerabilities is difficult to track and remediate.

As the list of publicly disclosed vulnerabilities has grown each year, so have organizations' backlogs of unresolved vulnerabilities as they struggle to keep pace. A 2022 survey conducted by security vendor Rezilion and the Ponemon Institute found that 66 percent of respondents cited having a backlog of more than 100,000 vulnerabilities, and that they're only able to patch less than half of those vulnerabilities. Another study published in 2022 by security vendor Qualys found that there remains a gap between organizations' mean-time-to-remediate (MTTR) vulnerabilities and malicious actors' abilities to exploit them. In our roles both in organizations and as members of society, we, as cybersecurity practitioners, simply cannot keep up with the growth of vulnerabilities associated with our digital ecosystem, nor the malicious actors who are actively exploiting them.

Contributing to the problem of the growing publication of vulnerabilities and malicious actors exploiting them is the reality that organizations can't identify the important components of the noise. Despite there being over 25,000 known vulnerabilities published in 2022, less than 1 percent of all these known vulnerabilities were exploited by malicious actors. This means that organizations are spending energy, effort, and resources on addressing vulnerabilities that never actually get exploited by malicious actors, and are trying to make sense of and prioritize the ones that have been or are likely to be exploited.

As we will point out throughout the text, in addition to organizations struggling to keep up with patching flaws in software and systems, there are a myriad of other factors that complicate an organization's ability to address vulnerabilities. These include challenges with proper asset visibility and inventory, ensuring secure configurations are in place to prevent system exploitation by malicious actors, the pervasive use of third-party and open source code, configuration missteps, and the addition of the human factors in vulnerability management.

Malicious actors increasingly are gaining efficiency at chaining together vulnerabilities and taking advantage of the pervasiveness of software in modern society, driven by widespread efforts at digital transformation. Efforts such as DevSecOps that promise to "shift security left" have their own challenges like noisy findings by modern vulnerability scanning tools, cognitive overload on often-understaffed security teams, and worldwide shortages of cybersecurity talent.

Given the prevalence of vulnerability chaining, digital transformation, DevSecOps, and software supply chain security concerns, vulnerability management is more important now than ever. Without an updated and modern approach to handling vulnerabilities, organizations will continue to be buried in vulnerabilities with little context. Our approach addresses cloud environments, large and small development programs, and the combination of hybrid and multicloud deployments. This approach focuses on not just the technology and methodologies of vulnerability management, but also the humans and organizations involved in the activities.

So let's begin.

What Does This Book Cover?

This book covers the following topics:

Chapter 1: Asset Management This chapter addresses fundamental activities such as asset management, which includes physical and mobile asset management, as well as software asset inventory and dealing with complex cloud, hybrid, and multicloud environments. There will also be coverage of tooling to facilitate asset management.

Chapter 2: Patch Management This chapter covers the fundamentals of patch management, including both manual and automated patch management, as well as the benefits and trade-offs between the two. It discusses software patch management, including open source management, and the various roles and responsibilities for patch management between different teams within the organization.

Chapter 3: Secure Configuration While patching known vulnerabilities are a core of vulnerability management processes, there is also the need for secure configurations. This chapter discusses the role of regulations and frameworks in secure configurations, as well as resources such as the NSA and CISA Top 10 cybersecurity misconfigurations publication. It also discusses industry-leading configuration resources such as CIS Benchmarks and DISA STIGs.

Chapter 4: Continuous Vulnerability Management Vulnerability management is far from a snapshot in time or once-and-done activity. This chapter discusses the concept of continuous vulnerability management and continuous monitoring. It discusses resources such as CIS and NIST controls that tie in to continuous vulnerability management and their associated tasks and activities.

Chapter 5: Vulnerability Scoring and Software Identification A major part of vulnerability management is identifying software and properly prioritizing vulnerabilities. In this chapter we cover both, including long-standing vulnerability scoring methodologies, as well as emerging vulnerability intelligence resources to help organizations more effectively prioritize vulnerabilities such as the Exploit Prediction Scoring System (EPSS) and the CISA Known Exploited Vulnerability (KEV) catalog.

Chapter 6: Vulnerability and Exploit Database Management Vulnerabilities are captured and stored in vulnerability databases. In this chapter, we cover widely used vulnerability databases such as the NIST National Vulnerability Database (NVD), as well as emerging databases such as Open Source Vulnerabilities (OSV) and others that address gaps in databases such as NVD. We also cover the role of exploit databases and how they can be used for both good and harm, depending on the user.

Chapter 7: Vulnerability Chaining It's often said that defenders think in lists while attackers think in graphs. This is because attackers are often looking to chain vulnerabilities together to move laterally through environments or make their way toward sensitive resources. In this chapter, we discuss the concept of vulnerability chaining, as well as provide examples and gaps in the industry when it comes to focusing on vulnerability chaining.

Chapter 8: Vulnerability Threat Intelligence This chapter covers the role of vulnerability threat intelligence and advanced techniques such as threat hunting. We also discuss integrating threat intelligence into vulnerability management programs, including not just technologies but also people and process.

Chapter 9: Cloud, DevSecOps, and Software Supply Chain Security The modern threat landscape is complex, including cloud, a push for DevSecOps, and increasing attacks on the software supply chain. In this chapter, we go deep into these topics, including multi- and hybrid cloud containers, as well as the role of open source software and the systemic risks across the software supply chain.

Chapter 10: The Human Element in Vulnerability Management Most conversations about vulnerability management focus on the technical aspects, such as software and applications. However, behind all that technology are humans, operating in complex socio-technical environments, dealing with psychological stressors and challenges such as decision and alert fatigue. This chapter covers the human element of vulnerability management, including leading research on the topic from one of the authors.

Chapter 11: Secure-By-Design At the heart of vulnerability management is an uncomfortable truth, that the process of "patch faster, fix faster" is broken. Organizations continue to struggle with mounting vulnerability backlogs and insecure products. This chapter discusses the push for secure-by-design/default software and products and some of the key players who advocated for this paradigm shift. It also discusses some of the challenges facing the need to make this fundamental change of how we operate in the digital world.

Chapter 12: Vulnerability Management Maturity Model We conclude the book with a chapter looking at how to begin down the path of creating a mature vulnerability management model. We discuss key recommendations and steps, from asset management to continuous monitoring and integrating human factors. We hope to empower readers to modernize their vulnerability management programs and ultimately lead to decreased organizational risk.

Who Should Read This Book

As the title implies, this book is intended for people who have an interest in vulnerability management, software, and digital and cyber physical systems. It is suited for various professional roles ranging from the C-suite (CISO, CTO, CEO, etc.) to security and software practitioners and aspiring entrants looking to better understand the vulnerability management practice and evolving landscape.

How to Contact the Publisher

If you believe you have found a mistake in this book, please bring it to our attention. At John Wiley & Sons, we understand how important it is to provide our customers with accurate content, but even with our best efforts an error may occur.

In order to submit your possible errata, please email it to our Customer Service Team at wileysupport@wiley.com with the subject line "Possible Book Errata Submission."

How to Contact the Authors

The authors would appreciate your input and questions about this book! Email Chris Hughes at chughes@resilientcyber.io and Dr. Nikki Robinson at dr.nikki.robinson@gmail.com.

Asset Management

Asset management is one of the most critical components of a vulnerability management program (VMP). Of all the fundamental building blocks of a successful VMP, it's crucial to get asset management right and complete before focusing on other aspects of vulnerability management.

Asset management is the listing or inventory of all hardware and software of an environment. Each environment has a different makeup of assets, including everything from mobile devices (e.g., laptops and cell phones) to application libraries and third-party software-as-a-service (SaaS) software. Without a comprehensive asset management program, organizations are limited in building mature VMPs with secure configuration, patch management, and continuous monitoring.

Asset management has evolved quite a bit over the last 10 years, with the advent of cloud infrastructure, increased use of SaaS, exponential growth of open source software use, and incredibly large and complex development environments. Years ago, asset management could be as simple as a spreadsheet with a list of asset names, tag numbers, and potentially an asset owner or IP address. Hardware and software inventories were kept separately and possibly managed by that same IT administrator. Yet with the increased use of cloud infrastructure, whether infrastructure-as-a-service (IaaS), platform-as-a-service (PaaS), or SaaS, traditional asset management methods are simply no longer viable. Using a spreadsheet to manage complex and dynamic assets is not maintainable or feasible to keep updated information available for management.

Traditional vulnerability management components are no longer able to mature with manual or incomplete asset inventories. It's increasingly difficult to manage dynamic assets such as containers, which are meant to come online and be torn down at will. These asset types require a dynamic asset management program—one that can be updated quickly and at scale with large-scale development projects. An asset library can no longer be solely used for managing mobile devices or hardware assets but must be capable of keeping updated information on ephemeral applications and tools.

Without a modern approach to asset management, organizations have limited visibility of the hardware and software used by employees, which can have several cascading effects. Without knowledge of a laptop, for example, there is no way to determine if it has proper monitoring software installed, if it's still in the employee's possession, if it's checking for updated patches, or if it's compliant with organizational policies. And if an organization does not have the ability to see what software is installed on what systems, they have no way of knowing the number of vulnerabilities it has, what its potential attack surface is, or what dependencies that software might have on other systems.

Other limitations of an immature asset management program are the "unknown unknowns." If there are hardware or software assets that aren't effectively managed or visible to IT operations staff, organizations do not know the scope of vulnerabilities, inherent risks, or the interconnectivity of devices and applications. These limitations make it impossible to prioritize and remediate vulnerabilities effectively. It also makes it difficult to determine if applications are at the right patch level, if the application's version is at end of life/support, and if there are outstanding vulnerabilities or missing configurations that could lead to cyberattacks like distributed denial-of-service (DDoS) attacks, malware, or ransomware.

Asset management can be performed in a variety of ways. Organizations are using IT operations software, vulnerability scanning tools, cloud inventories, and even other configuration management software like ServiceNow (www.servicenow.com). This type of software can not only keep track of assets, but can also tie tickets and ongoing management of those devices with a system owner. Smaller organizations might still be managing assets manually, which limits the maturity and capability of a VMP. In this chapter, we discuss the common limitations of asset management tools and processes, possible impacts of an immature asset management program, and what organizations can do to create a modern approach to asset management.

Physical and Mobile Asset Management

In traditional data centers, asset management consists of the physical components in server racks—for example, networking devices, servers, power management, and any other physical devices in the organization. However, organizations have moved to a much more digital workforce, utilizing multiple mobile devices per employee. One employee might have a tablet, laptop, and smartphone, and use primarily online applications for collaboration versus solely working on a physical desktop located in an office setting.

Many organizations are moving to hybrid work environments where employees are working between an organization's office and their home or an off-site location. This type of work environment complicates the management of these devices, given that they may or may not be connected to the organization's virtual private network (VPN) or potentially cloud assets and servers. This setup has increased the challenge of managing and tracking mobile devices.

In modern organizations, managing all these mobile devices requires an asset management solution to handle all the operating systems (OSs) and types of applications required for online collaboration. A mobile toolkit includes asset management and inventory software, as well as configuration management, usually performed by a mobile device management (MDM) solution. This tool provides a management console to catalog each mobile device and assigns policies and security configurations as determined by the organization.

Several SaaS solutions are also available as well as tools provided by the mobile carrier. For example, mobile solutions provided by Apple (e.g., iPhones and iPads) have their own asset management solution like Jamf software. Other devices or applications, however, can be managed by MDM solutions like Miradore and Citrix Endpoint Management.

Because most organizations are moving away from on-premises data centers, there are fewer servers and network devices requiring asset management. With the advent of the cloud, more organizations are migrating their physical assets to a cloud infrastructure and using more ephemeral servers like containers. Yet on-premises data centers still require an asset management solution to provide full visibility to all systems. And it's not just for security reasons—they also must manage systems and ensure they are properly online and functioning without hardware failures. All the physical assets could be providing warning indicators of cyberattacks, and if not monitored properly, an organization could be missing critical data to determine risk.

While physical risk management is typically focused on mobile devices, there has been an increased "return to work" effort across large organizations. It means that physical assets and MDM could grow in complexity and include a mix of bring-your-own-device (BYOD) and corporate-owned assets. Such complexity might require integration with either multiple products or the use of two separate applications to manage the physical assets, versus more configuration settings on laptops and tablets. Because most organizations use a tool for inventory and a separate tool for configuration management, this complexity adds another layer for system owners to review and manage assets for consistency.

Consumer IoT Assets

Another category of assets that has become a major risk for organizations is Internet of Things (IoT) devices. With the interconnectivity of devices, IoT could be anything from a thermostat to a treadmill, home automation devices, or wearable devices like smartwatches. Because many organizations, particularly healthcare and medical organizations, use Wi-Fi or wireless connections, employees may have the option to connect their wearable devices to the local network.

Allowing these potentially vulnerable IoT devices to gain access to the network causes many concerns. The National Institute of Standards and Technology (NIST) has published a consumer's guide on the risks and potential security concerns around IoT devices. The NIST guide, "IoT Cybersecurity Criteria for Consumer Labeling Program," came out in early 2022 and details a growing need for more consumer cybersecurity information around risks of IoT devices. The Biden–Harris administration recently released additional guidance around consumer labeling to ensure consumers understand risks associated with products (see www.white house.gov/briefing-room/statements-releases/2023/07/18/biden-harris-administration-announces-cybersecurity-labeling-program-for-smart-devices-to-protect-american-consumers/#:~:text=This%20new%20labeling%20program%20would,trustworthy%20products%20in%20the%20marketplace).

Based on an article by Mary K. Pratt in TechTarget titled "Top 10 security threats and risks to Prioritize" on page (www.techtarget.com/iotagenda/tip/5-IoT-security-threats-to-prioritize), there are numerous ways that IoT devices can pose risk to organizations. One of the biggest threats to all organizations that is highlighted in the article is the increased attack surface. Similar to mobile devices and increased teleworking or mobile workforces, the more devices that connect to the network, the more risks and possible attack vectors there are. Organizations must have a good grasp of what IoT devices may exist on their network, by using either network scanning or sniffing to detect rogue or unexpected IoT devices. *Sniffing* is a technique used by hackers to detect if there are unsecured devices or systems that may be exploitable. There are many ways to detect attacks in an environment and these are covered at length in later chapters.

Software Assets

Software inventories have become an increasingly important topic. While this area will be covered in depth in a later chapter, it's important to cover the basics here. Recent attacks and zero-days against SolarWinds, Log4J, and MOVEit have been big motivators for understanding the software landscape and attack surface. To understand large attack surfaces, organizations need to catalog and inventory their use of software tools, libraries, and dependencies. A *zero-day* is a vulnerability that was previously unknown in software or hardware that can be majorly exploitable.

Without a proper software inventory, organizations may scramble to find zero-days in their applications, which leaves little time for remediation and more time for attackers to exploit vulnerabilities. With many organizations leveraging larger and more complex development environments, software asset discovery and continuous monitoring become a crucial aspect of risk management.

For example, if an organization has limited visibility into which libraries developers are adding, removing, patching or not patching, their security team will be unable to determine risk and prioritize patching and remediation. If any libraries and dependencies go undetected, or are not reported automatically to an inventory tool, the organization would be unaware of the number and severity of vulnerabilities that do exist.

Another concern is the possibility of using open source software that may not be patched or maintained regularly. And the larger the development environment, the more possibility there is for unknown and undetected vulnerabilities and missing secure configurations.

Cloud Asset Management

With digital transformation, agile software development, and an increasing focus on artificial intelligence (AI), the move to the cloud for systems is an integral step of managing infrastructure and complex development environments. More organizations are considering multicloud or hybrid cloud environments using either two cloud providers or potentially a private and public cloud deployment with the same provider. Multicloud environments allow for more resiliency and scalability, whereas private and public cloud options (i.e., a hybrid cloud) allow organizations to keep specific assets apart from the public cloud infrastructure.

Figure 1.1 provides a simple explanation of the differences between hybrid and multicloud environments. A hybrid cloud setup uses a combination of a private and public cloud option, but typically within the same cloud service provider (CSP). A multicloud solution uses two or more different CSPs to host the infrastructure.

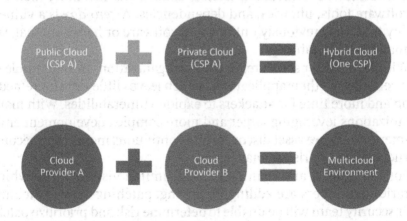

Figure 1.1: Hybrid vs. multicloud environments

Figure 1.1 shows the unique characteristics of multicloud environments compared to hybrid cloud environments. Hybrid cloud is made up of one public cloud and one (or more) private cloud environments while using the same CSP, whereas a multicloud solution uses a combination of private and public cloud environments across multiple CSPs.

Multicloud Environments

In some multicloud environments, an organization may need multiple cloud providers. One example is the need to run production and non-production workloads in one cloud environment and use a second cloud for resiliency and quick transfer in the event of network or regional failure in one of their providers. Another example is to run production and nonproduction workloads in one cloud environment and have backups and long-term storage for recovery in the event of data loss in another cloud environment.

Unfortunately, using multiple cloud providers complicates an asset management strategy. One of the biggest concerns of using multiple cloud providers in a multicloud strategy is that collecting, automating, and keeping track of assets between both environments may require multiple tools. There are more modern organizations using a multicloud strategy and third-party tools can sync data between those disparate workloads. Tools like CloudSphere are working to solve secure configuration and inventory concerns by collecting and maintaining asset data. But this means that each cloud environment may need to open various ports and create service accounts to manage the information. It would be incredibly easy to lose sight of the ephemeral systems of each environment unless they were mirrored.

Hybrid Cloud Environments

A hybrid cloud solution could potentially be used for similar reasons, but the architecture is quite different. A hybrid cloud utilizes both public and private cloud environments. Organizations, for example, might use this strategy to store certain high-impact data and assets in the private cloud, while keeping lower-impact items in a lower-cost public cloud environment. This may complicate asset management in a few ways, but it can also be beneficial for organizations looking to strategize spending and budget over time. Hybrid cloud environments can also be a great solution for organizations who want to keep intellectual property

(IP), personally identifiable information (PII), or other sensitive data in a private cloud, while keeping other data and workloads that are less critical to the business in the public cloud environment.

Figure 1.2 highlights the various layers within an organization for which you should build an IT infrastructure. The top layer includes everything from the platform to cloud management and infrastructure, as well as the overall networking architecture. The mid-layer includes the infrastructure operations applications, development environment, and the major security components that continuously monitor the environment. A sovereign cloud environment is one where the provider stores each organization's data within their own country.

Top Layer	Mid-Layers	Cloud Layer
App Platform	App Development	Private Cloud
Cloud Management	Management Level	AWS/GCP
Cloud/Edge Infrastructure	Infrastructure/Ops	Oracle
Security/Networking	Security Level	Sovereign Clouds
Work Anywhere	End-User Space	Edge Computing

Figure 1.2: IT infrastructure layers

Figure 1.2 illustrates the differing layers in platform services in cloud environments. In the top layer, there are services like cloud and edge computing, management interfaces, as well as the application platform. The middle layers are composed of development environments, infrastructure operations, as well as the largest security components. The cloud layer is really the platform itself, whether it's Amazon Web Services (AWS) or Oracle.

One of the main concerns in using hybrid cloud solutions is the potential limitations between the private and public cloud environments. These limitations include the sheer complexity of managing two separate cloud environments as well as the security concerns of using two separate cloud environments and manually implementing the same controls. Another possible solution would be to run the same tool in both environments to segment the networks and aggregate the data elsewhere. But allowing access to the private cloud from the public cloud could increase the risk of compromise between both environments.

Third-Party Software and Open Source Software (OSS)

Many traditional asset management tools did not account for third-party software or open source software (OSS) being used in modern organizations. But the rampant use of OSS has complicated the asset management and software library processes and the ability to calculate risk.

As displayed in Figure 1.3, software assets are used across the various enterprise layers. Starting with the business layer, applications like Java and Log4j (i.e., OSS components) build the foundation for development environments. Additional software in the presentation and service layers may be required to integrate and communicate to build complex applications.

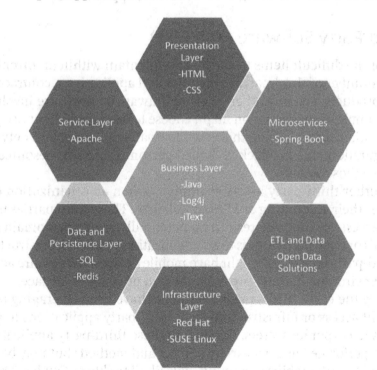

Figure 1.3: Various enterprise layers

Figure 1.3 outlines the various layers that work together across an enterprise. The business layer is the backbone of the rest of the layers, and it has major connectivity between all the other enterprise environments—everything from the data and persistence layer that contains databases, to the infrastructure layer using Red Hat and OS components. Each piece of this matrix works together to create a comprehensive platform to support business functions.

Due to the increased OSS use, organizations are witnessing the dependencies and intricacies of how OSS works in complex and large application environments. Many developers leverage OSS because of the mean time to delivery, meaning the developer can spend less time rebuilding code that already exists by using tools that other developers have built. Lowering their time spent coding and providing some consistency in their applications allows developers to spend their time on more complex and nuanced development cycles. Yet with the increased use of OSS comes the need to catalog and understand what types of libraries and tools are being used within the applications.

Third-Party Software (and Risk)

One of the difficult items to collect and maintain within an inventory is the number of third-party companies and applications, contractors, SaaS products, and any other external software or hardware involved. For example, an organization might choose to use a firewall service provider rather than running their own firewall appliances and network configuration, due to a lack of skilled personnel or other resources to manage those assets.

Another third-party assets example is when an organization outsources their accounting or IT helpdesk firm. These third parties must have access to corporate resources, potentially requiring domain credentials or open ports/access to an organization's SaaS or infrastructure. A third-party contractor might have mobile devices that require access to an environment, thus spreading the potential attack surface.

Since the early 2020s, malicious actors have been leveraging open account access or infrastructure from third-party applications to gain access to corporate secrets. Cataloging these third-party applications can be performed using a variety of tools and methods but may be discovered by vulnerability scanning tools like Tenable or Qualys. Therefore, it's critical for organizations to determine what method is best for discovering and monitoring these third-party applications in the environment to protect themselves from risk.

Accounting for Open Source Software

Static lists will not capture changing versions, patches, or removal of any OSS within an environment. Organizations must move to dynamic asset discovery and categorization because of the possibility for human error and missed assets with a manual process. Every missed asset is a possible entry point for an attacker with exploitable vulnerabilities or misconfigurations. The process should be as automated as possible—allowing developers to consistently change their applications without running into major hurdles with configuration management activities.

Using something like GitHub or another open source tool (made for developers) is a possible solution for dynamic OSS application inventories. The recommendation is to use the open source repository that the developers are already using, whether that's GitHub, GitLab, or another platform. The most important component of each of these options is to have a consistent process known among all developers.

Documentation and the standard operating procedure (SOP) for OSS inventory management is just as important as the tools that perform inventory management. These options allow developers to manage OSS, are usually cross-platform, and provide additional functionality over the standard cloud inventory management systems. There are also several "for purchase" options, and organizations should carefully weigh their own unique needs *before* selecting a product.

On-Premises and Cloud Asset Inventories

While many small to medium businesses (SMBs) are choosing to create cloud environments from the start, there are still many organizations who have on-premises environments or who are choosing smaller on-premises data centers to manage specific data. Because there's still a mix of solutions for organizations, this complicates the tooling landscape for managing hardware and software appropriately. Hardware in data centers includes everything from servers to network devices, as well as all the IoT devices that may tie into the corporate network. Software incorporates everything from SaaS products like email services, to the actual tools and libraries used by developers like Python and Tomcat.

In reviewing Figure 1.4, it's easy to see how complex physical data centers can be compared to their cloud environment competitors. Physical data centers require power management, servers, racks, cables, and physical storage devices like storage area networks (SANs).

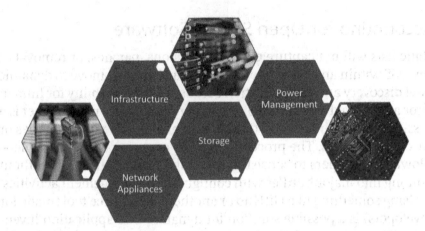

Figure 1.4: Physical data centers

Source: pixelnest/Adobe Stock Photos, khamkula/Adobe Stock and shymar27/Adobe Stock.

On-Premises Data Centers

In on-premises environments, assets are a mix of hardware and software, in addition to any other SaaS products that the organization is using. Part of the trouble is that many organizations who have on-premises environments are also supporting workloads in the cloud.

It's rare to find a tool to manage all of an organization's systems and applications and parse the information into one spot. But organizations should work toward using as few tools as possible, while also balancing the needs of an ever-changing hardware and software landscape.

Because hardware fails and must be replaced over time, having a tool like Microsoft Configuration Manager may be good for both inventory and patch management. Organizations can benefit from this automation and reduce the overhead of manual patching and remediation activities.

Figure 1.5 shows the vast difference between on-premises and cloud environments. On-premises environments require appliances and physical devices like firewalls and physical servers that will sit in a server rack, whereas cloud environments will require additional tooling to look at static and dynamic application scanning, web application firewalls, and more software devices.

In Figure 1.5, it is easy to see how different on-premises and cloud environments are, based on the types of hardware and software supported. In a data center, there are hardware firewalls and network switches, as well as all of the physical servers that would sit in a server rack. However, in a cloud environment, there would be web application firewalls (WAFs), cloud-native tooling, as well as containers and virtual servers.

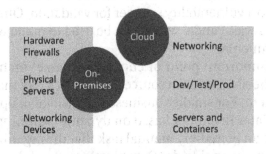

Figure 1.5: On-premises vs. cloud environments

Tooling

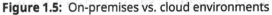

There are multiple tool options to determine whether assets—physical or virtual, hardware or software—are available for on-premises and cloud environments. For most organizations, a combination of inventories from cloud systems and application libraries may need to be consolidated into one platform. A few tools are available today that will catalog and categorize hardware, software, continuous integration/ continuous delivery (CI/CD) pipelines, SaaS, and cloud platform inventories into one dashboard.

But there is hope; asset management is a moving target that must be evaluated any time new products or devices are brought on board. Just like patch management, monitoring and logging, and all other cybersecurity activities, asset management must be an iterative and continuous process.

Asset Management Tools

To begin, tools like Salesforce, ServiceNow, Microsoft Configuration Manager, and others, have been standard IT asset management tools for many years. Many large organizations leverage ServiceNow or a similar ticketing system because of its ability to catalog assets and assign tickets for maintenance and operations to those assets and their respective owners. However, this may not be an option for SMBs. Smaller organizations may need to leverage open source tools or the inventory management systems that come with their CSP. If you're using a small cloud environment, whether private or public, it makes more sense to leverage the CSP's in-house capabilities and compare those results to a vulnerability scanner for validation. One possible open source tool is Asset Panda, which can be used to manage inventory for cloud environments.

The most important point of choosing an asset management tool, whether off-the-shelf or open source, is to select a tool that's scalable for the environment. For smaller businesses, consider an option that automatically updates inventory based on dynamic scanning. Otherwise it could become an incredibly manual task that the organization may not have enough personnel to do. Organizations should consider the best option for their environment as well—if there's a large development environment with test, development, and production in place, use a tool that covers ephemeral devices and dynamically updates. Doing so provides a real-time view of the environment instead of using a tool that requires manual input.

Vulnerability Scanning Tools

Organizations typically have a vulnerability management tool in place that serves as a vulnerability scanner and secures configuration validation, in addition to many other functions like reporting and asset discovery. These tools can also be used to validate inventory alongside configuration management tools like ServiceNow. Vulnerability scanning tools should not be the only source of truth, and assets should be checked regularly by the owners and operators of ephemeral systems.

Given the dynamic nature of development environments, automation should be used wherever possible to capture and remove systems when they are no longer required. Outdated systems with years of vulnerabilities take an incredible amount of time for administrators to sort through and determine what is truly vulnerable. To save time and resources, asset discovery should be automated and validated using at least two tools.

Off-the-shelf tools like Tenable or Qualys can double as an inventory checking tool to ensure that all assets are being scanned for vulnerabilities and secure configurations. Most of these tools serve double duty to validate that the servers, applications, and other systems in place are being scanned properly. If an asset is missing from the scanner, the tool can be updated with proper IP ranges, or even be set up to discover unknown assets by scanning the entire network. Daily or weekly reports can then be configured to notify system administrators and account owners of these new or unexpected servers and systems.

Cloud Inventory Management Tools

Cloud inventory management is easier with AWS or Google Cloud Platform (GCP) because they have inventory built into the management console. This is in stark contrast to managing a data center inventory where assets need to be managed with some additional tool or managed via a spreadsheet. Major cloud providers have made it much easier to identify, manage, and organize assets, even over multiple cloud accounts. There are an incredible number of benefits to using cloud systems, including the built-in categorization for containers, servers, workers, nodes, and more.

AWS has the AWS Systems Manager Inventory, GCP has the Cloud Asset Inventory, and Microsoft Azure uses an inventory system called Change Tracking and Inventory in their Azure Automation suite. These cloud inventories provide the ability to categorize systems and include tagging or metadata for system type, system-specific drivers or components, as well as instance details and network configuration. Microsoft's tracking and inventory tools leverage Log Analytics to monitor and manage assets.

Cloud providers have integrated several essential components into their inventory systems, so a traditional inventory tool may not even be capable of tracking their inventory. For example, the ability to leverage log analysis within an inventory system provides cloud engineers and security analysts with the ability to review logs without switching from an inventory management system to a security information and event management (SIEM) tool.

Organizations benefit from these cloud inventories based on their ease of use, "single pane of glass" to review assets, and lower administrative overhead to manage multiple tools. A "single pane of glass" means that there is one dashboard or panel that a group of security tools can be part of. This allows an organization to review one website instead of administrators or analysts having to log in to multiple tools and use numerous dashboards. Using a cloud environment may also reduce the number of separate tools required to manage the infrastructure, also reducing risk and cost to the organization.

Figure 1.6 illustrates the increasing complexity when starting with an asset inventory system, as well as the additional tools and considerations for the whole environment. Having an inventory management system is the backbone to building a comprehensive security tooling strategy.

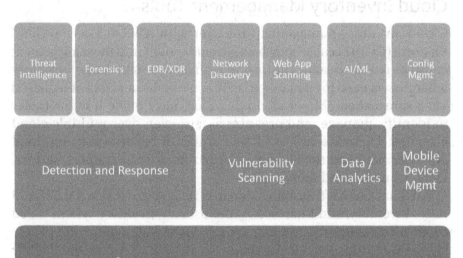

Figure 1.6: Complexity of an asset inventory system

Ephemeral Assets

One of the major challenges in modern IT infrastructure and cloud environments is *ephemeral assets*, which include containers, nodes, workloads, and several types of modern container technologies. The typical life span of these system types can be anywhere from minutes to hours to days, and they only come online to serve a scalability purpose. For example, a new worker node may come online during business hours to support the increased workload from major website traffic. That node may go offline at 5 p.m. and a new instance is then brought online the next morning at 8 a.m. So, how can an organization's inventory systems and containers stay online for minutes or hours? Easy; they can utilize any number of the cloud-native tools and automation when bringing servers and containers online to keep their assets up-to-date.

Accounting for ephemeral assets is a growing requirement for organizations, but it is incredibly difficult because accounting for these systems by hostname or IP is not sufficient. Because they're only online for minutes or hours, asset inventories must be dynamic and account for IP ranges and expected hostname ranges, versus a static hostname or IP. Many cloud environments can monitor these assets, but vulnerability scanners and endpoint detection and response (EDR) solutions must be configured properly to monitor entire IP spaces and use dynamic scanning to capture all systems.

If there are static IPs or hostnames in those scans, these scans will be insufficient for finding vulnerabilities and providing an accurate view of the vulnerability landscape. Organizations will need to not only review their inventory tool, but also their vulnerability scanners and any other security tools to ensure the entire organization is accounting for ephemeral assets.

Sources of Truth

Many security teams, developers, and platform engineers use multiple sources of truth to validate vulnerabilities, secure configurations, and asset/inventory management activities. A *source of truth* is the ability for an organization to aggregate data into a single dashboard or tool to verify that (in this case) the assets are configured properly. This would be a combination of multiple tools and utilizing that "single pane of glass" mentioned previously. If a team is using a single tool for all these activities—for example, using a vulnerability scanner to double as an inventory record system—the team might be missing out on assets that either cannot or do not get scanned by those tools. One concern would be whether the team is using a tool that does not have the functionality or ability to identify and manage certain types of assets.

For example, it's possible that some vulnerability scanners aren't able to inventory or find vulnerabilities on containers or infrastructure as code (IaC). Because of this limitation, organizations must understand the full functionality and capability of the tools that they use for specific purposes. A vulnerability scanner without the ability to find vulnerabilities in a container would not be sufficient for a cloud workload that consists of only containers.

Organizations should have a primary source of truth—a configuration management tool that they can rely on for enterprise asset discovery and management. However, a VMP should have a second source of truth to validate that the proper assets are in place, being patched consistently, and scanned regularly by both the vulnerability scanner and the EDR solution. The ability to validate between two tools provides clarity for teams and prioritization to investigate any inconsistencies between the tools.

Asset Management Risk

Asset management is the basis of any vulnerability management program. Without a comprehensive understanding of all possible assets across an organization, it's impossible to understand the organization's risk landscape or to even prioritize vulnerability management activities. The "unknown unknowns" are typically the highest risk to any organization, because without an understanding of assets there's no way to know which vulnerabilities are still exploitable on the network. Without any visibility, the risk of an organization moves from a "known known" to an "unknown unknown."

Log4j

An excellent example of the need for proper software inventories is the incident that occurred in December 2021 called Log4j, or Log4Shell. Based on the guidance from the Cybersecurity and Infrastructure Security Agency (CISA), CVE-2021-44228 was a remote code execution (RCE) that malicious actors leveraged to gain access to systems, conduct a ransomware attack, and exfiltrate data (www.cisa.gov/news-events/news/apache-log4j-vulnerability-guidance).

The UK's National Cyber Security Centre (NCSC) noted just how prevalent Log4j was based on the open source nature of the tool and how developers needed such a tool for logging functionality (www.ncsc.gov.uk/information/log4j-vulnerability-what-everyone-needs-to-know). The NCSC also noted, however, how difficult it was for organizations to determine or identify that Log4j was in their environment.

This article also mentions the increased need for the communication required between vendors and developers. The Center for Internet Security (CIS) released an article discussing the severity of the vulnerability, rated a 10.0 on the Common Vulnerability Scoring System (CVSS; www.cisecurity.org/log4j-zero-day-vulnerability-response).

One of the major challenges with this incident was the inability for organizations to find and detect Log4j instances within their pipelines or development environments. Any delay in patching this vulnerability left precious time for malicious actors to exploit this vulnerability. Because the vulnerability was made public, it was possible for actors and hackers to exploit the vulnerability in the time it took organizations to identify whether they had Log4j in place. This example highlights the need to understand the software, libraries, and dependency components of any development environment. Organizations must have a dynamic library of all software components, both off-the-shelf and OSS. OSS will be covered more in-depth in later chapters, but the Log4j incident highlights the harmony required between asset management and OSS.

Missing and Unaccounted-for Assets

This section might seem redundant—but enterprise risk around assets is tied very closely to unknown or unaccounted-for hardware and software assets. Without the proper inventory or management of devices, servers, containers, and applications, organizations cannot account for those risks. Any server that's unaccounted for is most likely not being patched, missing secure configurations, and ultimately increasing the risk for the whole environment. That server could become the entry point for an attacker or actor to gain access to privileged credentials or compromise the entire network. Each hardware or software asset that's unaccounted for is a potential entry method, providing the ability to gain a foothold in the environment.

It's also impossible to monitor servers and systems for compromise if they are not in the EDR or asset inventory lists. Administrators and security analysts would be unaware of such compromises and not be able to monitor and review potential alerts on unmanaged devices and applications. If there is malware, a potential compromise, or even a system that's being leveraged to gain access to other systems, it may go undetected and unnoticed until the asset comes into the inventory management system.

Detecting hardware and software assets necessitates both tools and processes to detect, monitor, and bring those assets into alignment. An organization's asset management team should be heavily involved in the process and policy, continuously monitoring for unaccounted-for and missing assets.

Unknown Unknowns

In the world of vulnerabilities, there are *known knowns, known unknowns*, and *unknown unknowns*. What is of major concern to any organization are the unknown unknowns. Based on the 2022 article by Nathan Wenzler from Tenable, unknown unknowns are a major concern when understanding an enterprise risk landscape (www.tenable.com/blog/finally-finding-the-unknown-unknowns-across-your-entire-attack-surface).

These unknown unknowns (henceforth known as UUs) are typically items classified as zero-day or being actively exploited in the wild by the time that they're disclosed. These types of vulnerabilities are incredibly difficult to plan for within a VMP. But VMPs should have their own processes and people in place to manage events and be prepared when these vulnerabilities are found.

One example of a UU is the SolarWinds attack that took place in September 2019. The U.S. Government Accountability Office (GAO) in 2021 noted that the SolarWinds attack was the largest hacking campaign against both government and private organizations (www.gao.gov/blog/solarwinds-cyberattack-demands-significant-federal-and-private-sector-response-infographic). What is interesting is the SolarWinds attack was just the beginning for software supply chain attacks and the understanding that even patches can contain malicious code, leaving organizations vulnerable to UUs.

To plan for such events, organizations should have a strategy and procedure to handle UU events like zero-days and highly exploitable vulnerabilities. Using resources like the CISA Known Exploitable Vulnerabilities (KEV) catalog and the National Vulnerability Database (NVD), organizations can set up alerts for when possible exploitable vulnerabilities have been released. These processes tie well together with an incident response (IR) plan and any cyber-resiliency tooling and procedures.

Patch Management

Patch management is one of the major areas of concern when it comes to what servers, systems, and applications exist in any on-premises or cloud environment. And of course, without a thorough understanding of what hardware and software assets exist, an organization will have an ineffective patch management program. If an asset program is missing any systems or devices, it will be impossible to determine what patches are missing, leading to unknown risks.

To create an effective patch management strategy, an organization must first understand the levels of OSs, applications, libraries, container versions, and so on. Each of these pieces helps create a complete picture of their vulnerabilities and allows organizations to prioritize remediation activities.

An example of the complexity of software asset patch management is the migration from one OS to another. Chances are that an organization who's migrating from one server version to another (e.g., Windows Server 2019 to 2022 or Red Hat Enterprise Linux [RHEL] 8 to 9) will be managing two levels of patch sets. The administrators will need to download and install patches for both version levels, meaning that they will need to ensure that the proper patches are being both downloaded and installed properly. This necessity doubles administrative overhead unless the team leverages some automation or automatic patching for servers and applications.

Patch management will be covered more in-depth in the next chapter, but the connection between inventory management and patch strategy is undeniable.

Increased complexity with patch management starts when an organization cannot reboot or patch systems outside of maintenance windows. Many environments will require some customization and considerations for service level agreements (SLAs), customer requirements, maintenance windows, and stability of the environment. There will always be unique requirements, but organizations must have a patch management strategy to combat these complexities. Recommendations include building resiliency into systems that are considered unstable, patching test and development environments first for monitoring, and instituting a rollback plan for any patches or secure configuration changes.

Recommendations for Asset Management

There are several recommendations for organizations, large or small, to get a handle on their assets. Whether on-premises, cloud-based, multicloud, or any combination of software and hardware assets, organizations must start with the people who will manage those assets. The people-process-technology aspect of asset management is an important combination of having the personnel who own and manage the assets, installing the proper tooling in place for inventory systems, and understanding the processes to discover, manage, and organize their assets. This section covers multiple areas for organizations to consider when creating an asset management program.

Asset Manager Responsibilities

The people part of the people-process-technology trilogy is just as important as the tools and processes used for inventory management. An account owner might be designated to manage the cloud infrastructure, an operations team may be in place to manage the OS and application layers, and a security team may be in place for vulnerability management. But without properly identifying who will own the asset inventory tooling and processes, organizations may spend hours, days, or weeks trying to find the proper technology owner. This wastes company resources and time, and potentially compiles risk for vulnerable systems without an owner.

Designating a primary and secondary asset manager helps alleviate some of these potential concerns. A primary asset manager should be making the decisions about the frequency of vulnerability scanning, continuous monitoring, provisioning and decommissioning of systems, and the categorization of the data. For a thorough understanding of how to catalog and understand asset management, any organization can start with the Risk Management Framework (RMF) from NIST.

The NIST RMF is a framework used to help organizations understand and determine their security and risk management activities. There are seven steps to the RMF: preparation, categorization of systems, selection of security controls, implementation of controls, assessment, authorization of a system for use, and finally monitoring of the selected controls. This framework is a starting point for any organization to determine risk in their environments and continuously monitor to ensure the proper security controls are in place.

A secondary asset manager provides backup, can perform an additional check for unexpected devices, or aids in understanding workloads to determine expected versus unexpected systems. Having a secondary manager also provides an extra layer of security when the primary leaves the company, goes on vacation, or simply needs another pair of eyes on an incident. Having an additional pair of eyes on missing devices can provide context as well.

Asset Discovery

Asset discovery is the continuous monitoring component of any asset and configuration management program. With the increased complexity and incredible speed at which systems are built, brought online, and put into production, organizations need to continuously detect and monitor new systems. This ensures that any team is aware of expected versus unexpected (or rogue) devices on their network. As mentioned previously, having assets that are unknown increases risk and there is no accounting for vulnerabilities, missing configurations, or even understanding if rogue devices have been placed on the network.

To start an asset discovery process, you will need the right tools in place. Use discovery tools to regularly scan for expected assets, or use the dynamic scanning process that exists in your current tools. For example, vulnerability scanners may have special scans to monitor the entire network and report on any new and unaccounted-for systems and servers. These reports should be run daily and alerts should be set up for any unexpected devices.

After these reports are put in place, a process should be enacted to determine why a system wasn't accounted for and who the system's owner is, and to catalog that asset properly. For cloud environments, the in-house inventory system is a good starting place and should be compared to any of the other scanning or inventory tools that the team employs. This asset discovery program is a balance of tools and processes to ensure that no rogue or unexpected systems are online.

Part of IT project management is asset discovery and the ongoing management of the asset and configuration management processes. To align with the asset discovery tooling, the processes must pick up where the tooling leaves off. To do so, proper alerting and notifications should be installed to notify the appropriate system or account owner. This alert or notification should trigger a process to assign the right technical owner, bring the system into alignment with the organization's inventory, and then have continuous monitoring and vulnerability scanning occurring. Similarly, if an unexpected server is brought online and discovered, an incident response process should be triggered to notify the security team and contain or investigate it, as appropriate.

Getting the Right Tooling

Asset management is part of everyone's responsibility. Leveraging a tool like ServiceNow for asset and configuration management is part of the puzzle but not the entire picture. Each organization has their unique requirements, but it is important for the IT, development, and management teams to come together to select a tool that will work for today and for five years from now. When organizations are first formed, it's a perfect time for the IT, security, and architecture staff to come together to decide on a solution. But asset inventory tooling will not necessarily grow and scale with the organization; the tooling should be reviewed and measured over time for success.

Organizations many years ago maintained data centers or server rooms. Then "the cloud" became a viable solution for many businesses to reduce cost and speed up access to development resources. It created a more agile and scalable environment that allowed organizations to move away from physical data centers.

Now organizations are leveraging hybrid or multicloud solutions to increase scalability even further. To reduce risk, and administrative overhead of OS-level infrastructure, organizations are now moving to infrastructure as code or low-code solutions to manage their platforms and infrastructure. Each step of the way, organizations are looking to reduce cost and overhead, and allow for lower risk and a smaller attack surface.

Figure 1.7 shows the progression over the years from on-premises and physical infrastructure, through the great cloud migration, and now to infrastructure as code.

As an organization grows, the asset inventory and configuration management tools need to grow too. For example, an organization that manages one server rack in a local data center has very different business requirements than a multicloud environment. The right tool needs to be scalable and grow with the organization, but that's not always possible. So as other security tools and vulnerability scanners are being reviewed for efficiency, the asset inventory tool should be reviewed at the same time. If deficiencies or missing functionalities exist, consider the cost of ripping and replacing before choosing a new tool. An example of when an organization does a "rip and replace" is when a company removes one vulnerability scanner and replaces it with another vulnerability scanner from a different vendor. One example is removing Tenable Security Center and replacing it with a Qualys suite of tools. This would require the removal of servers and infrastructure, and applying all new permissions and access for the new tooling. The cost and management of these tools is just as important as the automation and reduction in overhead.

Any IT or security team should also be aware of asset inventory tooling that could potentially lead to confusion, mismanagement, or inconsistent information.

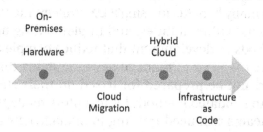

Figure 1.7: Progression of organizational management over the years

Digital Transformation

Digital transformation should be aligned with an asset management provisioning and decommissioning process. In a 2021 article by Michael Pease from NIST, he noted that digital transformation (DX) is divided into three phases: digitization, digitalization, and digital transformation (www.nist.gov/blogs/manufacturing-innovation-blog/supporting-digital-transformation-legacy-components). Basically, this means bringing data to the business using more digital assets and transforming the business to move away from legacy systems. Digital transformation requires enhanced technical skills to manage dynamic and emerging technologies (see Figure 1.8).

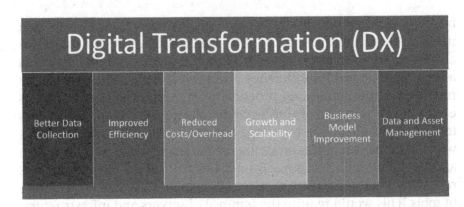

Figure 1.8: Digital transformation (DX)

Speaking of legacy systems, organizations will see the decommissioning and removal of many legacy applications, systems, devices, and appliances as they move toward a more DX strategy. Improving a DX strategy means having the ability to remove and decommission end-of-life (EoL) and legacy applications quickly and efficiently.

There are so many benefits to using a DX strategy, including lowering risk, removing old vulnerabilities, and implementing newer applications and methods of development that reduce complexity. However, with DX comes the need to manage newer systems that the current workforce may not be prepared for based on their current skillset. Along with using updated methods for inventory management, IT and development teams will need training to manage new and emerging technology.

Establishing and Decommissioning Standard Operating Procedures

A final recommendation for organizations is the process behind the inventory management tooling. For asset discovery and management, the processes and procedures are just as important for both auditing and an overall understanding of the environment. The establishment of service documents should outline the inventory component of bringing systems online, whether they are servers, containers, or applications. This document, known as the standard operating procedures (SOPs), provides the steps to validate that the system is checking the right inventory tool and is being properly scanned by the vulnerability scanner of choice.

The SOPs ensure that no system is brought online without some visibility by the administrative and operations team. Similarly, a decommissioning process will ensure that any system taken offline or removed is documented properly and removed from the inventory as appropriate. Having systems showing as still online and vulnerable can be confusing and waste time for operations teams, versus spending time on real live vulnerabilities.

Decommissioning and removing EoL products is an essential part of the asset management program. Organizations can determine their own schedule for validating if their systems are online or offline, but within minutes of a system coming online, it should be scanned before being put into production or set as externally facing.

Protection of new systems is paramount to ensuring that vulnerable or misconfigured systems do not enter a production environment without being cataloged and scanned. Without these processes in place, systems that are vulnerable may be set to be decommissioned but stay online and accessible to malicious actors, opening an organization to risk. Having an asset inventory and management program is not just good IT practice, but a risk management activity to protect the business.

Summary

This chapter encompassed a number of topics within asset and inventory management. It began with the physical components of organizations like on-premises data centers and mobile device management, then covered the challenges of managing that physical infrastructure. Moving from physical environments, the chapter covered all aspects of cloud assets and software management managed in hybrid or multicloud environments. Risk was discussed across all types of environments, focusing on how important it is for organizations to understand their assets to determine the appropriate risk level for their infrastructure. Starting with a proper asset and inventory management program is crucial, especially as organizations then consider a patch management process, which will be discussed in the next chapter.

2

Patch Management

A ny good patch management program consists of automatic and manual patching processes and techniques. Given the dynamic nature of infrastructure, it should be a continuous process of evaluating what's working, what's being patched, and what's missing. Without a strong vulnerability management program, systems can become outdated or reach EOL. Similarly, without a scheduled and regimented plan, systems will be left vulnerable for days, weeks, or longer to zero-day vulnerabilities like what happened at MOVEit or SolarWinds.

Foundations of Patch Management

Despite all the industry buzz about the latest flashy zero-day vulnerability, malicious actors are regularly targeting "vintage vulnerabilities"—vulnerabilities with existing patches that are known to be exploited in the wild (www.rezilion.com/blog/report-vintage-vulnerabilities-never-go-out-of-fashion). This is due to the fact that, despite being known to be exploited and having existing patches, organizations still struggle with remediation capacity, on average only being able to remediate 1 out of 10 new vulnerabilities per month. Figure 2.1 displays the layers of patch management activities that would take place in any IT infrastructure, whether cloud or on-premises.

Each organization must determine what patch management process will work best for them, but the basics include a comprehensive inventory; maintenance windows, tools, or processes to automate patching; and processes for reboots or taking systems offline for testing.

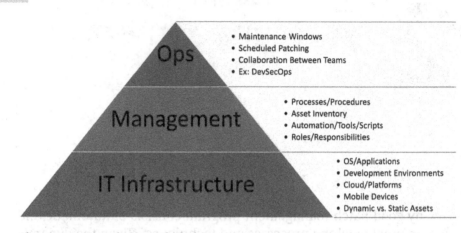

Figure 2.1: Foundations of patch management pyramid

A patch management plan must also include high-availability or redundancy concerns to ensure that systems are patched and backed up to keep them online for customers. It's typical for service level agreements (SLAs) to include an outlined maintenance window or allotted time frame for patching and other activities. This also includes a rollback plan or backup strategy for when patches may cease functioning or cause service disruption.

Manual Patch Management

Manual patching is any patching in an environment that requires an individual to download and install a patch, reboot servers based on organizational requirements, or investigate patching for servers that falls outside of normal maintenance windows. Typical organizations will have a combination of manual and automated patching due to the reality that not all activities can always be automated, and implementation might vary, based on organizational and technical considerations.

Although it's ideal to have as much automation in place as possible, there will always be a need for manual patches. For example, an organization may have an application that requires 99 percent uptime. The team would then need to apply patches to a development environment, then perform user acceptance testing (UAT), and finally apply patches in production. While there might be some automation for patch application, rebooting the servers and testing might still be a manual task (in the early stages of a patch management program) before patching subsequent production servers.

Another common use for manual patching is testing one-off patches when a zero-day vulnerability is announced. Depending on the vulnerability's severity, it could be possible to download and automatically install patches, but accelerated testing and remediation would still need to occur. With a condensed timeline, groups may not want to alter the automation in place to account for a one-off situation or unique patch that doesn't follow their regular patch cadence.

Risks of Manual Patching

As previously mentioned, a combination of automated and manual patching is more of a reality for organizations than having all patch management activities automatically done using tools. But with any manual activity, there are risks. One of the first concerns is human error. Any IT administrator or systems engineer is balancing engineering, operations, and security tasking.

As with any other role, a systems administrator juggling many systems, responsibilities, projects, and tasks is prone to mistakes here and there. These mistakes could lead to:

1. Missing patches for exploitable vulnerabilities
2. Misconfigured settings
3. Additional system-compromising vulnerabilities

Figure 2.2 highlights the risk level if a team is solely managing patches by manually downloading and installing them per system.

Another potential risk of manual patching is the sheer amount of effort needed to download patches, install and test them, and have fully updated systems in production. In automated patching, typically any outstanding hotfixes, rollups, or individual patches are downloaded and installed based on a predetermined schedule. The added time to manually install patches means additional risk for possible vulnerability exploitation.

On the flip side, if no test environment exists for patching and manual patches must be installed on production systems, there's a major risk to operations. Security is a balance of risk management and operations, per the Confidentiality, Integrity, and Availability (CIA) triad. If there's a requirement for customer systems to be operational 99 percent of the time, administrators and system owners will spend additional time in testing before applying patches to production.

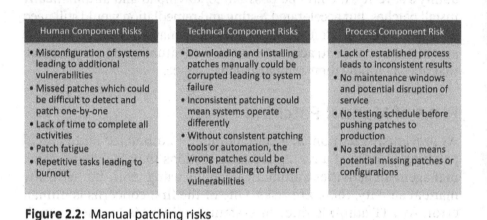

Human Component Risks	Technical Component Risks	Process Component Risk
• Misconfiguration of systems leading to additional vulnerabilities • Missed patches which could be difficult to detect and patch one-by-one • Lack of time to complete all activities • Patch fatigue • Repetitive tasks leading to burnout	• Downloading and installing patches manually could be corrupted leading to system failure • Inconsistent patching could mean systems operate differently • Without consistent patching tools or automation, the wrong patches could be installed leading to leftover vulnerabilities	• Lack of established process leads to inconsistent results • No maintenance windows and potential disruption of service • No testing schedule before pushing patches to production • No standardization means potential missing patches or configurations

Figure 2.2: Manual patching risks

Systems administrators could consider a phased rollout of patches throughout the environment. This path could alleviate some concerns with functionality or operability concerns. It would also provide limited interruption to the environment at large, limiting the impact of patching operations.

Manual Patching Tooling

Some tools allow administrators to perform patch management activities without fully automating a solution, using capabilities that will automatically download and install patches based on the system's type. One example would be using Ansible for either Linux or Windows servers or both. Administrators can leverage Ansible playbooks to download and install updates while still requiring manual intervention for reboots. Figure 2.3 details how Ansible works in a cloud environment, including infrastructure and networking requirements.

For Windows, it's as simple as creating scheduled tasks (if you're old school), or you can leverage Ansible. Other tools like ManageEngine and even SolarWinds can manage patches for Windows as well. However, SolarWinds comes at a cost, and if it isn't already used in the environment for server management, you should leverage the capabilities of newer Windows servers, including centralized management.

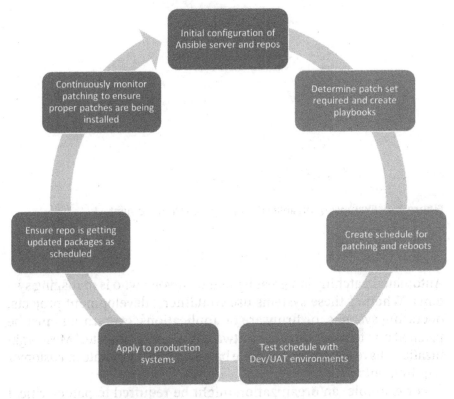

Figure 2.3: How Ansible works

Another paid option is Microsoft Configuration Manager, which, like SolarWinds, is a great option if it's already being utilized for other capabilities. But using it solely to manage patches could be a costly solution. Any solution is dependent on customer requirements, the ability to connect to the Internet to automatically download patches, and who manages the patches on the systems.

If the team is quite experienced and understands the environment's nuances, there might be little need to purchase expensive patching solutions. However, if the team is more junior and newer to the environment, it could be beneficial to augment any manual patching with a more automated solution like Ansible. There are several open source repositories and references that administrators can leverage to reduce the manual tasking required. Figure 2.4 provides an example of a simple Ansible playbook to automate patch installation.

```
---
- name: Patching Playbook
  hosts: all
  tasks:
  - name: Patching initiation
    shell: /var/tmp/update.sh
    async: 10
    poll: 0
  - name: Verifying server state once it's back
    wait_for:
      host: "{{ inventory_hostname }}"
      state: started
      delay: 60
      timeout: 600
      port: 22
      delegate_to: localhost
```

Figure 2.4: Example of Ansible script for patch management

Automated Patch Management

Automated patching is a great benefit to anyone who is managing systems. Whether these systems use containers, development projects, operating systems, or firmware or applications, everything must be patched due to the reality that software is never "complete." Most organizations have a patching schedule based on their corporate or customer requirements.

For example, an organization might be required to patch critical vulnerabilities within 15 days (about 2 weeks), and high-severity vulnerabilities within 30 days (1 month). To accomplish these timelines, automated patching is a must to accurately and effectively apply required patches. Because of the massive number of vulnerabilities released each day—roughly 85 a day based on recent reports (www .linkedin.com/posts/jgamblin_2023-ytd-cve-stats-total- number-of-cves-activity-7136354512683859968-YjfK?utm_ source=share&utm_medium=member_desktop)—administrators must reduce manual tasking to maintain constant patching activities.

Another organization might be required to report vulnerabilities or patching status to a third agency or prepare those findings for audits. In that scenario, it's even more valuable to have some automation in place as well as documentation to outline the process. Patching automation is as much about the tools and techniques as it is about the alignment of processes and practice.

Automated patching can not only reduce the potential for oversight or errors that may arise with manual patching activities, but can also help with the constant reality most organizations face, which is a shortage of cybersecurity talent and resource constraints.

Benefits of Automated vs. Manual Patching

As Figure 2.5 shows, there are some incredible benefits to utilizing automated patching tools and techniques versus solely relying on manual patching methods:

Manual   # Automated

Manual
More time spent on patching efforts versus overall operations/building enhancements
Patching cycles may take longer because of the amount of time to patch each system one-by-one
Vulnerabilities may linger for months or years because of the amount of time to patch

Automated
Reduced administrative overhead and more free time for admins to work on innovation/ops
Faster and more efficient patching cycles to meet organizational or customer expectations
Reduced time to remediation leaving less risk in the environment

Figure 2.5: Benefits of automated vs. manual patching solutions

Reduced Administrative Overhead   It's well established that the time that administrators, engineers, and developers have to patch systems is limited. These operations teams are typically juggling many different tasks and projects, while also working to patch and remediate vulnerabilities within a predefined timeline.

Faster and More Efficient Patching Cycles   Without having some automation in place, patching simply takes more time. Additional time is required for downloading and installing the patches, especially when across multiple environments. In any complex environment, automated patching is a must to keep up with the multitude of patches released at the operating system (OS), application, and container levels. In development environments, there will likely be development, UAT, and production levels as well.

Reduced Time to Remediation   Based on the sheer volume of vulnerabilities identified daily, without automation, teams will need weeks or months to remediate vulnerabilities. However, by using additional tools, scripts, or playbooks, the time from vulnerability identification to remediation can be reduced significantly.

Reducing the time to remediation is critical, as organizations are often in a race with attackers seeking to exploit new or known vulnerabilities faster than organizations can remediate them. Known as the *minimize the attack* or *exploitation* window, this time frame can help mitigate the risk of an organization being breached or compromised as part of a security incident. It can also bolster an organization's case that they're performing due diligence with mitigating known vulnerabilities and risks.

Combination of Manual and Automated Patching

However, the true solution lies somewhere between manual practices and automated solutions. There will not be any one right solution for a team, especially due to the intricacies between infrastructure, operations, and development. However, the best way to build a comprehensive patch management program is to start by building a Roles and Responsibilities Matrix. This simple activity allows teams to understand what they are responsible for and start building the tools and practices around it. Each team can align their patching activities, which not only reduces risk, but can also build relationships between teams.

Building a comprehensive patch strategy including all teams helps teams align their goals and missions regarding an overall vulnerability management program. Each may be able to leverage the same automation and implement the same days/times for patching to limit downtime and reduce remediation time.

The balance of automation and manual patching can be a shared experience between teams, including sharing scripts and playbooks. Overall, the strategy is just as important as the teamwork. Sharing automation techniques with other teams that may not be as mature in patch management will grow the teams, align strategy, and ultimately provide a more secure environment. The recommendation here is to build a patch management repository where teams can share information, instead of groups working in silos and potentially impacting one another's work.

Risks of Automated Patching

Several risks associated with automation have more to do with operations than security (see Figure 2.6). For example, automating the patching and rebooting servers without testing could lead to broken functionality or even corruption in the patch sets themselves. Patches include not only security features but also enhancements and potentially resolve other software issues.

Automated Patching Risks

Potential downtime without proper testing	Patches may not be the only component for remediation	Skillset and proficiency with patching
• If teams do not have a test environment, they risk corrupting servers or breaking functionality on production systems	• Some vulnerabilities require a patch and a configuration – which may not be automatically installed with a script or tool	• Not all teams are proficient in patch management and may need training or additional assistance to build automation into their systems

Figure 2.6: Risks of automated patching

The first risk is the impact to operations and associated downtime for users due to patch activities. Because patching one application may have a dependency on another, it could take an application down or impact functionality. This is why it's so critical for teams to test patches as much as possible in a separate environment or create a rollback plan before patching systems. Additionally, organizations have been adopting strategies, such as Blue/Green deployments, where changes are made to one version of a running system. For example, green may be the production environment, patches are made to the blue environment, and then configuration changes are made to route traffic to the staging, or blue, environment, making it the production environment moving forward.

An additional patching risk is that the patch doesn't resolve the vulnerability alone and requires configuration changes. An example would be a Microsoft patch to fix a vulnerability that also requires an Active Directory (AD) Group Policy or registry key change. This complexity could leave open vulnerabilities simply because remediation instructions aren't always clear.

A final risk is that if teams aren't proficient with patching, they may not read the details of the Common Vulnerabilities and Exposures (CVE) ID to understand what's needed for full remediation. If there's a lack of knowledge of how patching works, it could be the beginning of a large vulnerability backlog, which is incredibly difficult to return from.

Patch Management for Development Environments

As organizations move to larger and more diverse development environments, patching in development environments becomes an even higher priority for operations teams. Development-level patching includes everything from the OS level (e.g. Red Hat Enterprise Linux [RHEL]) to the application layer (e.g., Tomcat, Python, and other libraries) and other tools (e.g., Bootstrap, Java, or Jenkins).

Newer roles such as DevOps and DevSecOps are more prevalent and include responsibilities from software development, security engineering, and infrastructure operations. These new roles require additional skillsets across each discipline to provide harmony in operations and security.

Anything external facing is at a higher exploitation risk and would be at the top of the patch management list. And with any application, there will be external-facing components requiring some additional testing before the patches are installed.

Open Source Patching

Most developers use some level of open source software (OSS) within their applications. In fact, studies show that modern codebases are composed of up to 60 to 80 percent OSS code overall. OSS allows teams to focus on the actual development and engineering aspects, without having to reinvent every function type. For example, why create a logging tool when a team could leverage Log4j?

OSS provides a lot of flexibility and adaptability whereas simply purchasing software or building it could take additional time and resources. With stretched budgets and condensed timelines, it makes sense to use as much free software as possible. However, OSS patching can be tricky, especially when using tools or libraries that aren't updated often.

As we'll discuss in Chapter 9, "Cloud, DevSecOps, and Software Supply Chain Security," studies from organizations like Synopsys have found that 88 percent of modern codebases contain OSS components that have had *no* new development in 2 years, and 85 percent of codebases contained OSS that was *more* than 4 years out of date. Further complicating the issue is the fact that 25 percent of all OSS projects have *one* developer contributing code, and 94 percent of projects have 10 or fewer active contributors. In fact, Sonatype's 9th Annual State of the Software Supply Chain report (www.sonatype.com/state-of-the-software-supply-chain/introduction) found that only 11 percent of all OSS overall seems to be actively maintained.

Multiple OSS projects are used widely but are only maintained by a small group of developers. For example, Log4j was managed by three developers and because it wasn't a paid product, they didn't have the time or resources to patch and manage it over time. When the Log4j exploit was released at the end of 2022, it took time to obtain a patch due to its smaller team and limitations on their availability.

While major exploits like Log4j don't occur all the time, there is a possibility for an attacker to use OSS to develop malware or attacks. They know that these projects aren't always maintained, and because Log4j was so successful, it's possible that another opportunity like this exists in other software. Teams must be aware of the exploitation potential for any OSS that isn't actively maintained.

Not All Software Is Equal

In this section, we'll discuss some of the complexities of managing OSS patches internally and the varying responsibilities between development and operations teams. We'll also discuss the need for clear roles and responsibilities, such as ownership of patch management.

Managing OSS Patches Internally

The first part of managing OSS patches internally within the development, operations, or security teams is to understand what applications and libraries are actively being used. Creating an OSS application library would be beneficial to understand the OSS projects being used, what they are used for, who has responsibility for them, and what version is on which system.

The next step would be to integrate OSS patching within a normal patch management window. Patch management plans aren't just for vendor-related software but also for any OSS. Within Linux and Windows environments, it could be as simple as creating a patch playbook within Ansible to download and install those patches.

To reiterate, whether it's OSS or vendor-related applications, both the process and tooling aspects are equally important to the patch management program's success.

The final step would be the vulnerability scanning and reporting of those servers and containers to ensure that the patches are being properly applied. These reports could be used to determine if a particular OSS component hasn't been upgraded in some time or doesn't have any newer patches available. Security teams can then determine risk for any OSS components that are no longer being maintained, to evaluate alternatives or decide to accept the risk of using the components.

Managing OSS dependencies in modern environments is very complex and tedious and is often referred to as "dependency hell." As a sign of embracing automation and tooling, the industry is seeing the increased adoption of tools such as Dependabot (`https://github.com/dependabot`) and Renovate (`https://github.com/renovatebot/renovate`), which help facilitate automated dependency updates. These tools can be integrated into existing developer workflows, and they are supported by widely used development platforms such as GitHub.

Responsibilities of Infrastructure vs. Operations Teams

There's a long-standing debate in the technology industry that exists between infrastructure and operations teams about who is responsible for what. Infrastructure teams are typically responsible for the underlying hosting and management that is the foundation upon which all applications, servers, and containers sit. They may also be responsible for some patching, secure configuration, and even identity and access management (IAM). In a data center, infrastructure teams would manage the data center, while operations teams would remain focused on the daily care of the servers and operations on top, including resolving downed servers, application errors, or any other user functionality concerns. These teams may also be responsible for high availability (HA). However, this paradigm is changing with the advent of cloud computing, infrastructure as code (IaC), and methodologies such as GitOps that declaratively provision and manage digital infrastructure using practices leveraged from software development. Increasingly, the industry is adopting a "you build it, you own it" mantra, where many development and engineering teams find themselves responsible for the systems they've developed, designed, and put into production. There is also a concurrent push over the last decade for DevOps, breaking down the silos between development and operations teams.

Who Owns Patch Management?

It's a tricky question—who owns patch management? And at what level? Hardware devices, hosts, applications, containers, and so forth are all going to potentially require different individuals to be responsible for patching. One example is an application that uses a database. The development team might be required to patch and configure the application, but a separate database administrator (DBA) could be responsible for the database. And yet another team could be responsible for the infrastructure-level patching, or the OS or hosts on which the systems rely. For example, when there are patches for Oracle servers, who would install them?

While not a simple answer, it could be the DBAs simply because they're performing the regular database maintenance and should know the expected behavior before and after patches are applied. The expected system performance and operations are important to validate once changes have been made. So, it's possible that once DBAs apply the fixes, they may work together with the development team to ensure that application functionality hasn't changed.

Each situation will be different, but the best way to run patch management programs is to align teams with patch strategies and coordinate efforts. Create a Responsible, Accountable, Consulted, and Informed (RACI) matrix, also known as a *responsibility assignment matrix*, and document what roles each team will play. Without this, team members could point fingers at another team who should be responsible for patching, leading to confusion and delays in remediation. The RACI matrix in Figure 2.7 shows an example of how teams can create their own matrix to organize patching.

Roles	Patching OS / Infra	Patching Apps	Operations OS / Infra Layer	Operations App Layer	Monitoring OS / Infra	Monitoring App Layer
Operations	R, A	I	R, A	I	I	N/A
Development	I	R, A	I	R, A	N/A	I
Security	I	I	I	I	R, A	R, A

Action	Icon
Responsible	R
Accountable	A
Informed	I

Figure 2.7: Example of RACI matrix for infrastructure and operations

Separation of Duties

After creating a RACI matrix, teams should also consider the classic concept of separation of duties. IT and security teams would keep separate duties to ensure that checks and balances are in place. For example, the infrastructure team would handle the underlying patching and secure configuration, while the security team would run vulnerability scans and validate that all security expectations are met.

IT and development teams may share some responsibilities when it comes to patching, but there would also be a secondary set of checks performed by another team for testing and ensuring functionality across systems. Patching at an OS level may affect the top-level applications or databases, so it would be important to have a multi-tier patch management plan.

Separating duties provides two main benefits to any patch management strategy. The first benefit is that not one person is responsible for every task of patching and validating each setting as it's complete. This allows team members to not be responsible for every task and risk burning out, missing a patch or configuration, or having too many tasks to juggle at once.

The second benefit is enhanced in-depth security using multiple tiers of individuals who will implement and validate that the vulnerabilities are remediated. Without at least two pairs of eyes to ensure that patches were implemented, it is possible that they could fail, and that the implementer may not know without a second validation step. This could be done with a vulnerability scanner with reporting sent to both the operations and security teams. The security engineer or analyst could then review the findings and notify the IT staff if any patches were unsuccessful.

Tools and Reporting

Tools are the backbone of any patch management program, regardless of what technology is used in the environment. Reporting is the second part of the program that provides validation and organization vulnerability data for users. Tooling and reporting work together to install, manage, and continuously monitor patches.

Common patch management tools like Microsoft's Configuration Manager or SolarWinds require some additional configuration and can be costly. Entire engineering roles are dedicated solely to managing those tools given the complexity of cloud environments and software products. Reporting can be done in any of the tools mentioned previously and customized for the individual receiving that report.

For example, a security engineer might want to see every vulnerability, regardless of its severity or exploitability. However, a developer might only be interested in their specific applications and not the vulnerabilities on the infrastructure side.

For reporting, a manager would only be interested in the assets under their area of responsibility (AOR), while an executive would only be interested in the top five vulnerable systems or the top three most exploitable vulnerabilities. Each unique data set can be built into a reporting tool to give job roles their own reports. This solution reduces the amount of irrelevant information in reports, cutting down on time needed to remediate or spend time on vulnerabilities that are not a high priority.

Patching Outdated Systems

There may be many reasons why an organization is using EOL or end-of-support (EOS) software. EOL software or hardware is no longer being patched or fixed by the vendor. It's common that there would be a timeline for a particular OS or application to be supported and then retired for newer versions.

One example is the support of Windows Server 2012 until October 2023. After that date, customers could purchase extended support from Microsoft for a year or two while they worked on a transition plan to a later version like Windows Server 2019 or 2022. But if a customer doesn't purchase extended support, they will be left with potentially vulnerable software that will not be patched.

One of the largest risks that leaves behind exploitable vulnerabilities is outdated patches. As mentioned previously, most organizations follow a timeline for remediating vulnerabilities within a certain time frame. Along with unsupported software, the other major risk is the use of open source software, if the developers/maintainers aren't maintaining and updating their products and projects. Each of these scenarios leads to major unknown vulnerabilities and risks.

End-of-Life Software

Organizations may need to keep older software because of customer requirements or the complexity of applications. It's possible in a development project that the team would be hesitant to upgrade certain libraries or dependencies due to the code's rework. However, this would be a mistake. The earlier the planning begins for upgrading or migrating to a new environment, the sooner the teams can identify problems in functionality that require additional testing. Figure 2.8 shows end-of-life software listing examples.

EOL
- If support is not purchased, the product becomes EOL
- No patches, hotfixes, and as vulnerabilities become known and exploited, there will be no fixes for them

EOS
- Extended support for a year
- After EOS – no more patches, hotfixes, or feature enhancements

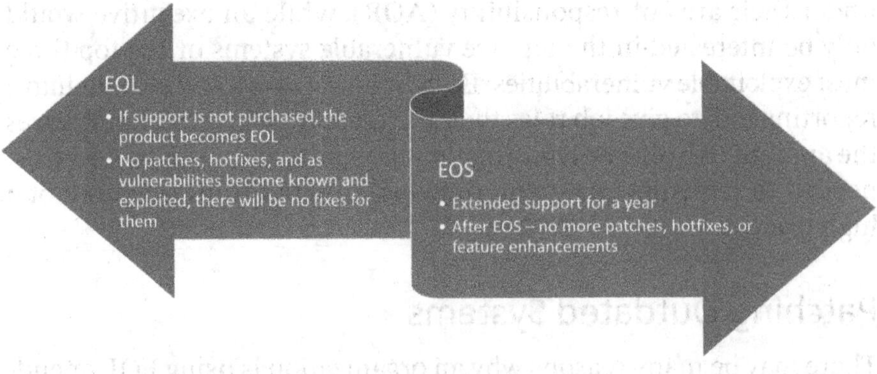

Figure 2.8: End-of-life software listing examples

There are incredible risks associated with unsupported or EOL software and hardware. Because these outdated systems are no longer being patched or maintained, no more fixes for bugs or exploitable vulnerabilities exist, with unknown vulnerabilities remaining. This adds to the list of unknown unknown risks, leaving an organization potentially vulnerable to a common attack against unpatched systems known as remote code execution (RCE), unauthenticated access, or other exploitable vulnerabilities.

In RCE, an attacker could leverage an RCE to inject malware or malicious code into a web application or infrastructure. RCE vulnerabilities exist across several types of applications, OSs, and other devices, which are highly exploitable and easier for attackers to leverage, in order to gain initial access into a system.

It's essential to have a plan for EOL and EOS software and hardware long before the software has reached its end of life. Otherwise, organizations might be at risk from EOL products in the environment while transitioning away from older software. One example would be the migration of applications and services to an RHEL 9.x server, while maintaining the old environment on an RHEL 7.x. Typically, these types of projects take time and require several teams to be engaged.

Unpatched Open Source Software

One of the risks with using any OSS application or package is that some of them aren't maintained, based on the limited developers and team who manage an open source project. Each application, library, or tool will be dependent on whomever maintains that repository. Several open source projects started because developers wanted to share their work with the world and make repetitive tasks easier for others.

But therein lies the risk—these projects are available for free, and are maintained as the developers have the time and ability to work on them outside of their normal jobs. If OSS looks like it hasn't been updated in 3 months or 3 years, it would be important to reach out to the owners of the repo to determine if it is still actively maintained. Without a response, teams can assume that any vulnerabilities found in the software may not be patched quickly.

With this risk, it is incredibly important for an organization to keep a library of all OSS applications and components used in their environment. Without it, it could be a lengthy process to determine risk, or even find where the libraries and tools are being used. Each security team should be aware of what OSS is used, where it is installed, and if it is currently required. Most organizations struggle with a comprehensive inventory of OSS components used in their environments, whether for internally developed software or components contained in software they consume from third parties (either self-hosted or consumed over the Internet such as software-as-a-service [SaaS]). For example, the Cyber Safety Review Board (CSRB) review of the Log4j incident revealed that some U.S. federal agencies spent tens of thousands of aggregate hours just trying to figure out where the Log4j component existed in their systems.

All outdated or unused OSS should be updated or removed from the environment as quickly as possible, which can also help minimize the attack surface of applications and the software for malicious actors to exploit.

Another key consideration and distinction when dealing with OSS compared to proprietary software is, when you're working with a vendor, you typically have service level agreements (SLAs) and time-lines associated with maintaining software, providing updates, and disclosing vulnerabilities. Unlike proprietary software vendors, OSS maintainers aren't software suppliers, and OSS is generally free for use as is, meaning that consumers have no assurance of the vulnerabilities or defects being addressed in any formal and rigid timeline. Organizations consuming OSS need to be aware of this distinction and be prepared to implement compensating controls for vulnerable OSS software without patches available, as well as potentially forking the code and implementing remediations themselves. Despite this being the reality, most organizations don't have a strong understanding of this distinction and defer to relying on the OSS maintainers, failing to realize they are ultimately responsible for any OSS they're consuming and utilizing.

Residual Risk

Residual risk is any risk that is left over from any vulnerability management activities, including the application of patches and hotfixes, which are quick engineering updates or secure configurations. This residual risk could be accepted, mitigated, or transferred to another party.

It is important to note that not all patches can be implemented on all systems, simply because of the requirements by customers or other circumstances. Residual risk is a component of any vulnerability management program and must be accounted for by creating exemptions or accepting specific risks in the environment.

The worst thing a team can do, however, is to be overwhelmed by the sheer volume of vulnerabilities or work that it would take to "catch up" or remediate all the outstanding vulnerabilities. *Decision paralysis* is when an individual is incapable of making a timely decision based on the sheer volume of data to input at one time. To this end, teams should be aware of this concept and provide adequate space to make complex decisions on risk.

Common Attacks for Unpatched Systems

According to statistics from a Cybersecurity and Infrastructure Security Agency (CISA) article, there is a serious need to focus on updated vulnerability management practices to reduce risk (www.cisa.gov/news-events/news/transforming-vulnerability-management-landscape). Leaving systems with exploitable vulnerabilities expands the possible attack surface. With a larger attack surface, an attacker has multiple routes into systems. Each vulnerability left unmitigated is a possible entry point, leaving an opportunity for an attacker to conduct vulnerability chaining attacks. Vulnerability chaining will be explored in depth later in Chapter 7, "What is Vulnerability Chaining?"

Another common attack method against unpatched systems is targeting any unauthenticated login access to servers and conducting a compromise, or then conducting a privilege escalation attack. These types of attacks can be found in a variety of software and aren't exclusive to any one type of application or vendor.

These two attack vectors are particularly devastating, given the possibility to gain remote access or elevate privileges to gain access to more systems. If there is no network segmentation or other mitigating controls set in place, exploiting these vulnerabilities would make it relatively easy to move to other systems. One example is gaining access to a web application server and then laterally moving to a database or another server containing business or financial information. Even with these few examples, it's easy to see how unpatched systems are a massive attack vector and how they can be used frequently to gain unauthorized access to systems.

One area that can greatly assist unpatched systems, if they cannot be patched due to application or legacy system requirements, is mitigating controls. Mitigating controls offer additional protection to limit the "blast radius," or the potential damage done to systems. For example, if network segmentation is put in place to limit access to databases, a malicious actor might be able to compromise a frontend web server, but might be unable to leverage it to gain access to the database due to limited connectivity between the web server and database.

Another example of mitigating controls is the concept of least privilege, or limiting the number of permissions that users have within a system. Limiting root access to Linux servers, or disabling root access, requires that each user log in with far fewer permissions or less access than administrators. While an attacker might still be able to conduct privilege escalation, it will be far more difficult for the attacker to do that without being detected by logging and monitoring.

Prioritizing Patching Activities

Any IT project is going to require juggling operations, maintenance, and ongoing innovation and engineering projects. One common example would be an organization deciding to upgrade from an EOL version of RHEL to the latest on new containers. Another common example would be the upgrade of Windows servers from 2016 to the latest 2022 server version. These migration types typically include maintaining an old environment while building a new one.

Of course, with these types of situations, there will not be an increase in staff to build the new systems. The same team who is managing the production environment might also be developing new containers and applications. These administrators and developers will need to double up their work to keep up on patching activities in both environments.

To help prioritize patch management, organizations should be leveraging automation as much as possible to limit the amount of manual intervention (and time) required by administrators and engineers. Before even beginning to prioritize patch management, a full asset and application inventory should be considered so that teams understand their highest-priority assets.

First, any OS and application patching that can be automated should be tested and put into production to handle the majority of vulnerabilities with the least amount of effort. At this stage, the teams can also create prioritization for development and testing systems, then patch production systems after. An example is patching dev on a Friday morning, then after a week of testing, patching all production systems, the following Thursday evening.

Second, organizations should look at third-party applications that may not automatically be pulled into repos or their patch management system. Administrators and engineers should create alerts or notifications from the vendors to be notified as patches are released. These applications should be built into the patch management process and may be organized around normal patching schedules.

Finally, there should be continuous monitoring and improvement of this process over time. Both the operations and security teams should be reviewing vulnerability reports to ensure that patching is happening as expected, and if not, that the process and tooling are adjusted.

Patching is not a one-time activity—it must be iterated and improved over time. As long as teams understand their responsibilities in regard to patching, it will go a long way in terms of helping them to adjust to integrating these activities into their daily routines.

Risk Management and Patching

Risk management programs and patching should not be done as siloed activities, or without interaction between responsible teams. Some larger organizations have separate risk management teams and programs. While this might work in a larger business, smaller organizations should be conducting risk management activities in coordination with their regular maintenance and operations activities.

For example, it would make no sense to prioritize patching database servers that no longer contain sensitive or proprietary data when there are higher-risk databases attached to web application servers with no network segmentation. Without this knowledge, siloed teams might deprioritize other patching efforts that could potentially cause high risks to the organization.

Each team should consider the risk associated with any outstanding vulnerabilities and how they want to conduct their patching schedules.

If a team decides to patch all externally facing assets first, then they can deal with patching infrastructure and databases or storage second. However, note that a healthcare organization would prioritize protected health information (PHI) over a database server that might be used for testing.

One final thought on patching and risk management: As with vulnerability management concepts, it is a continuous and iterative process. It isn't a one-time exercise, but it must be done horizontally and vertically throughout the organization.

Building a Patch Management Program

This chapter has outlined several of the risks, concerns, and considerations for building a comprehensive patch management program. The biggest theme throughout has been the classic concept of people, process, and technology. The reason this concept is still so prevalent is due to how it comprehensively captures all aspects of an organization. This concept works well in building a patch management program because classic practices (like manual patching alone) do not work.

The harmony between the people (e.g., development, operations, and security), process (e.g., standard operating procedures [SOPs] or policies), and technology (e.g., configuration managers and vulnerability scanners) is essential to a successful program. Without alignment between all three, organizations are at risk for all the concerns listed previously: exploits, zero-day vulnerabilities, and unknown unknowns.

Building that alignment isn't going to happen overnight but can be done in steps to build maturity into any organization. Figure 2.9 illustrates what teams should be involved, how to integrate tooling, and how processes can be the glue between both when building or maturing a patch management program.

People

The aspects of people, process, and technology will be seen throughout the book, but here it's important to note who is responsible for patch management. The decision as to who is responsible for patch management is integral to the successful patching of systems across the enterprise.

It is possible that the system owners, administrators, developers, security engineers, or even third parties might be responsible for patching their own individual components. For everyone involved in the patch management process, they must understand their own responsibilities and timelines for applying patches.

| People | Operations, Engineers, Security, Architects, Administrators, Management |

- Harmony between the people who manage systems means that each person is aware of changes, knows the patch management schedule, and coordinates activities together.

| Process | Standard Operating Procedures, Security Policies and Guidance, Patch Management Guide |

- Harmony of process means that it aligns with the people who need to manage systems – be concise, provide actionable guidance, and be adaptive to changes in technology, regulations, and standards.

| Technology | Ansible, Configuration Manager, ServiceNow, SolarWinds |

- Harmony of technology means that each tool or application is coordinated during patching activities. Any automation is coordinated and aligns with the processes and procedures outlined.

Figure 2.9: Alignment of people-process-tech

Process

For practitioners, they might have their own set of SOPs, or processes defined for the technical implementation of patches and associated playbooks or scripts. Their timelines and schedules might align with the requirements from customers or other guidelines—for example, they must remediate critical vulnerabilities within 4 days.

For management and executives, processes might be more in line with the customer requirements or any federal mandates that may be applicable to their area of business. A healthcare organization might have different requirements than an IT contractor company. The leadership teams might create a policy to travel down to all other management and practitioners to implement via technical methods.

Technology

The technology for patch management will be at the discretion of the people behind the regular patching and management of systems. This includes anything from using third-party tools like Configuration Manager or ManageEngine, to creating scripts or playbooks with Ansible or PowerShell.

Each of these components would be selected by the administrators and, if requiring funding, would be approved by the leadership. Ideally, administrators and engineers would have the ability to manage multiple OSs, containers, or applications with the same tool. However, administrators and engineers might need to come up with creative technical solutions.

Summary

Organizations need to have a comprehensive patch management strategy. This strategy includes building an asset inventory, in addition to understanding missing patches and how patches will be deployed throughout the environment. Patch management truly requires harmony between people, process, and technology. Organizations should focus on removing EOL and EOS, preparing for regular patching cadence, and building rollback and backup plans for when things go wrong. In addition, organizations should have expected patching and maintenance windows.

3

Secure Configuration

While some vulnerabilities are inherent to software and services and intrinsic aspects of a digital environment, others are tied to how a specific product, software, or service is configured. This chapter covers the topic of secure configurations and discusses various aspects such as regulatory frameworks, common misconfigurations, and industry secure configuration guidance.

Regulations, Frameworks, and Laws

Regulatory frameworks and laws play a significant role in advocating for the industry adoption of best practices and secure configurations. For example, the Center for Internet Security (CIS) Benchmarks align closely and map to frameworks such as the National Institute of Standards and Technology (NIST) Cybersecurity Framework (CSF), the Payment Card Industry Data Security Standard (PCI DSS), and the Health Insurance Portability and Accountability Act (HIPAA).

In the defense space, there are requirements for utilizing the Department of Defense's (DoD) Defense Information Systems Agency (DISA) Security Technical Implementation Guides (STIGs) where possible, and to utilize vendor- and industry secure configuration guidance in the absence of STIG availability. The reason is that most products and software don't come to customers and consumers in a "hardened" state. This is due to the inherent give and take between concepts such as usability and security. Suppliers are often trying to make products as feature-rich, capable, and easy to use as possible, whereas security practitioners are often looking to make products secure and difficult to exploit, with a minimized attack surface. These two priorities often are at odds, as features get disabled, configurations get hardened, and systems get "locked down" to minimize the exploitation of their systems, software, and products by malicious actors.

It isn't uncommon for users to use hardening guides from suppliers directly or other industry organizations such as CIS or DISA, as well as security vendors and independent experts. This often involves making configuration changes to enable an application or product to be more secure and to disable features and functions that may be exploited by attackers.

That said, we are seeing a push from sources like the Cybersecurity and Infrastructure Security Agency (CISA) to pivot within the industry, advocating for suppliers to provide secure-by-design/default products, and have them hardened upon delivery to customers and consumers. Instead of hardening guides, suppliers would provide "loosening guides" to help customers make configuration changes to enable features and functionality that might increase risk, and to inform consumers of the risks of making such configuration changes.

NSA and CISA Top Ten Cybersecurity Misconfigurations

While cybersecurity headlines are often dominated by the latest zero-day or other notable vulnerability in a vendor's software/product or open source software (OSS) library, the reality is that many significant data breaches have (and will) continue to be due to misconfigurations. As defined by NIST, a misconfiguration is:

> *An incorrect or suboptimal configuration of an information system or system component that may lead to vulnerabilities.*

It's why the National Security Agency (NSA)/CISA recently released their Top Ten Cybersecurity Misconfigurations (https://media .defense.gov/2023/Oct/05/2003314578/-1/-1/0/JOINT_CSA_ TOP_TEN_MISCONFIGURATIONS_TLP-CLEAR.PDF). These misconfigurations were identified through extensive red and blue team assessments and threat hunting and incident response team activities.

If you're like most cybersecurity professionals, many of these items should come as no surprise and might even seem simple. But as the saying goes, just because something is simple doesn't mean it's easy, and in modern complex digital environments doing these fundamentals at scale may be daunting.

Their publication emphasizes how pervasive these misconfigurations are in large organizations, even ones with mature security postures, and also emphasizes the need for software suppliers to take a secure-by-design/default approach, which is something CISA in particular has been advocating for and has published a document discussing (www .cisa.gov/securebydesign).

For those interested in secure-by-design/default, one of this book's authors has covered the topic in previous articles such as "The Elusive Built-in not Bolted-on" (https://resilientcyber.substack .com/p/the-elusive-built-in-not-bolted-on) and "Cybersecurity First Principles & Shouting Into the Void" (https://resilientcyber .substack.com/p/cybersecurity-first-principles-and).

With that said, let's dive into the Top Ten items the NSA and CISA identified. As their publication points out, these are in no way prioritized or listed in order of significance, as each one on its own can be problematic and lead to a pathway of exploitation by attackers.

Default Configurations of Software and Applications

One wouldn't think in 2024 that we would be discussing the risks of insecure default configurations of software, but here we are. Issues like default credentials, permissions, and configurations are still a common attack vector that is exploited.

For example, having default credentials in widely used commercial-off-the-shelf (COTS) software and products creates a situation where malicious actors who can identify those credentials can exploit the systems and environments that haven't changed those defaults. These defaults are often widely known and easy to find by even the least skilled malicious actors, as they are often published by the manufacturers themselves. This can allow attackers to identify credentials, change administrative access to something they can control, and pivot from compromised devices to other networked systems.

In addition to default credentials on devices, CISA points out that services can have overly permissive access controls and vulnerable settings by default. They specifically call out items like insecure Active Directory

(AD) Certificate Services, legacy protocols/services, and Server Message Block (SMB) services.

For those unfamiliar with the CISA Known Exploited Vulnerabilities (KEV) Catalog, it's an authoritative source of vulnerabilities that have been exploited in the wild. You can find a digital visualization of it at www.cisa.gov/known-exploited-vulnerabilities-catalog, representing the leading vendors on the KEV Catalog and their number of known exploited vulnerabilities.

If it seems like Microsoft has a large presence among the vulnerabilities listed, it's because Microsoft products are also the most common that the assessment teams encountered throughout their activities. Default credentials aside, Microsoft also reigns supreme atop the CISA KEV Catalog. They are also the recent target of the Cyber Safety Review Board (CSRB) due to Chinese hacks of Microsoft Exchange and prompts from some elected officials (www.bleepingcomputer.com/news/security/us-cyber-safety-board-to-analyze-microsoft-exchange-hack-of-govt-emails). Sometimes being first isn't quite so glamorous (see Figure 3.1).

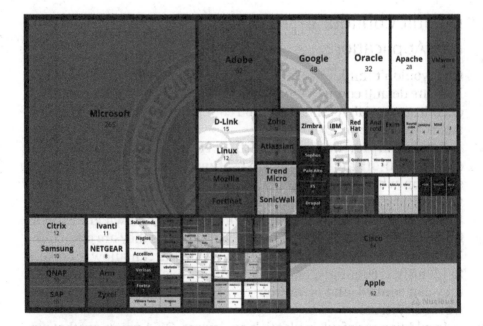

Figure 3.1 CISA KEV flag

Source: Patrick Garrity/2023// last accessed on 19 January 2024.

Improper Separation of User/Administrator Privilege

Despite industry-wide buzz about things like zero trust, which is rooted in concepts such as least-privileged access control, this weakness still runs rampant. The NSA/CISA publication calls out excessive account privileges, elevated service accounts, and nonessential use of elevated accounts.

Anyone who has worked in IT/cyber for some time knows that many of these issues trace back to human behavior and the general demands of working in complex environments. Accounts tend to aggregate permissions and privileges as people rotate through different roles and tasks, and these permissions rarely, if ever, are cleaned up.

Sources such as the Verizon Data Breach Investigations Report (DBIR) (www.verizon.com/business/resources/reports/dbir) yearly demonstrate that credential compromise remains a key aspect of most data breaches, and these overly permissive accounts sit, lying in wait, as a rich target for malicious actors to abuse.

Insufficient Internal Network Monitoring

If a tree falls in a forest and no one is around to hear it, does it make a sound? Similarly, if your network is being compromised and you lack visibility, awareness, and associated alerting, are you able to do anything about it?

No.

The NSA/CISA publication demonstrates that organizations need to have sufficient traffic collection and monitoring to ensure that they can detect and respond to anomalous behavior. As the publication discusses, it isn't uncommon for assessment and threat-hunting teams to encounter systems with either insufficient networking and host-based logging, or to have these measures in place but not properly configured and monitored to be able to respond to potential incidents when they occur.

This lack of configuration and monitoring allows malicious activity to go on unfettered and extends the dwell time of attackers in victims' systems without detection. To bolster network monitoring and hardening, the publication recommends that readers check out CISA's document, "CISA Red Team Shares Key Findings to Improve

Monitoring and Hardening of Networks" (www.cisa.gov/news-events/cybersecurity-advisories/aa23-059a).

Lack of Network Segmentation

Another fundamental security control that makes an appearance is the need to segment networks, a practice that again ties to the broader push for zero trust. By failing to segment networks, organizations are failing to establish security boundaries between different systems, environments, and data types.

Without boundaries, malicious actors can compromise a single system and move freely across other systems without encountering friction and additional security controls and boundaries that could impede their nefarious activities. The NSA/CISA publication specifically calls out challenges where there's a lack of segmentation between IT and operational technology (OT) networks, putting OT networks at risk, which have real-world implications for security and safety in environments such as industrial control systems (ICSs).

The problem can be further exacerbated with cloud environments due to their multi-tenant nature, allowing a malicious actor to compromise a single account/environment or service but have a cascading impact across other victims. This challenge was discussed by one of the authors in an article titled "Troublesome Tenants" (https://resilientcyber.substack.com/p/trouble-in-the-neighborhood), where he used Wiz's Cloud Isolation Framework to examine the issue in cloud environments.

Poor Patch Management

Patching is everyone's favorite activity in cybersecurity, right? CISA's Top Ten publication points out that failing to apply the latest patches can leave a system open to being exploited by malicious actors who target known vulnerabilities.

The challenge there is that even for organizations who are performing regular patching, sources such as the Cyentia Institute (www.cyentia.com) have pointed out that organizations' remediation capacity—their ability to patch and otherwise remediate vulnerabilities—is subpar. Organizations on average can only remediate 1 out of 10 new vulnerabilities per month, placing them in a perpetual situation where vulnerability backlogs continue to grow exponentially, demonstrating

why others such as Ponemon and Rezilion found (www.rezilion.com/
wp-content/uploads/2022/09/Ponemon-Rezilion-Report-Final
.pdf) that organizations have vulnerability backlogs ranging from
several hundred thousand to millions. See Figure 3.2.

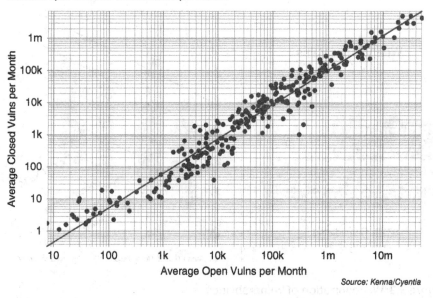

Ration of open to closed vulnerabilities per month.

Source: Kenna/Cyentia

Figure 3.2 Ratio of monthly open to closed vulnerabilities
Source: Wade Baker / 2023 / (www.linkedin.com/feed/update/urn:li:activity:
7071571847460311040) / last accessed on 19 January 2024.

Couple that with findings from Qualys on attackers' abilities to
exploit vulnerabilities 30 percent faster than organizations can remediate them, and it's a recipe for disaster—remember, attackers only
need to be right once (see Figure 3.3).

Issues cited include a lack of regular patching as well as using unsupported operating systems and firmware, meaning that these items
simply don't have patches available and are no longer supported by
vendors. I would personally add the need for organizations to ensure
that they're making use of secure open source components and using
the latest versions, which is also something that many organizations
struggle with and which is helping contribute to the increase in software supply chain attacks.

We will also discuss extensively in Chapter 5, "Vulnerability Scoring and Software Identification," how organizations should prioritize

known exploited vulnerabilities (e.g., CISA KEV) and vulnerabilities that are highly probable to be exploited (e.g., Exploit Prediction Scoring System [EPSS]; https://resilientcyber.substack.com/p/a-look-at-the-exploit-prediction). CISA and the NSA make similar recommendations in their guidance.

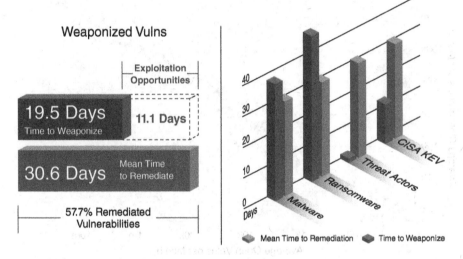

Figure 3.3 Weaponization of vulnerabilities

Source: Qualys TRURISK Threat Report 2023 (www.qualys.com/forms/tru-research-report) / last accessed on 19 January 2024.

Bypass of System Access Controls

We've discussed the need for access controls quite a bit, but some situations allow malicious actors to bypass system access controls. The guidance specifically points out examples such as collecting hashes for authentication information like pass-the-hash (PtH) attacks, and then using that information to escalate privileges and access systems in an unauthorized manner.

Weak or Misconfigured Multifactor Authentication Methods

In this misconfiguration, we again see CISA and the NSA discuss the risk of PtH-type attacks. They point out that despite the use of multifactor authentication (MFA) such as smart cards and tokens on many government/DoD networks, there's still a password hash for the account, and malicious actors can use the hash to gain unauthorized access if MFA isn't enforced or properly configured. This problem, of course, can exist in commercial systems as well, where YubiKeys or digital form factors and authentication tools are used.

Lack of Phishing-Resistant MFA

Despite the industry-wide push for MFA for quite some time, we face the stark reality that not all MFA types are created equal. This misconfiguration and weakness points to the presence of MFA types that are not "phishing-resistant," meaning they're vulnerable to attacks such as subscriber identity module (SIM) swapping. CISA directs readers to resources such as their fact sheet "Implementing Phishing-Resistant MFA" (www.cisa.gov/sites/default/files/publications/fact-sheet-implementing-phishing-resistant-mfa-508c.pdf).

Insufficient Access Control Lists on Network Shares and Services

It's no secret that data is the primary thing malicious actors are after in most cases, so it isn't a surprise to see insufficiently secured network shares and services on this list. The guidance states that attackers are using comments, OSS tooling, and custom malware to identify and exploit exposed and insecure data stores.

We, of course, see this occur with on-premises data stores and services too. But the trend has accelerated with the adoption of cloud computing and the rampant presence of misconfigured storage services by users, coupled with cheap and extensive cloud storage, enabling attackers to walk away with stunning amounts of data in terms of both the data's size and the number of individuals impacted.

The guidance also emphasizes that attackers not only can steal data, but that they can also use it for other nefarious purposes like intelligence gathering for future attacks, extortion, identification of credentials to abuse, and much more.

Poor Credential Hygiene

Credential compromise remains a primary attack vector, with sources such as Verizon's DBIR citing compromised credentials being involved in over half of all attacks. The guidance specifically calls out issues such as easily crackable passwords or cleartext password disclosure, both of which can be used by attackers to compromise environments and organizations.

We would add that with the advent of the cloud and the push for declarative infrastructure-as-code and for machine identities and authentication, we've seen an even more explosive abuse of secrets, which often includes credentials and is cited well in sources like security vendor GitGuardian's "The State of Secrets Sprawl" report (https://res.cloudinary.com/da8kiytlc/image/upload/v1646148528/GitGuardian_StateOfSecretsSprawl2022.pdf), which one of the authors discussed in "Keeping secrets in a devsecops cloud-native world" (www.csoonline.com/article/572425/keeping-secrets-in-a-devsecops-cloud-native-world.html).

This problem is also why we continue to see vendors implement secret management capabilities into their platforms and offerings. This continues to impact even the most competent digital organizations as well, such as Samsung, who saw over 6,000 secret keys exposed in their source code leak.

Unrestricted Code Execution

This one is straightforward, with the recognition that attackers are looking to run arbitrary malicious payloads on systems and networks. Unverified and unauthorized programs pose significant risks as they can execute malicious code on a system or endpoint and lead to its compromise, facilitating lateral movement and the spread of malicious software across enterprise networks. The guidance mentions that this code can take various forms, such as executables, dynamic link libraries, HTML applications, and macros in office applications.

Mitigations

For the sake of brevity, we won't be laying out all of the recommended mitigations in this article, but we definitely recommend that those interested read the source document from the NSA/CISA. Note that several of the recommendations are specific to the assessed environments (e.g., Windows-specific).

The mitigations are broken out into two sections: one aimed at network defenders, and the other at software manufacturers/suppliers.

We wanted to spend some time on the supplier angle, because it aligns with the language of the latest National Cybersecurity Strategy (which one of the authors has covered in the article `https://resilientcyber` `.substack.com/p/striving-towards-an-implementing`) when it comes to pushing the onus for mitigating vulnerabilities onto those best positioned to do something about it (i.e., the least-cost avoider in economic speak).

Rather than the burden of vulnerabilities falling on customers and consumers, software suppliers, in many cases, are arguably better positioned and equipped to address them, rather than externalize that cost/risk onto downstream customers and consumers.

The NSA/CISA publication once again points to their secure-by-design/default publication titled "Shifting the Balance of Cybersecurity Risk: Principles and Approaches for Secure by Design Software" (`www.cisa.gov/resources-tools/resources/secure-by-design-and-default`).

So, let's walk through some of the recommended mitigations for suppliers.

Default Configurations of Software Applications

The NSA/CISA publication points to recommendations such as embedding security controls into product architecture from the start *and* throughout the software development life cycle (SDLC). It references the NIST Secure Software Development Framework (SSDF), which we discuss in Chapter 11, "Secure-by-Design." It also calls for security features to be provided "out of the box" and to be accompanied by "loosening guides."

Of course, this aligns with recent heat that some vendors, such as Microsoft and other cloud service providers (CSPs), have taken from industry and government leaders for charging for logging tier capabilities, leaving customers in the dark during widespread incidents unless they had the right licensing tier/subscription. The concept of loosening guides puts the onus on suppliers to produce secure products, rather than customers and consumers needing to use hardening guidance to make a product or system secure after purchasing it.

It, of course, is a delicate dichotomy between functionality and security, and one that has been a problem since the inception of software and digital systems. Additional recommendations include eliminating default passwords that apply universally across product lines and considering the user experience consequences of security settings.

This latter recommendation is particularly refreshing because it considers the user experience and the cognitive burden on users, which, as we know, can lead to work-arounds and behavior that violates security policies like what we see with "shadow IT," which is systems, software, and infrastructure that exists outside of the governance of the security team or department.

Improper Separation of User/Administration Privilege

This mitigation includes challenges around excessive account privileges for users and service accounts, as well as the routine use of elevated accounts when it isn't essential.

Recommendations for suppliers include designing products so that the compromise of a single security control doesn't compromise the entire system, which is commonly referred to as "limiting the blast radius." Additionally, there are recommendations to generate reports automatically on inactive administrative accounts or services.

Insufficient Network Monitoring

Here again, we see the call for software suppliers to provide high-quality audit logs to customers at no extra charge. While it's debatable what qualifies as high quality, we think most would agree that customers shouldn't be forced into scenarios where they have to cough over additional money to do things like investigate an incident or respond to a data breach.

Poor Patch Management

This misconfiguration/weakness sees mitigations in the form of embedding controls through the product architecture from the onset of development and throughout the entire SDLC, again pointing to using the SSDF, following secure coding practices, performing code reviews, and testing code to identify vulnerabilities.

There's also a call to ensure that published Common Vulnerabilities and Exposures (CVEs) from suppliers include a root cause analysis (RCA) and associated Common Weaknesses Enumeration (CWE) identification, so that the industry can perform analysis of system design flaws and seek to systematically resolve them. Following this approach can slow the pace of the cyclical "identify and patch" pain cycle we all know too well and allow for eliminating entire classes of vulnerabilities in systems/software.

As we've discussed previously in this chapter, customers/consumers only have the capability to remediate 1 out of 10 new vulnerabilities a month, and vulnerability backlogs are ballooning out of control from hundreds of thousands to even millions of un-remediated vulnerabilities in large complex enterprises. Until we begin to resolve systemic vulnerabilities and weaknesses at their source, this isn't likely to change and will continue to leave organizations drowning in vulnerability backlogs, cognitive overload, and burnout. When the attacker only needs to be right once, sitting on a trove of hundreds of thousands to millions of vulnerabilities makes their chances of getting lucky high.

Wrapping up the CIS Misconfigurations Guidance

While on the surface misconfigurations and weaknesses may seem intuitive to security professionals, the reality is that these issues continue to wreak havoc across the IT/cybersecurity landscape, contributing to the majority of data breaches and security incidents. As modern IT systems only become more complex, the idea of simply doing the "basics" continues to become more elusive due to complexity, coupled with human factors such as cognitive overload.

That said, by striving to address the misconfigurations and weaknesses discussed in this guidance, consumers can mitigate some of the largest attack vectors in their environments that lead to compromises from malicious actors. Likewise, if software suppliers focus on addressing the issues identified in the NSA/CISA publication, they can systemically drive down common misconfigurations and weaknesses that leave a wake of security incidents across downstream consumers and customers.

CIS Benchmarks

Another critical and widely recognized resource for secure configuration of software and products is the Center for Internet Security (CIS) Benchmarks. These benchmarks are prescriptive guidance for secure configuration over 25 vendor product families, and they are created in a consensus-based model of collaboration between cybersecurity experts and the vendors themselves. As of this writing, the benchmarks number over 100 different secure configuration guidelines.

The CIS Benchmark community includes over 12,000 IT and cybersecurity professionals who collaborate and contribute to the CIS Benchmarks. The CIS Benchmark portfolio ranges from a variety of products and software such as operating systems, cloud infrastructure and services, desktop and server software, mobile devices, network devices, and even multifunctioning print devices.

Like many approaches to security, the CIS Benchmarks have various levels/profiles, depending on the rigor needed and use case. They use a Level 1, Level 2, and STIG profile tiering of their benchmarks. Level 1 is a base recommendation that's typically easier to implement and won't significantly impede the performance of a system or software or impact business functionality. Level 2 profiles rally around the long-standing "defense-in-depth" cybersecurity best practice and are aimed at higher assurance environments with more rigorous security requirements. It is stated that Level 2 profiles can negatively impact systems, software, and business if not properly implemented because the configurations can impede the system's performance in some cases. The final tier of the CIS profiles is the STIG profile, which is used in the DoD for securely configuring systems and software.

Given the potential impact to production environments and business operations, CIS recommends that organizations initially apply their chosen CIS Benchmark(s) to test environments to assess the potential impact prior to applying them in production.

Many organizations and industries cite the CIS Benchmarks as part of security and compliance requirements, requiring systems and environments to be configured in accordance with the CIS Benchmarks. The benchmarks range across some of the most popular vendors and software such as Microsoft Windows, Linux, VMware, and Kubernetes, and major CSPs such as AWS, Microsoft Azure, and Google Cloud.

Much like the DISA STIGs discussed in the next section, many security vendors have released tooling to help aid with the implementation of the CIS Benchmarks, as well as conducting assessments to verify the compliance posture of systems and software with the benchmarks. Increasingly with virtualized computing such as virtual machines and cloud with machine images and instances, providers have also begun releasing "hardened" images, which are preconfigured to align with CIS Benchmark configurations in advance, to help expedite the compliance efforts of customers and consumers.

DISA Security Technical Implementation Guides

Unlike the CIS Benchmarks that are developed by commercial industry, the DoD Defense Information Systems Agency (DISA)

Security Technical Implementation Guides (STIGs) are developed by the DoD entity known as DISA. They focus on secure configurations for hardware and software that are used as part of DoD IT networks, systems, and data.

DISA STIGs number in the hundreds, and like the CIS Benchmarks, range across software, routers, operating systems, and other devices. STIGs are used to ensure that software and systems used by the DoD are hardened beyond the default vendor configurations. As we have discussed, default vendor configurations often focus on usability and customer experience, sometimes at the expense of more secure default configurations.

For higher assurance and regulated environments such as the DoD, that balance may look different due to a lower risk tolerance, warranting more secure configurations and implementations.

DISA STIGs follow a quarterly update and release cycle; however, the schedule can change, depending on the threat landscape. They often are updated based on activities such as major version changes for software or products, as well as the emergence of new vulnerabilities that must be addressed to mitigate risk to DoD systems and data.

Much like the CIS Benchmarks, DISA STIGs have varying compliance levels. These come in the form of Severity Category Codes (CATs) and go from 1 to 3. CAT 1 compliance levels are focused on the configurations that pose the most risk in terms of exploitation and impact. CAT 2 includes vulnerabilities that can potentially result in a security issue, and CAT 3 vulnerabilities are often considered low risk and low severity but could impact the defenses of a system, network, or data if not resolved.

The DoD and DISA have various tools they use and offer to facilitate the implementation and assessment of STIGs in DoD environments. These include tools such as the Security Content Automation Protocol (SCAP) Compliance Checker (SCC), which can help with assessing systems for compliance with the STIG and implementation gaps, as well as the Assured Compliance Assessment Solution (ACAS), which can help with scanning networks and environments to identify the STIG compliance level of devices and systems in the environment. Additionally, several proprietary software vendors and security tools have rolled out support for DISA STIGs, allowing DoD system owners and security practitioners to conduct assessments for STIG compliance and automate activities with implementing STIG configurations.

Summary

In this chapter, we discussed the role of secure configurations. While known vulnerabilities can lead to exploitation and attacks, so can misconfigurations or the lack of secure configurations, which is especially prevalent in cloud-native environments. We covered industry-leading guidance such as the CIS Benchmarks and DISA STIGs, as well as CISA and the NSA's publication on the Top Ten cybersecurity misconfigurations. In the next chapter, we will discuss the concept of continuous vulnerability management, and how vulnerability management needs to be an ongoing and iterative activity.

4 Continuous Vulnerability Management

Vulnerability management is a constant activity, not a static snapshot in time. New vulnerabilities emerge, configurations change, assets are exposed, permissions are modified, and the list goes on. A static snapshot–in-time approach to vulnerability management will leave you blind to the dynamic risk landscape in which we operate.

However, that's exactly how many organizations have traditionally approached the activity of vulnerability management: performing time-boxed activities, such as vulnerability scans, at intervals such as monthly, quarterly, or even annually, and having a false sense of security using this approach.

Meanwhile, malicious actors are continuously seeking to identify vulnerabilities, exploit weaknesses, and compromise vulnerable systems, software, and products. In fact, continuous vulnerability management is even listed as a Center for Internet Security (CIS) Critical Security Control, currently number 7 on the list of controls in CIS Critical Security Controls version 8. This harsh reality requires a more dynamic, iterative, and ongoing approach to vulnerability management, and that's where continuous monitoring (ConMon) comes into play.

Modern vulnerability management programs take into account the dynamic nature of the landscape. They are implementing processes and technologies, underpinned by competent expertise to facilitate this ongoing activity.

In this chapter, we discuss aspects of ConMon for vulnerability management, as well as some technologies and resources on the topic, and why this approach is critical for modern vulnerability management programs.

CIS Control 7—Continuous Vulnerability Management

As mentioned in the chapter's introduction, continuous vulnerability management is listed as control number 7 in CIS Critical Security Controls v. 8. Within that control are various sub-controls that we will discuss in this chapter, as well as the details of what performing these activities are and why they are critical to mitigating organizational risk and operating an effective modern vulnerability management program.

Before diving into the specifics of this control and the associated sub-controls and activities, let's look at the official CIS overview of the control:

> *Develop a plan to continuously assess and track vulnerabilities on all enterprise assets within the enterprise's infrastructure, to remediate, and minimize, the window of opportunity for attackers. Monitor public and private industry sources for new threat and vulnerability information.*

CIS points out that it's necessary not only to perform continuous vulnerability management due to new vulnerabilities emerging, threats becoming present, and configuration changes introducing risk, but also to have a detailed understanding of the organization's risk posture over time and to track the effectiveness of vulnerability management and remediation activities.

CIS proposes an iterative process of seven specific activities, which should be established and then repeated indefinitely, to ensure that organizational vulnerabilities are continuously addressed. Let's take a look at each of these activities.

Establish and Maintain a Vulnerability Management Process

While this one may seem intuitive, the reality is that many organizations don't have a codified and adhered-to vulnerability management process. Vulnerabilities may be identified and addressed with an ad hoc cadence without a defined approach, schedule, and repeatable process. The vulnerability management process should be documented and encompass *all* enterprise assets, which may include endpoints, servers, cloud environments and instances, and more, depending on the nature of the enterprise's technology stack.

These documented processes should be regularly revisited. CIS recommends these processes be undertaken annually or when significant changes occur, to ensure that no changes need to be made to account for shifts within the enterprise, technologies, and organizational operations.

We also recommend revisiting the processes to ensure that they are leveraging current industry-best practices, resources, and methodologies as they evolve. For example, if your vulnerability management process still revolves around legacy vulnerability base scoring systems (e.g., Common Vulnerability Scoring System [CVSS]) for prioritization, it might be time to modernize your vulnerability management process.

Establish and Maintain a Remediation Process

Having a vulnerability management process is great, and of course, is key to identifying vulnerabilities. But without a comprehensive and effective remediation process in place, you've simply identified risk and aren't doing anything to address it.

CIS recommends developing a risk-based remediation strategy that's documented and reviewed frequently for improvements. This remediation strategy can be revisited to see how the organization is doing on resolving identified vulnerabilities and what improvements and optimizations can be implemented. Organizations should also ensure this strategy isn't created in a vacuum.

While the security team often identifies the risk, they very rarely actually "own" the risk. System owners, developers, and engineers have a system-specific context and need to be engaged in both documenting the remediation process and performing the actual remediation activities.

Perform Automated Operating System Patch Management

As we've discussed, the pace of vulnerabilities is only accelerating, and the idea that organizations can do activities like patch management effectively in a manual fashion, in an enterprise of any significant size and complexity, is simply impractical.

This is why CIS and industry-standard best practices recommend performing automated operating systems (OSs) patch management. They recommend performing this monthly at a minimum but ideally at a faster cadence. Minimizing the time between a patch becoming available and its implementation decreases the potential window of exploitation, where malicious actors can take advantage of known vulnerabilities that have a patch available but go unmitigated.

For operating systems, there are various vendor and well-known tools that can help automate this activity and streamline OS patch management in complex environments, as long as the organization has an accurate asset inventory and a mature patch management process. As we discussed in Chapter 2, "Patch Management," most organizations struggle to have an accurate and maintained asset inventory.

Perform Automated Application Patch Management

Much like operating systems, applications require automated patch management as well, whether it's applying patches for proprietary vendor applications or using the latest version of an open source software (OSS) application. Organizations also need to leverage automation to keep the pervasive footprint of OSS dependencies and components up-to-date. We've discussed some tools in Chapter 2 like Renovate and Dependabot, which can help automate the process of keeping dependencies updated for OSS components.

Studies from organizations like Sonatype have found that organizations routinely use outdated components, even when more secure updated components are available, which is often due to the challenges of keeping dependencies updated at scale. Developers even refer to this activity as "dependency hell" due to the frustration with trying to manage dependencies in complex modern applications.

On the proprietary software front, having vendor applications in your environment that have known vulnerabilities but remain unpatched can be a recipe for disaster, leaving vulnerabilities ripe for exploitation by attackers. Again, the key is minimizing the exploitation window, which, in turn, can minimize organizational risk.

However, studies demonstrate that, as an industry, we have known vulnerable software, applications, and components throughout our environments even when patches are available, often due to the challenges of doing patch management at scale across an expansive portfolio of proprietary and open source software.

Perform Automated Vulnerability Scans of Internal Enterprise Assets

A key part of being able to remediate vulnerabilities is understanding they exist. CIS recommends performing automated vulnerability scans of internal enterprise assets on a quarterly basis or more frequently. We suggest doing it on a much more frequent basis, such as weekly. New vulnerabilities emerge regularly, and depending on when a vulnerability is published, identified, and eventually remediated, a quarterly scan approach could leave exposed assets vulnerable for several months.

One key distinction that CIS makes is between internal enterprise assets and externally exposed assets, which we will touch upon next. While there is merit to the approach of focusing on externally exposed enterprise assets, internal assets that are vulnerable also pose risks. For example, once a malicious actor is inside a network or enterprise, they often look to move laterally across vulnerable and misconfigured assets to impact additional systems and get to sensitive data they are after.

The cybersecurity industry has increasingly moved to adopt zero-trust methodologies, which do away with the concept of a hardened perimeter and a "squishy" vulnerable internal environment. Every vulnerable system is part of the potential attack surface.

Perform Automated Vulnerability Scans of Externally Exposed Enterprise Assets

Next up on the list of CIS activities is performing automated vulnerability scans of externally exposed enterprise assets, meaning assets that are exposed to the Internet and reachable either publicly or more broadly than strictly "internal" assets. Given that these assets are often reachable from public actors over the Internet, they are potentially at more risk than internal systems that might reside in private IP address ranges or be behind compensating security measures like web application firewalls (WAFs) and boundary protection devices. For this reason, these assets often get prioritized for vulnerability remediation over internal assets.

Remediate Detected Vulnerabilities

Great; you've created a vulnerability management and remediation process, implemented automated patch management for operating systems and applications, and implemented automated vulnerability scans to continuously identify new vulnerabilities on your assets, as well as to understand trends associated with the effectiveness of your vulnerability management process. Now you must do the work, meaning you must remediate the vulnerabilities that you've identified.

CIS lists the activity of remediating detected vulnerabilities using your processes and tools on a monthly or more frequent basis. Obviously the smaller the remediation window, the narrower the exploitation window, but we know that most organizations are dealing with constraints like competing priorities, incentives, and resources.

Furthermore, organizations with mature vulnerability management processes should be utilizing vulnerability intelligence sources that we've discussed such as the CISA Known Exploited Vulnerabilities (KEV) Catalog, as well as exploitation probability using the Forum of Incident Response and Security Teams (FIRST) Exploit Prediction Scoring System (EPSS). Organizations should also be coupling this with organization-specific context for assets, such as the data types involved, system and organizational criticality, and any compensating controls that might be in place to mitigate risks.

Continuous Monitoring Practices

Another cross-reference to continuous vulnerability management is NIST SP 800-53, Security and Privacy Controls for Information Systems and Organizations (https://csrc.nist.gov/pubs/sp/800/53/r5/upd1/final). As of this writing, this publication is in its fifth revision. NIST SP 800-53 is used by various compliance schemes and frameworks, such as NIST SP 800-171, the Federal Risk and Authorization Management Program (FedRAMP), and Cybersecurity Maturity Model Certification (CMMC). NIST SP 800-53 is a catalog of security and privacy controls for information systems and organizations to protect operations, assets, and individuals.

In this section, we take a look at some of the NIST 800-53 controls and control families that focus on vulnerability management activities and

ConMon. These controls also cross-reference other frameworks like the Cloud Security Alliance (CSA) Cloud Controls Matrix (CCM), and the CIS Critical Security Controls that we discussed in the previous section.

NIST SP 800-53 lists CA-7: Continuous Monitoring, which falls within the Security Assessment Authorization control family. While the CA-7 control itself focuses on broader continuous monitoring, including security controls and the overall cybersecurity program, it also focuses on vulnerabilities and vulnerability management.

In NIST SP 800-53, vulnerability scanning falls under the Risk Assessment control family and is titled RA-5: Vulnerability Monitoring and Scanning (`https://csf.tools/reference/nist-sp-800-53/r5/ra/ra-5`). It includes controls and control enhancements that increase through the system categorizations of low, moderate, and high. In this section, we look at some activities within the SP 800-53 RA-5 control, as well as some of the additional activities captured in the control enhancements (CEs), which tend to be used for more sensitive systems, such as those categorized as moderate or high.

RA-5 involves some fundamental activities related to vulnerability monitoring and scanning, including regularly monitoring and scanning for vulnerabilities in both the system and the hosted applications at an organizationally defined frequency. Much like CIS, there are also calls to automate parts of the vulnerability management process using tools to enumerate platforms, software flaws, and misconfigurations, as well as the potential vulnerability impact (often discussed as severity). NIST recommends performing these activities at an organization-defined frequency based on the security categorization of the systems in scope. Any tools used as part of vulnerability monitoring should regularly be updated, as new vulnerabilities emerge and new vulnerability scanning methods emerge as well, to ensure that no known vulnerabilities go unidentified.

The frequency and comprehensiveness of vulnerability scans should be dictated by the security categorization of the system per NIST. This is based on Federal Information Processing Standards (FIPS) 199, the security categorization process, but in industry terms it should be driven by the business criticality of the system(s) involved and the sensitivity of the data they involve as well. Systems that are critical to business continuity and revenue will drive tighter frequencies of activities than noncritical business systems, which may not contain sensitive data, for example.

While organizations might use traditional vulnerability scanning tools for endpoints and servers, increasingly organizations are using tools like static application security testing (SAST), dynamic application security testing (DAST), secrets scanning, and more, integrated into continuous integration/continuous delivery (CI/CD) pipelines and automated as part of the software development life cycle (SDLC). These activities integrate vulnerability scanning into every software release, especially prior to the introduction to production environments or products. This ties to industry-wide themes, such as shifting security "left" in the SDLC and application security and product security.

RA-5 includes various control enhancements, such as updating tool capabilities, frequency of scanning, and depth of coverage. It also includes automating trend analysis to determine if vulnerability backlogs are trending downward, representing a positive impact, or growing, depicting a struggle to keep up with the vulnerability footprint and hygiene of an environment. NIST also recommends reviewing historical audit logs to determine if a vulnerability that has been identified in systems has been previously exploited.

As we discussed in Chapter 3, "Secure Configuration," it isn't just known vulnerabilities that can introduce risk to organizations. The need for securely configured systems, products, and software is also crucial. This is why NIST also lists CM-3: Configuration Change Control as a related control to continuous monitoring. This control involves activities such as ensuring system configurations are controlled, reviewing and documenting proposed configuration changes, and capturing and regularly reviewing configuration changes. Unauthorized configuration changes to a system can introduce vulnerabilities, which attackers can exploit.

Much like the previous controls we discussed, CM-3 has various control enhancements as well. These include controls such as automated notification and documentation of system changes and even blocking changes from occurring until authorized. They also include activities such as ensuring a security representative is part of groups like a configuration change control board (CCB), and implementing an automated security response to unauthorized system changes.

We would like to note that we aren't fans of CCBs in large complex environments with multiple independent development and product teams. A CCB often functions as a bottleneck, slowing down development velocity, as well as being sidestepped due to being too cumbersome. The CCB is often disconnected directly from the work and the context of proposed changes, and therefore is often not in a position to be able to valuably weigh in on proposed changes. That said, there is undoubtedly a need for governance and oversight of configuration changes; otherwise vulnerabilities can emerge and risk can be introduced.

Summary

In this chapter, we looked at the concept of continuous vulnerability management and continuous monitoring. We reviewed examples like NIST and related control baselines and frameworks that introduce fundamental activities such as continuous monitoring, vulnerability management, and continuous configuration management. In modern dynamic IT and software environments, changes are occurring rapidly, new vulnerabilities are being discovered and disclosed, and the legacy approach of snapshot-in-time activities related to vulnerability and configuration management is insufficient to address organizational risk. Organizations must have continuous vulnerability and configuration management processes and innovative tooling in place to keep up with the evolving threat landscape.

5

Vulnerability Scoring and Software Identification

No conversation about vulnerability management would be complete without discussing vulnerability scoring methods. *Vulnerability scoring* is used to assign values, either quantitative or qualitative, to aid in vulnerability prioritization and remediation efforts. The cybersecurity industry has a variety of vulnerability scoring methodologies in current use. Some have been around for years, whereas others were more recently developed and adopted in the ecosystem.

In this chapter, we discuss both the pros and cons of various scoring systems. Some of them might be improved and may lend themselves to automation, whereas others are more valuable for manual analysis and scoring. As the landscape of vulnerabilities continues to grow and evolve, so does the vulnerability scoring ecosystem, as organizations seek more efficient and effective methods to allocate resources when it comes to managing vulnerabilities.

Common Vulnerability Scoring System

First up in our discussion of vulnerability scoring systems is the widely used, well-known, and long-established Common Vulnerability Scoring System (CVSS). CVSS originated in 2005 with its initial version 1 and was shortly thereafter adopted by the Forum of Incident Response and Security Teams (FIRST), where it now resides as part of the CVSS Special Interest Group (SIG). Check out www.first.org/cvss for more on this.

Since its release in 2005, CVSS has undergone various iterations and, as of this writing, is in the process of its v4.0 release. Previous versions include 2 in 2007, 3.0 in 2015, and 3.1 in 2019, all addressing critiques and making improvements from previous versions, as it looks to bolster its value to the community as one of the leading vulnerability scoring methodologies. CVSS SIG co-chairs Dave Dugal and Dale Rich published a presentation discussing the chronology of CVSS, challenges and goals of v4.0, and best practices for effectively making use of CVSS (see https://csrc.nist.gov/csrc/media/Presentations/2023/update-on-cvss-4-0/jan-25-2023-ssca-dugal-rich.pdf).

Before we dive into CVSS, how it works or can be used, as well as some of its critiques, it is worth noting that prior to CVSS the industry used incompatible and custom rating systems to try to communicate vulnerability severities. Despite many valid critiques of CVSS and how it is often used, it is inarguably the most formalized and widely adopted system for vulnerability scoring in the industry as of this writing.

In terms of adoption and use, CVSS has been used by the National Institute of Standards and Technology (NIST) for years. NIST's National Vulnerability Database (NVD) is the most widely used vulnerability database in the ecosystem and is leveraged by everything from small organizations and vendors to the U.S. federal government and Department of Defense (DoD) and international entities as well.

CVSS is in the process of moving to version 4.0, so let's examine it and some of the key differences from previous versions.

CVSS 4.0 at a Glance

At its core, the aim of CVSS is to output a numerical score indicating the severity of a vulnerability among the broader collection of known vulnerabilities.

There are four metric groups in CVSS 4.0: Base, Threat, Environmental, and Supplemental, each of which we will discuss further very soon. The Base score is based on the intrinsic characteristics of a vulnerability and doesn't change over time.

Unlike the immutability of the Base score, the Threat metric can adjust the Base severity based on factors related to threats, including the existence of either proof-of-concept exploits, which are non-harmful and used to demonstrate the existence of a security weakness or full-blown known exploitation in the wild.

After the Threat metric group is the Environmental metric group, which customizes the Base and Threat severities based on the unique aspects of the computing environment and architecture in which the vulnerability exists. It also can include factors that influence the score such as organizations having mitigating controls in place, or the business context on the criticality of the system(s) that the vulnerability could impact if exploited.

Last up is the Supplemental metric, which allows for the consideration of extrinsic attributes of a vulnerability to further enhance context and make scoring more accurate.

Because the four metric groups often rely on information known by different parties, it is common for the Base and Supplemental metrics to be provided by the organization that maintains the vulnerable product or a neutral third party such as security researchers. On the other hand, information such as threat and environmental context is known by the impacted organization or consumer, so these metrics often factor into scoring.

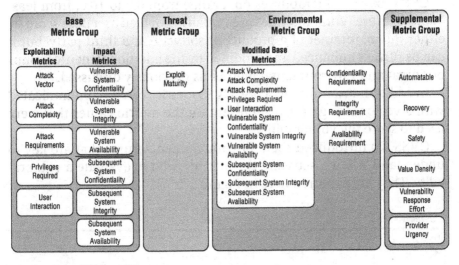

Figure 5.1: CVSS metrics

Figure 5.1 shows each of the four metric groups and their set of metrics that are taken into consideration to facilitate scoring. As we mentioned previously, the Base metric group has intrinsic characteristics for a vulnerability that do not change over time or across environments and organizations. The Base metric group includes two subgroups: Exploitability metrics and Impact metrics. Exploitability is focused on the difficulty of exploiting a vulnerability and the technical means to do so, whereas Impact metrics are focused on the direct consequence of a successful exploit.

The second metric group is Threat, which has characteristics specific to vulnerability and associated threats that can and do change over time, but they aren't necessarily tied to a specific environment where the vulnerability belongs. This group focuses on things such as the existence of exploits, either as proof-of-concepts or active-known exploitation.

Environmental metrics are the third metric group and are focused on a specific user's environment. It serves as one of the best metric groups to make vulnerability scoring organizationally specific and actionable. It considers factors such as mitigating controls and business criticality of impacted systems and software to influence scoring.

The fourth and final metric is the Supplemental metric group, which factors in extrinsic attributes of a vulnerability. This lets consumers add significant local context to the scoring and analysis.

CVSS scores vulnerabilities on a range from 0.0 to 10.0, from least to most severe. Vulnerabilities are initially provided as a **Base** score by either the maintainer of a product or software or a third party, but it can be further enhanced and modified by the additional metric groups of Threat and Environmental metrics as previously discussed.

In addition to a numeric score, CVSS metrics can be communicated with a vector string of text representing the metric values that were used to score the vulnerability.

CVSS 4.0 introduced the following nomenclatures that are key to understand when discussing the metrics used to evaluate a vulnerability. They are captured here in Figure 5.2.

CVSS Nomenclature	CVSS Metrics Used
CVSS-B	Base metrics
CVSS-BE	Base and Environmental metrics
CVSS-BT	Base and Threat metrics
CVSS-BTE	Base, Threat, Environmental metrics

Figure 5.2: CVSS nomenclature

This nomenclature helps quickly communicate the metrics used to analyze and score a vulnerability and can be captured in the vector string as well such as AV:N/AC:L/Au:S/C:P/I:P/A:N, which can demonstrate things such as attack vector and complexity in a shorthand fashion. This helps consumers understand what metrics were used to produce the output score. For example, is it just a Base metric (e.g., CVSS-B), or does it include Threat and Environmental metrics (e.g., CVSS-BTE)?

While the NVD provides the Base score for CVEs, the CVSS consumer is responsible for the Threat and Environmental metrics, because only the consumers have the context related to their specific systems and environments. It isn't possible for NVD to have insight on things such as system criticality, data sensitivity, and compensating controls like the CVSS consumer does, so those metrics to further refine scoring are best suited for the CVSS consumer to apply. The below image demonstrates the process and workflow for a new CVE to make it into the NIST NVD (see Figure 5.3).

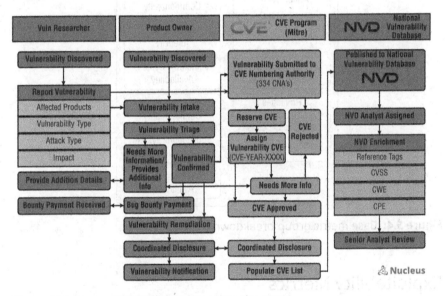

Figure 5.3 How a CVE Makes it's Way Into the NVD

Source: Patrick Garrity of Nucleus Security

If the Threat and Environmental metrics are not used, the resulting score defaults to a "not defined" value, making it easy to understand what metrics went into the resulting score by ensuring the metrics are represented in the final CVSS string.

Now that you have a high-level understanding of the various metrics and nomenclature, let's take a deeper dive into those metrics.

Base Metrics

As discussed, the Base metric group represents the intrinsic characteristics of a vulnerability, and they do not change over time or environments. Within that Base metric group are two sets of metrics: Exploitability and Impact. See Figure 5.4.

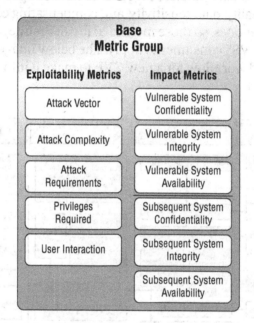

Figure 5.4: Base metric group breakdown

Exploitability Metrics

Exploitability metrics are the characteristics of the "thing that is vulnerable," as defined in the CVSS 4.0 specification. They're often referred to as the *vulnerable system*, which means exploitability metrics get assessed in relation to the vulnerable system. Base metrics also make assumptions regarding what a malicious actor knows about weaknesses of the target system and its associated configurations. Such weaknesses may include the following:

Attack Vector First up under Exploitability metrics is the Attack Vector (AV). This is the context of how a vulnerability is exploitable.

The metric value is influenced by various factors, most notably how accessible the systems are. CVSS 4.0 orients around four specific metric values for AV: Network, Adjacent, Local, and Physical. These four values indicate if the vulnerable system is exploitable over a network, such as being remotely exploitable if connected to the Internet, or if it is only exploitable over a specific networking protocol or network proximity (adjacent) such as with Bluetooth, or exploitable only from a specific IP subnet or local area network (LAN).

Attack Complexity   This complexity represents actions a malicious actor must take to evade or circumvent existing built-in security controls or mitigations to get a working exploit. It represents the level of complexity of the attack and is directly tied to actions the attacks must take to overcome mitigations or protective controls set in place to impede their attack. Potential values include Low or High, with Low being no measurable action required to exploit the vulnerability and High requiring an active evasion or circumvention of measures that may hinder the attack.

Attack Requirements   In many cases, specific deployment or execution conditions or variables must exist for the attack to be enabled; this is represented by the Attack Requirements. Unlike Attack Complexity, these requirement conditions exist naturally and are not mitigating controls intentionally set in place to impede attacks. Their value may be either Present or None, indicating whether or not specific conditions must be present for the attack to succeed.

Privileges Required   In many vulnerability exploitations, the attackers need specific privileges in the environment. Privileges Required represents that scenario. The potential values are None, Low, and High, with None representing scenarios where an attacker can exploit the vulnerability without privileges and escalate from there, up to High, which represents scenarios requiring administrator-level control to be successful.

User Interaction   It isn't uncommon for attacks to require unwitting involvement from a human user. This is captured in the User Interaction metric. Potential values include None, Passive, and Active, with None being no interaction needed from a user, Passive being limited interaction from a user, and Active requiring a user to perform specific actions to enable the exploitation.

The next group of metrics under the Base metric group is Impact metrics. These metrics capture the effects of a successfully exploited vulnerability. Let's look at the Impact metrics.

For anyone familiar with the longstanding Confidentiality, Integrity, and Availability (CIA) triad in cybersecurity, it should come as no surprise that the first trio of metrics under the Impact metrics are Confidentiality, Integrity, and Availability:

Confidentiality   This metric measures the extent to which information access is disclosed to unauthorized users. The potential values for this metric are None, Low, and High, with either no loss of confidentiality, some loss, or a total loss. Low loss could include scenarios where the attacker can only access a subset of the information, which doesn't cause a serious system loss, whereas a High loss would have a direct and serious impact. The Confidentiality metric includes an additional metric, SC, for potential impacts to subsequent systems, for example, if a subsequent system was impacted as part of the attack.

Integrity   Next up in the CIA triad is Integrity, which CVSS defines as the trustworthiness of information. Integrity is impacted by unauthorized modifications. Potential values, again, are None, Low, and High. The impacts are similar to those with Confidentiality, in the sense of either having no loss, no serious impact, or serious consequences to the impacted system(s).

Availability   Closing out the widely popular CIA triad is Availability, which CVSS defines as loss of availability of the impacted system and can include examples such as consuming network bandwidth, exhausting system resources, and degrading system performance. Again, the metric's possible values are None, Low, and High, which represent no impact to availability, reduced performance, or a partial denial of service, or total loss of availability. All of these potential metrics can be applied to subsequent systems as well.

Threat Metrics

One significant change from CVSS 3.1 to 4.0 is the replacement of the Temporal metric group with the Threat metric group. This group consists of a single metric, Exploit Maturity (see Figure 5.5). It's essentially a measurement of the current state of exploit techniques or code availability for a specific vulnerability to which the CVE applies.

Figure 5.5: Threat metric group

As discussed previously, Exploit Maturity is based on the current state of exploit techniques or the availability of exploit code in the wild. The maturity of an exploit can have a significant influence on the likelihood of exploitation. This metric is left to the CVSS consumer to populate based on the information they have on the maturity of the exploit in the wild. Typically, organizations will utilize threat intelligence sources to provide information related to Exploit Maturity. The potential values for this metric are Unreported, Proof-of-Concept, Attacked, and Not Defined. These range from no knowledge of reported exploit attempts for the vulnerability, to a proof-of-concept publicly available but lacking known exploitation attempts, all the way to Attacked, which means threat intelligence sources can confirm attempted exploitation of the vulnerability is occurring or has already succeeded. Not Defined is for exploits where a maturity has not been explicitly provided.

Environmental Metrics

Moving on from the new Exploit Maturity metric group, next we have Environmental metrics (see Figure 5.6). This group allows CVSS consumers to customize the score using their specific organizational context. This can include information such as the criticality of the asset to the organization, mitigating controls in place, and other unique organizational factors that can and should influence the vulnerability scoring.

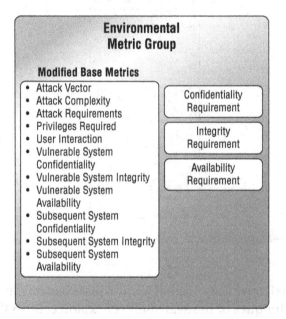

Figure 5.6: Environmental metric group

It's worth noting that currently many organizations do not make use of the Environmental metric group, which would add organization-specific context, and instead just consume CVSS Base scores from NVD. This widespread lack of environmental context leads to prioritizing vulnerabilities, which may not pose the most risk to the organization and could lead to both reduced vulnerability management effectiveness as well as wasting resources in terms of time and human capital. We discuss this further in the section on the Exploit Prediction Scoring System (EPSS), which is also often used without organization-specific context being applied.

You'll notice the Environmental metric group builds on metrics from the Base metric group. The Environmental metrics allow the CVSS consumer to customize the resulting score, depending on the importance of the asset to the organization in terms of the CIA triad we discussed previously. Each organization may have specific needs that drive the criticality of Confidentiality, Integrity, or Availability of its systems and data, and the Environmental metrics allow for that unique context.

The authors strongly recommend that organizations utilizing CVSS make use of the Environmental metric group to ensure that the scoring of vulnerabilities considers their unique organizational context and helps prioritize vulnerabilities that pose the most risk to their organization and their systems and data. The widespread lack of applying environmental context remains among the most damning critiques of the CVSS in the industry.

That said, applying environmental context per vulnerability is much easier said than done. As we have discussed, many organizations have vulnerability backlogs ranging from thousands to hundreds of thousands, and even millions. The practicality of individually assigning modified environmental context scoring across that level of vulnerabilities, using human cognition, is simply untenable for most organizations, hence the widespread use of CVSS Base scoring.

Supplemental Metrics

Last in the list of CVSS metric groups is the Supplemental metric group (see Figure 5.7), which is an optional metric group used to describe and measure additional extrinsic attributes of a vulnerability. This, like the Threat metric group, is left to the CVSS consumer to implement and determine, and it may look different for each CVSS consumer based on their unique organizational context. It is worth noting that Supplemental metrics do not have an impact on the final calculated CVSS score, but instead leave it to the CVSS consumer to assign an importance to each metric and enable them to convey additional extrinsic characteristics of the vulnerability.

Let's take a look at the available metrics in the Supplemental metric group and how they may be used:

Safety This metric represents the degree of impact to the safety of a human actor or participant who can be injured as a result of vulnerability exploitation. The metric represents the increasing convergence of software with physical systems, often referred to as *cyber-physical systems*, as well as software within critical systems in various fields such as manufacturing and medical devices, which can pose direct safety threats to human life. The potential values are Not Defined, Negligible, or Present; Negligible might include minor injuries, whereas Catastrophic might include multiple lives lost.

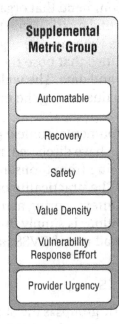

Figure 5.7: Supplemental metric group

Automatable This metric deals with the potential for exploitation activity to be automated across multiple targets by an attacker. CVSS uses the widely recognized Kill Chain (www.lockheedmar tin.com/en-us/capabilities/cyber/cyber-kill-chain.html) with an emphasis on steps 1–4, which are reconnaissance, weaponization, delivery, and exploitation. (See the section "CISA SSVC Guide" later in this chapter for more on the Kill Chain.) The potential values are Not Defined, No, and Yes. Obviously attacks that are automatable or known to already be automated and used in exploitation should be considered as part of vulnerability prioritization.

Provider Urgency While not all vulnerability communication occurs between product or software suppliers and consumers, much of it does. Utilizing provider urgency allows a CVSS consumer to account for things such as product security advisories, given that the supplier is the one best positioned to provide an assessment of urgency related to their products. Potential values are Red, Amber, Green, Clear, and Not Defined, in declining order of urgency. This particular metric may be increasingly important as we see more software supply chain attacks and malicious actors targeting software suppliers.

Recovery   Systems have varying levels of resilience and recoverability, which is represented in the Recovery metric. While some systems may have automated recovery as part of a failover or incident response, others might require manual intervention or be completely unrecoverable. The potential values for this metric represent that reality, with the options of Not Defined, Automatic, User, or Irrecoverable.

Value Density   This metric is used to describe the resources that attacks gain control over as part of the exploitation event. Potential values are Not Defined, Diffuse, and Concentrated, and represent the range of scenarios involving either a single resource or limited resources up to highly concentrated resources rich in value. The CVSS 4.0 specification mentions a central email server as a concentrated target, but other examples include an identity provider (IdP) or key management system.

Vulnerability Response Effort   Each vulnerability and exploitation brings with it a unique response effort level. The Vulnerability Response Effort metric captures this by allowing the CVSS consumer to take into consideration the level of effort required to respond. Potential values are Not Defined, Low, Moderate, and High, with impacts ranging from a trivial response effort to significant or difficult with implications for outages and service downtime.

Qualitative Severity Rating Scale

CVSS utilizes a Qualitative Severity Rating Scale to numerically rank vulnerabilities. If you've been in the cybersecurity career field for some time, you've inevitably heard organizational- or industry compliance–driven requirements around remediation timelines tied to vulnerability severities, such as seven days to remediate a critical vulnerability. These scores can be tied to Base, Threat, and Environmental scores, but as we have discussed, most organizations simply use the Base score. It is often provided to them via vulnerability scanning tools, which obtain the scores from sources such as the NIST NVD. The Qualitative Severity Rating Scale is shown in Figure 5.8.

Rating	CVSS Score
None	0.0
Low	0.1 - 3.9
Medium	4.0 - 6.9
High	7.0 - 8.9
Critical	9.0 - 10.0

Figure 5.8: Qualitative Severity Rating Scale

Vector String

One other key piece to be familiar with when working with CVSS is the use of the vector string. This is a text representation of a set of CVSS metrics. We've discussed items, such as metric groups, metric names, and possible values, and whether they were mandatory or not. These all can consolidate into a concise vector string, such as CVSS:4.0/AV:N/AC:L/AT:N/PR:H/UI:N/VC:L/VI:L/VA:N/SC:N/SI:N/SA:N.

Exploit Prediction Scoring System

While predicting the future isn't practical, emerging models such as the Exploit Prediction Scoring System (EPSS) are showing that data can drive some highly useful prioritization criteria. We know from previous discussions and elsewhere in the book that using CVSS alone for vulnerability prioritization isn't sufficient. In this section, we will take a look at the evolving EPSS model, and how it can be used to aid prioritization by projecting how likely a vulnerability is to be exploited in the next 30 days.

EPSS 3.0—Prioritizing Through Prediction

Many organizations, including the U.S. federal government and Department of Defense (DoD), utilize CVSS Severity Scores to help drive their vulnerability remediation timeline requirements. While CVSS is the most widely used vulnerability rating system for assessing the severity of vulnerabilities, it is often inappropriately used in isolation to prioritize risk from the vulnerabilities by prioritizing vulnerabilities based on their CVSS score alone, despite the reality that only 2–7 percent of vulnerabilities are ever known to be exploited in the wild, regardless of CVSS severity.

The introduction of EPSS attempts to aid in the vulnerability prioritization efforts by providing a numerical score of how likely a vulnerability is to be exploited over the next 30-day window. Oddly enough, both CVSS and EPSS are governed through FIRST but by separate SIGs.

EPSS aids practitioners and organizations who are looking to improve their vulnerability management activities. Studies have shown that organizations can only remediate between 5 and 20 percent of their vulnerabilities each month, leaving them in a situation where they are perpetually falling behind the number of published and emerging vulnerabilities due to their inability to remediate them all (https://learn-cloudsecurity.cisco.com/vulnerability-management-resources/vmc/prioritization-to-prediction-volume-8). This study was conducted by Cyentia Institute and Cisco.

Organizations aim to take approaches to prioritize vulnerabilities for remediation, but they have historically been inefficient and ineffective, all at a time when we constantly hear about the shortfall of cybersecurity talent and organizations struggling to attract and retain it. It has been found that using just a CVSS Severity Score to measure the risk of an individual vulnerability is equivalent to picking random vulnerabilities to fix, whereas focusing on vulnerabilities with actual exploitation proof or probability is far more effective at mitigating organizational risks.

A common vulnerability prioritization strategy called for in sources such as Payment Card Industry (PCI) and federal vulnerability management guidance is to remediate vulnerabilities within a predefined set of calendar days after initial detection, based on the CVSS Severity Scores. This often manifests in having *Critical* and *High* vulnerabilities, as categorized by CVSS, and prioritized for remediation within 7–30 days of initial detection. On the surface, this seems intuitive except for the issue that less than 10 percent of known vulnerabilities are actually *ever* exploited in the wild.

For example, security vendor Qualys found in their 2023 Qualys TRURISK Research Report (www.qualys.com/docs/qualys-2023-trurisk-threat-research-report.pdf) that despite there being 25,000 known vulnerabilities published to the NIST NVD in 2022, less than 5 percent of those were ever actually known to be exploited in the wild.

While organizations may prioritize vulnerabilities based on CVSS Severity Scores, those vulnerabilities may not be known to be exploited by sources such as CISA's Known Exploited Vulnerabilities (KEV) list (www.cisa.gov/known-exploited-vulnerabilities-catalog), and they may *never* be known to be exploited. While patches can also address factors such as functionality, from a vulnerability management perspective organizations are essentially spending precious time and resources remediating vulnerabilities that pose little to no risk while ignoring those that potentially do.

As an industry, we desperately need to focus on vulnerabilities that pose the most risk, and those that are likely to be exploited are a suitable place to start. This is where EPSS comes in.

Let's take a look at the EPSS 3.0 model and some of its improvements over previous versions.

EPSS 3.0

The best way to really dig into EPSS 3.0 and the evolution of EPSS overall is with the latest whitepaper titled, "Enhancing Vulnerability Prioritization: Data-Driven Exploit Predictions with Community-Driven Insights" (found at https://arxiv.org/pdf/2302.14172.pdf) that was produced by the EPSS SIG members from organizations such as Cyentia and the RAND Corporation. The EPSS team opens the discussion by citing an 82 percent performance improvement in EPSS 3.0 over previous versions as well as covering the evolving vulnerability landscape. The NIST NVD has continued to see huge growth, with a 24.3 percent increase in vulnerabilities in 2022 over 2021, totaling over 25,000 vulnerabilities in a single year. Despite this increase, organizations only have a median remediation rate of 15.5 percent, with one-fourth of the organizations remediating less than 7 percent of their open vulnerabilities per month. This creates a scenario where these organizations are perpetually drowning in increasing vulnerability backlogs, with some studies finding that the average organization has a backlog of over 100,000 vulnerabilities and climbing.

EPSS is striving to help organizations quickly prioritize these vulnerabilities by focusing on those with the highest probability of being exploited over the next 30 days. EPSS boasts the ability to help organizations minimize their burden of patching critical vulnerabilities with one-eighth of the effort of typical strategies using CVSS.

When it comes to exploits, EPSS utilizes a variety of sources such as FortiGuard, AlienVault Open Threat Exchange, the Shadowserver Foundation, and GreyNoise, which all use various techniques to identify exploitation attempts in digital environments around the globe. In addition to these sources, EPSS uses over 1,400 features for predicting exploitation activity. These include sources such as published exploit code, public vulnerability lists, offensive security tools, and the age of the vulnerability.

To prove their performance improvements with EPSS 3.0, the CVSS 3.0 performed testing to explore the increased effectiveness of the 3.0 model. They measured their performance improvement on predicting vulnerability exploitation over 30 days using the features we discussed previously, and they compared their performance results and metrics against previous EPSS versions as well as CVSS v3 Base scores.

Figure 5.9 illustrates their significant improvement. It shows all CVEs, including CVEs with scores above a threshold and CVEs that are actually exploited. As you can see, when contrasting CVSS v3.x with EPSS v1 and v2, EPSS v3 shows a significant improvement in terms of prioritizing the largest portion of exploited vulnerabilities. The black circles represent the number of vulnerabilities that need to be remediated under the given methodology, and the white circle represents the actual exploitation activity. As you can see, EPSS significantly outperformed the other models by helping users remediate the largest portion of the exploited vulnerabilities and minimize wasted resources and effort on non-exploited vulnerabilities.

Moving Forward

While the EPSS model is not perfect, it does present a strong data-driven approach to help organizations focus on vulnerabilities that pose the greatest threat based on probable exploitation activity (see Figure 5.10).

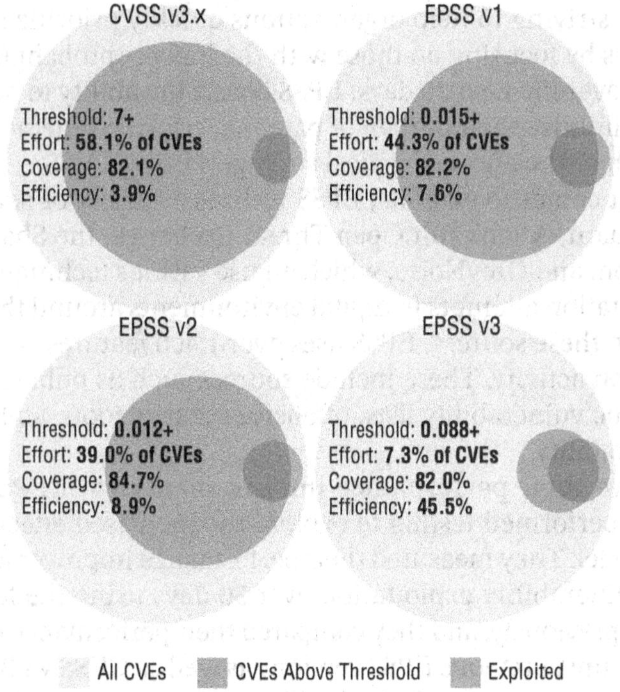

CVSS v3.x

Threshold: **7+**
Effort: **58.1% of CVEs**
Coverage: **82.1%**
Efficiency: **3.9%**

EPSS v1

Threshold: **0.015+**
Effort: **44.3% of CVEs**
Coverage: **82.2%**
Efficiency: **7.6%**

EPSS v2

Threshold: **0.012+**
Effort: **39.0% of CVEs**
Coverage: **84.7%**
Efficiency: **8.9%**

EPSS v3

Threshold: **0.088+**
Effort: **7.3% of CVEs**
Coverage: **82.0%**
Efficiency: **45.5%**

　　All CVEs　　　CVEs Above Threshold　　Exploited

Figure 5.9: CVE improvements

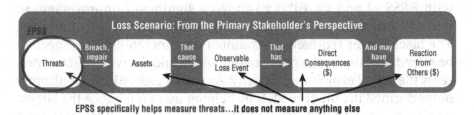

Loss Scenario: From the Primary Stakeholder's Perspective

EPSS

Threats　→ Breach, impair →　Assets　→ That cause →　Observable Loss Event　→ That has →　Direct Consequences ($)　→ And may have →　Reaction from Others ($)

EPSS specifically helps measure threats…it does not measure anything else

Figure 5.10: EPSS efficiency

We are also seeing an evolution of other industry resources, such as the long-standing CVSS, which we covered earlier in this chapter.

It's worth emphasizing that EPSS measures the threat associated with a published CVE, based on the probability that the CVE will be exploited in the wild in the next 30 days. It doesn't account for organization-specific context such as that related to assets or the business. That said, when organizations are drowning in a backlog of hundreds of thousands of open vulnerabilities, with the rate of discovered and published vulnerabilities only accelerating, starting with the vulnerabilities most likely to be exploited is a great foundation.

EPSS 3.0 brings a more comprehensive, efficient, and effective model to the industry looking to prioritize vulnerabilities that pose the greatest threat. It also offers a robust application programming interface (API) and resource that's open for anyone to access and consume as part of their vulnerability management program. For those looking to learn more, you can dig in at the EPSS FAQ page: www.first.org/epss/faq.

Stakeholder-Specific Vulnerability Categorization

As organizations look to optimize resources when performing vulnerability prioritization, another prominent option that has grown in the ecosystem is the Stakeholder-Specific Vulnerability Categorization (SSVC), which has been championed by organizations such as Carnegie Mellon's Software Engineering Institute (SEI) and CISA.

SSVC utilizes decision trees to aid in vulnerability prioritization and seeks to address some of the shortfalls and critiques of more prominent options such as CVSS. It was originally introduced to the community in a Software Engineering Institute (SEI) paper titled, "Prioritizing Vulnerability Response: A Stakeholder-Specific Vulnerability Categorization," by researchers Jonathan Spring, Eric Hatleback, Allen Householder, Art Manion, and Deana Shick in late 2019 (https://resources.sei .cmu.edu/asset_files/WhitePaper/2019_019_001_636391.pdf).

SSVC's use of decision trees includes the various elements of a decision, potential decision values, and potential outcomes. As pointed out by the original whitepaper, many organizations default to using CVSS Base severity scores as decisions when it comes to vulnerability prioritization, so the authors decided to rally around decisions as a more useful output than a simple severity score. It's worth noting that the CVSS SIG explicitly states that CVSS Severity Scores shouldn't be used solely for vulnerability prioritization, but that hasn't stopped the industry from using them in this fashion, including organizations as large as the U.S. federal government and the Department of Defense (DoD).

As the original SSVC whitepaper emphasizes, vulnerability context is critical, not optional. This means the temporal and environmental considerations for vulnerabilities matter (e.g., the environment they exist in and the system and context of the vulnerability), much more than just the Base severity score. At its core, SSVC is a qualitative framework for prioritizing vulnerabilities and provides decisions as outputs that are explainable. SSVC posits that decision trees are small enough for humans to manage in vulnerability management.

SSVC is compared against other vulnerability prioritization options, such as CVSS v3.0, parametric regression, and random forest, in Figure 5.11 (taken from the SSVC whitepaper, which can be viewed at www.cisa.gov/sites/default/files/publications/cisa-ssvc-guide%20508c.pdf).

	Outputs Are Decisions	Pluralistic Recommendations	Qualitative Inputs	Qualitative Outputs	Transparent	Explainable
Parametric Regression	✗	✗	✓	✗	✗	✓
CVSS v3.0	✗	✗	✓	✗	✗	✗
Bayesian Belief Networks	✗	Maybe	✗	✗	✓	✓
Neural Networks	✗	✗	✗	✗	✗	✗
Random Forest	✓	✓	✓	Maybe	✗	Maybe
Other Machine Learning	✗	Maybe	✗	✗	✗	✗
Boolean First Order Logics	Maybe	Maybe	✓	✓	✓	Maybe
Decision Trees (Small)	✓	✓	✓	✓	✓	✓

Figure 5.11: SSVC comparison

Source: Adapted from www.cisa.gov/sites/default/files/publications/cisa-ssvc-guide%20508c.pdf

The primary differentiator between decision trees (such as SSVC) and other vulnerability prioritization options is that the outputs are decisions, which are decisive, so they empower practitioners to take action on vulnerabilities in a defined order or value.

The authors of SSVC in the original research paper advocated that using decision guidance for vulnerability management should, at a minimum, consider the stakeholder groups, their potential decision outcomes, and the data necessary to make decisions at the relevant decision points.

As SSVC acknowledges, a variety of stakeholders are involved in vulnerability management and may include organizations developing, applying, or coordinating patches. After sufficiently identifying the stakeholders, you then need to enumerate the various decisions that can be made. These activities often involve things such as developing, applying, or coordinating patches, all of which are often conducted by various stakeholders, including those external to your respective organization.

Another important aspect that the SSVC whitepaper calls out is scope as it relates to decision points. Scope can include items like the boundaries of the impacted system. Defining scope, of course, can be challenging, because one system is often part of another, such as in the context of systems within systems.

While the initial SSVC whitepaper can be a bit theoretical and abstract, it makes sense to look at a practical example from an organization using SSVC. For our example, we will look at CISA, who has adopted and evangelized the use of the SSVC framework.

CISA SSVC Guide

CISA published a paper titled, "CISA SSVC Guide," which we'll use as our example to look at how organizations can leverage SSVC to aid in their vulnerability prioritization, remediation, and management efforts.

As the guidance mentions, the CISA SSVC utilizes decision tree models to assist in prioritizing their vulnerability response, much like the original SSVC whitepaper intended, but in this case, for U.S. government and critical infrastructure entities. However, as noted by CISA in their guidance, despite being published for U.S. government entities, any individual or organization can use SSVC to improve their vulnerability management practices.

The CISA guidance lays out four potential decisions that an entity leveraging their version of the SSVC has when becoming aware of a vulnerability; they are identified in Figure 5.12.

CISA also points out the topic of scope, which is determining, for example, if a vulnerability has a presence across multiple related systems and is accounted for as a single vulnerability or multiple vulnerabilities.

Track	The vulnerability does not require action at this time. The organization would continue to track the vulnerability and reassess it if new information becomes available. CISA recommends remediating **Track** vulnerabilities *within* standard update timelines.
Track*	The vulnerability contains specific characteristics that may require closer monitoring for changes. CISA recommends remediating **Track*** vulnerabilities *within* standard update timelines.
Attend	The vulnerability requires attention from the organization's internal, supervisory-level individuals. Necessary actions may include requesting assistance or information about the vulnerability and may involve publishing a notification, either internally and/or externally, about the vulnerability. CISA recommends remediating **Attend** vulnerabilities *sooner than* standard update timelines.
Act	The vulnerability requires attention from the organization's internal, supervisory-level and leadership-level individuals. Necessary actions include requesting assistance or information about the vulnerability, as well as publishing a notification either internally and/or externally. Typically, internal groups would meet to determine the overall response and then execute agreed upon actions. CISA recommends remediating **Act** vulnerabilities *as soon as possible*.

Figure 5.12: Potential SSVC decisions

Source: Adapted from www.cisa.gov/sites/default/files/publications/cisa-ssvc-guide%20508c.pdf

Another key aspect in the CISA SSVC is the state of exploitation—the evidence of active exploitation of a vulnerability. Unlike EPSS, this is not seeking to predict future exploitation but uses the information *currently* available at the time of the vulnerability analysis.

CISA's SSVC recommends using sources such as vendor vulnerability notifications, the NIST NVD, insights from Information Sharing and Analysis Centers (ISACs), and reliable threat reports that utilize CVE IDs or common names for a specific vulnerability. In this vein, SSVC is more akin to CISA's KEV catalog, because it focuses on the current state of exploitation, rather than the potential probability of future exploitation such as EPSS.

Potential exploitation decision values in the CISA SSVC are shown in Figure 5.13.

After determining the state of exploitation, CISA's SSVC examines technical impact. They compare it to CVSS's use of severity, which seeks to summarize the impact on the affected systems or assets if the vulnerability is present and exploited. CISA's SSVC takes a simplistic approach here, with only two potential options, as shown in Figure 5.14.

Value	Definition
None	There is no evidence of active exploitation and no public proof of concept (PoC) of how to exploit the vulnerability.
Public PoC	One of the following is true: (1) Typical public PoC exists in sources such as Metasploit or websites like ExploitDB; or (2) the vulnerability has a well-known method of exploitation. Some examples of condition (2) are open-source web proxies that serve as the PoC code for how to exploit any vulnerability in the vein of improper validation of Transport Layer Security (TLS) certificates, and Wireshark serving as a PoC for packet replay attacks on ethernet or Wi-Fi networks.
Active	Shared, observable, and reliable evidence that cyber threat actors have used the exploit in the wild; the public reporting is from a credible source.

Figure 5.13: Potential exploitation decision values

Value	Definition
Partial	One of the following is true: The exploit gives the threat actor limited control over, or information exposure about, the behavior of the software that contains the vulnerability; or the exploit gives the threat actor a low stochastic opportunity for *total* control. In this context, "low" means that the attacker cannot reasonably make enough attempts to overcome obstacles, either physical or security-based, to achieve total control. A denial-of-service attack is a form of *limited* control over the behavior of the vulnerable component.
Total	The exploit gives the adversary total control over the behavior of the software, or it gives total disclosure of all information on the system that contains the vulnerability.

Figure 5.14: Two options of technical impact

As you can see, the two options are partial or total. The former means that the threat actor has limited access over the impacted system, and the latter means the threat actor has complete and total control over the impacted software or system to which the vulnerability applies.

Another key aspect of the CISA SSVC decision tree process is determining if the exploit is not only available, but also automatable. Automation allows for much broader exploitation attempts by malicious actors and is a key consideration for how prevalent exploitation attempts may be across the ecosystem.

For this decision, CISA SSVC makes use of the widely popular Kill Chain from Lockheed Martin, which has seven steps, as shown in Figure 5.15.

RECONNAISSANCE

Harvesting email addresses,
conference information, etc.

WEAPONIZATION

Coupling exploit with backdoor
into deliverable payload

DELIVERY

Delivering weaponized bundle to the
victim via email, web, USB, etc.

EXPLOITATION

Exploiting a vulnerability to execute
code on victim's system

INSTALLATION

Installing malware on the asset

COMMAND & CONTROL (C2)

Command channel for remote
manipulation of victim

ACTIONS ON OBJECTIVES

With "Hands on Keyboard" access,
intruders accomplish their original goals

Figure 5.15: Lockheed Martin's seven-step Kill Chain

So, CISA's SSVC takes a binary approach to the assessment of an exploitation being automatable, oriented around the first four steps of the Kill Chain, as depicted in Figure 5.16.

Value	Definition
No	Steps 1-4 of the kill chain—reconnaissance, weaponization, delivery, and exploitation—cannot be reliably automated for this vulnerability.[1] Examples for explanations of why each step may not be reliably automatable include: (1) the vulnerable component is not searchable or enumerable on the network, (2) weaponization may require human direction for each target, (3) delivery may require channels that widely deployed network security configurations block, and (4) exploitation may be frustrated by adequate exploit-prevention techniques enabled by default (address space layout randomization [ASLR] is an example of an exploit-prevention tool).
Yes	Steps 1-4 of the kill chain can be reliably automated. If the vulnerability allows unauthenticated remote code execution (RCE) or command injection, the response is likely yes.

Figure 5.16: CISA's SSVC binary approach to assessment

As CISA points out, a variety of factors contribute to the automatability of exploitation, such as the complexity of the attack, the code needed to be written or configured by the attacker, as well as the common network deployment of the vulnerable system. If a vulnerability requires authentication, Internet reachability, or other specific criteria to be present or possible, then the ability to automate the exploitation of a specific vulnerability declines. However, as CISA also emphasizes, it isn't uncommon for malicious actors to chain vulnerabilities together to execute various steps or exploit multiple vulnerabilities as part of their overarching attack campaigns. Referred to as *vulnerability chaining*, it's a topic we'll discuss extensively in Section 5, "Vulnerability Chaining." It is not uncommon for malicious actors to use multiple vulnerabilities to achieve a desired outcome. One of the authors of this book, Dr. Nikki Robinson, conducted her doctoral thesis on the concept of vulnerability chaining and blindness.

Organizational context is as critical as other criteria for considering the prioritization of a vulnerability for remediation. CISA's SSVC approaches this from the concept of *Mission Prevalence*, meaning how critical a system or software is to the organization's mission. They discuss the concept of mission-essential functions (MEFs) as functions that relate to accomplishing an organization's mission. Organizations identify their MEFs as part of activities such as business continuity and disaster recovery planning activities. For example, if you're an e-commerce firm such as Amazon, your website's stability to enable customers to purchase products that contribute to your revenue is certainly an MEF.

MEFs are critical to normal operations where nonessential functions are not, although nonessential functions often support MEFs in various capacities such as logistics and financial operations, which may not be an organization's core competency but are key for it to continue to function. The potential decision values for Mission Prevalence are listed in Figure 5.17.

Value	Definition
Minimal	Neither *support* nor *essential* apply. The vulnerable component may be used within the entities, but it is not used as a mission-essential component, nor does it provide impactful support to mission-essential functions.
Support	The vulnerable component only *supports* MEFs for two or more entities.
Essential	The vulnerable component directly provides capabilities that constitute at least one MEF for at least one entity; component failure may (but does not necessarily) lead to overall mission failure.

Figure 5.17: Mission Prevalence potential decision values

While federal entities utilizing CISA's SSVC might not use the term *mission,* they inevitably have key organizational mission activities that they can designate as MEFs.

Moving on from Mission Prevalence, the next key consideration in the CISA SSVC is *Public Well-Being Impact.* CISA utilizes the Centers for Disease Control and Prevention (CDC) definition of well-being that includes the physical, social, emotional, and psychological health of humans involved. This is a nod to the increasing convergence of software and society, often what are called *cyber-physical systems,* and could be applied to not just governmental entities but also critical infrastructure as one example. Public well-being has a broader potential impact than the technological specific context usually considered under vulnerability management. But as software becomes increasingly integrated into every aspect of our society, it is also a necessary one.

CISA's SSVC looks at the impact in the context of minimal, material, or irreversible, and across diverse types of harm such as physical, environmental, financial, and psychological, as depicted in Figure 5.18.

Lastly, the criterion as defined by the CISA SSVC guidance is the *Mitigation Status,* which is a measurement of the degree of difficulty to mitigate the vulnerability. CISA looks at three different criteria—Mitigation Availability, System Change Difficulty, and Type, as depicted in Figure 5.19.

Considerations include whether a mitigation is publicly available or not, whether or not it is difficult to implement the mitigation, and whether it is a direct fix or merely a workaround to mitigate the risk in the interim until a permanent solution can be implemented.

Impact	Type of harm	Description
Minimal	All	The effect is below the threshold for all aspects described in material.
Material (Any one or more of these conditions hold.)	Physical harm	Does one or more of the following: • Causes physical distress or injury to system users. • Introduces occupational safety hazards. • Reduces and/or results in failure of cyber-physical system safety margins.
	Environment	Major externalities (property damage, environmental damage, etc.) are imposed on other parties.
	Financial	Financial losses likely lead to bankruptcy of multiple persons.
	Psychological	Widespread emotional or psychological harm, sufficient to necessitate counselling or therapy, impact populations of people.
Irreversible (Any one or more of these conditions hold.)	Physical harm	One or both of the following are true: • Multiple fatalities are likely. • The cyber-physical system, of which the vulnerable component is a part, is likely lost or destroyed.
	Environment	Extreme or serious externalities (immediate public health threat, environmental damage leading to small ecosystem collapse, etc.) are imposed of other parties.
	Financial	Social systems (elections, financial grid, etc.) supported by the software are destabilized and potentially collapse.
	Psychological	N/A

Figure 5.18: SSVC Impact Types

Factor	Value	Description
Minimal	Available	The mitigation is publicly available.
	Unavailable	The mitigation is not publicly available.
System change difficulty	Low	The system has an Integrated update process, and the mitigation does not require any unreasonable interruption to the normal function of the vulnerable component.
	High	Any of the following are true: • The system does not have an integrated update process. • Applying the mitigation will require exceptional downtime. • After mitigation, system functionality will be reduced below normally acceptable levels. • The regulatory environment may prevent application of mitigation.
Type	Fix	An official patch that remediates the vulnerability.
	Workaround	Some way of preventing exploitation that does not patch the underlying issue; this is often in the form of a reconfiguration of the vulnerable component or its environment.

Figure 5.19: Three criteria of Mitigation Status

Decision Tree Example

Given the governmental and critical infrastructure focus of CISA, it should come as no surprise that their notional implementation of an SSVC decision tree rallies around emphasizing the mission prevalence and public well-being decision points for prioritization while building on other metrics such as the maturity of exploitation, ability to be automated, and the technical impact of the vulnerability exploitation.

CISA points out that in addition to an expanded attack tree (see Figure 5.20), the data can also be tracked in a table format, which is represented in Figure 5.21.

The decision tree model lends itself to analyzing a specific vulnerability and walking through the various decision points and considerations, whereas a table format is more beneficial when tracking and triaging many vulnerabilities, leveraging the CISA SSVC model as a guide.

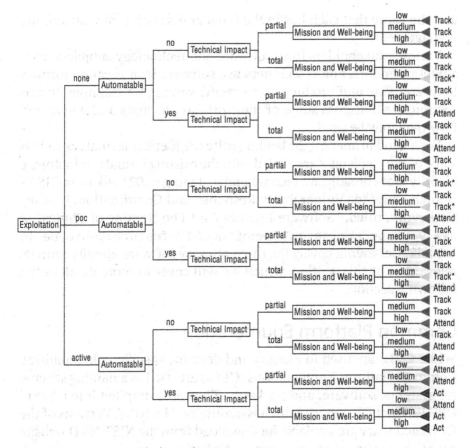

Figure 5.20: An expanded attack tree

Row Number	Exploitation	Automatable	Technical	Mission and Well-Being	Decision
1	none	no	partial	low	Track
2	none	no	partial	medium	Track
3	none	no	partial	high	Track

Figure 5.21: A table format of an attack tree

Source: https://csrc.nist.gov/projects/security-content-automation-protocol/specifications/cpe

Software Identification Formats

No conversation on vulnerability scoring and prioritization would be complete without also covering some of the primary software identification formats, their respective challenges and shortcomings, and the value that each has in the broader discussion of vulnerability management.

Various stakeholders from software and technology suppliers, consumers, vendors, and researchers use software identification formats to tie software and products to a specific vendor, for example. In this section, we'll discuss some of their primary formats and where and how they may be used.

For a good primer on the leading software identity formats as well as some of the challenges associated with the existing formats and software identity more broadly, we recommend watching a 2023 talk from CISA's Branch Chief for Vulnerability Response and Coordination, Lindsey Cerkovnik, titled, "Software Identity And The Naming of Things" at www.youtube.com/watch?v=wzo81uccSfU&feature=youtu.be. In her talk, Cerkovnik covers the three primary software identity formats relevant as of this writing, which we will cover in more detail in the following section.

Common Platform Enumeration

While CVEs are used to identify and describe specific vulnerabilities, Common Platform Enumerations (CPEs) are used as a naming scheme for systems, software, and packages. They are compiled into a broad CPE Product Dictionary, which is maintained by NIST. Versions of the CPE Dictionary are available for download from the NIST NVD website at https://nvd.nist.gov/products/cpe.

Products are identified by suppliers, and then a CPE name is submitted and approved to be included in the overarching Official CPE Dictionary. This way it can be used in searches for vulnerabilities, demonstrating the products and software it impacts. The NIST NVD uses CPEs when discussing the applicability of vulnerabilities and the products or software they impact. CPEs provide a standardized format for machine-readable representations of IT products and platforms. Prior to CPE's introduction, the industry lacked such a format and thus struggled to correlate vulnerabilities with specific products or platforms in the ecosystem.

As mentioned by NIST at https://csrc.nist.gov/projects/security-content-automation-protocol/specifications/cpe, CPEs can be leveraged by IT management tooling to collect information about installed products using the CPE name and to help make decisions regarding the assets based on the vulnerabilities impacting them.

As of this writing, the current version of CPE is 2.3. Its structure is captured in Figure 5.22, with its most fundamental purpose, naming, at the bottom of the structure with additional layers built on top of it.

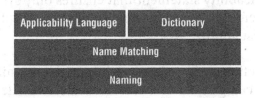

Figure 5.22: CPE 2.3's structure

Source: https://csrc.nist.gov/projects/security-content-automation-protocol/specifications/cpe

Let's look at the aspects of the CPE 2.3 structure and its various components:

Naming The Naming specification defines the logical structure of Well-Formed Names (WFNs), Uniform Resource Identifier (URI) bindings, and formatted string bindings, and the procedures for converting Well-Formed Names to and from the bindings.

Name Matching The Name-Matching specification defines the procedures for comparing WFNs to each other to determine whether they refer to some or all of the same products.

Dictionary The dictionary specification defines the concept of a CPE Dictionary, which is a repository of CPE names and metadata where each name identifies a single class of IT product. The dictionary specification defines processes for using the dictionary, such as how to search for a particular CPE name or look for dictionary entries that belong to a broader product class. Also, the dictionary specification outlines all the rules that dictionary maintainers must follow when creating new dictionary entries and updating existing entries.

Applicability Language The Applicability Language specification defines a standardized structure for forming complex logical expressions out of WFNs. These expressions, also known as *applicability statements*, are used to tag checklists, policies, guidance, and other documents with information about the product(s) to which the documents apply. For example, a security checklist for Mozilla Firefox 3.6 running on Microsoft Windows could be tagged with a single applicability statement that ensures only systems with *both* Mozilla Firefox 3.6 and Microsoft Windows Vista will have the security checklist applied.

The CPE Dictionary is updated nightly, and it is available for download as well as being available as a search-based website where individuals can run queries for specific products, applications, and software. You can also dig into the CPE 2.3 XML schema. All these additional resources are available at the NIST CPE website (https://nvd.nist.gov/products/cpe). You can also view the official CPE Dictionary statistics to see the annual growth of CPEs and the year-over-year growth of identified products, vendors, and entries as well as how many have been deprecated.

Package URL

Another prevalent software identification method is the Package URL, also known as PURL (https://github.com/package-url/purl-spec). While CPE is product-specific and is useful for identifying specific products and vendors, PURL is much more focused on third-party dependencies, components, and packages.

The reason this is key is based on studies from sources such as Synopsys. According to their previous versions of the Synopsys Open Source Security and Risk Analysis Report (www.synopsys.com/content/dam/synopsys/sig-assets/reports/rep-ossra-2023.pdf), 78 percent of modern codebases are increasingly made up of open source software (OSS) components. Not only were 78 percent of the 2,409 codebases audited composed of OSS components, but 97 percent of the codebases contained some level of OSS. Further concerning is the fact that almost 90 percent of the components had no new development in two years, and 85 percent of the components were more than *four years* out-of-date. (Check out Figure 5.23 for more information.)

This proliferation of OSS components and their associated risks is paired to the growth of software supply chain attacks, which may, of course, target specific vendors and products, but also are increasingly targeting the OSS components that software suppliers and organizations use in their applications and architectures.

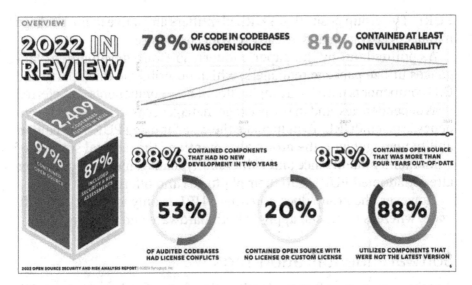

Figure 5.23: 2022 OSSRA Report summary
Source: https://cwe.mitre.org/about/new_to_cwe.html

To emphasize the growth of the risk associated with software supply chain attacks, software supply chain vendor Sonatype produced a 2023 State of the Software Supply Chain report, www.sonatype.com/state-of-the-software-supply-chain/introduction that found there was a 742 percent average annual increase in software supply chain attacks over the previous three years and over 3.4 *billion* vulnerable downloads each month. Their report also found that nearly *one trillion* more packages were downloaded from the most popular package repositories than the previous year, reiterating the explosive growth of OSS and software package consumption, and further emphasizing the key role of PURL for software identification.

The increased adoption of OSS, coupled with the growth of supply chain attacks, means the need for effective software and hardware identification is critical. However, as it stands currently, the NIST NVD only supports CPE, which as we have discussed is product- and vendor-specific.

One group, who goes by the name the SBOM Forum, has begun to declare that the NVD needs to grow beyond using CPE as the sole identifier. In a paper titled "A Proposal to Operationalize Component Identification for Vulnerability Management" (https://owasp.org/assets/files/posts/A%20Proposal%20to%20Operational ize%20Component%20Identification%20for%20Vulnerability%20 Management.pdf), the group proposes that the NVD adopt the use of

PURL. The group posits that PURL identifiers are native to the package manager ecosystem and already in widespread use.

As pointed out by the paper, modern software development languages utilize package managers, which describe the third-party and OSS components used by an application. These components are referred to as dependencies, and in the package manager ecosystem, each dependency is given PURL. To help make the case for using PURL for vulnerability management, the group also mentions that several sources of vulnerability intelligence and vulnerability management vendors have already adopted PURL into their platforms and offerings.

However, the group does note that PURL is only applicable to software, whereas CPEs can apply to both hardware and software.

Software Identification Tags

Another common software identification format, although it's experiencing less use due to CPE and most notably the growth of PURL, is the Software Identification (SWID) format (https://csrc.nist.gov/projects/Software-Identification-SWID). SWID is an International Organization for Standardization (ISO) standard that defines a structured metadata format for describing software products.

SWID seeks to help organizations effectively manage their software inventories in a structured fashion, by using what are known as *tag files* to describe specific releases of software products. SWID tags can be used throughout the entire software product life cycle, from installation to decommissioning.

Organizations other than ISO have also advocated for the use and adoption of SWID tags. NIST, for example, recommends SWID's use to entities such as software producers and standards bodies and mentions the use of SWID tags in their various guidance and publications.

Common Weaknesses and Enumerations

While CPE provides a standardized schema for discussing specific products, vendors, and software, the Common Weaknesses Enumeration (CWE) provides a common language for discussing software security vulnerabilities found in applications, software, and systems.

CWE is an effort run by MITRE and leveraged by entities such as the NIST NVD. As defined by MITRE, "CWE is a community-developed list of software and hardware weakness types. It serves as a common language, a measuring stick for security tools, and as a baseline for weakness identification, mitigation, and prevention efforts."

In the CWE context, a weakness is defined as "a condition in a software, firmware, hardware, or service component that, under certain circumstances, could contribute to the introduction of vulnerabilities."

While CPEs and CVEs are unique identifiers for products, software, or vulnerabilities, CWEs provide a common language to discuss prevalent weaknesses in systems and software through specific categorizations, such as buffer overflows, handler errors, and validity problems.

CWE has ties to MITRE's work with the U.S. Department of Homeland Security (DHS) and NIST, looking to enumerate software weaknesses tied to real-world vulnerabilities. Released in 2006, the original list and taxonomy have continued to grow in both depth and diversity, supporting use cases for mobile applications, operational technology, Internet of Things (IoT), and more.

Much like the Open Worldwide Application Security Project (OWASP)'s famous "Top 10" list of specific vulnerabilities and threats for domains such as software and AI, there is a "CWE Top 25 Most Dangerous Software Weaknesses" list that represents the most common and impactful software weaknesses. (Check out https://cwe.mitre.org/top25/archive/2022/2022_cwe_top25.html). To create the CWE Top 25, the CWE team utilized CVE records from the NIST NVD, along with CVSS scores for CVEs, and compared that information against the CISA KEV catalog. For the 2022 Top 25 list, they analyzed over 37,000 CVE records over the previous two years. The CWE Top 25 ranks the CWEs and shows their ID, name, and score along with the number of KEVs with which they are associated.

More broadly, NVD integrates CWE into the scoring of the CVEs. NVD then goes on to categorize and differentiate CVEs based on the type of vulnerability they represent, using the CWE classifications.

CWEs are represented with a unique ID chosen at the time of assignment, such as CWE-<ID>, along with a descriptive name for each CWE. As stated in the CWE guidance, for a CWE to be published on their site, it must include name, summary, and references among other information, as detailed in Figure 5.24.

CWE supports a variety of use cases, from providing the common language covered previously for developers and security researchers to discuss security weaknesses, to organizations evaluating security tooling to determine their ability to discover weaknesses around the CWE taxonomy.

Required CWE Element	Associated Information
Name	The name includes (1) the intended behavior, (2) the mistake (i.e., weakness), (3) the affected resource (if relevant), and (4) the affected technology (if relevant).
Summary	The summary is one or two sentences that describe the weakness focusing on the mistake that is made.
Extended Description	The extended description is one or two paragraphs further describing how the weakness can be a problem. It is intended for the audience that may not understand how the weakness can be a problem.
Modes of Introduction	The Mode of Introduction provides how and when the weakness may be introduced (e.g., by product lifecycle phase).
Potential Mitigations	Potential Mitigations are one or more techniques that will eliminate and/or reduce the frequency or impact of the weakness.
Common Consequences	Common Consequences are the typical negative security impact (or impacts) that occurs if this weakness can be exploited by an attacker.
Applicable Platforms	Applicable Platforms specifies the programming languages, operating systems, architectures, and technologies in which this weakness is usually found.
Demonstrative Examples	Demonstrative Examples illustrate the weakness through code, explanatory text, and/or diagrams.
Observed Examples	Observed Examples are publicly reported vulnerabilities (e.g., CVE Records) in real-world products that exhibit the weakness.
Relationships	Relationships are the other CWEs related to the weakness.
References	References include one or more citations, with URLs, for academic papers, white papers, blog posts, slide presentations, or videos that describe the weakness.

Figure 5.24: Required CWE elements

Source: https://cwe.mitre.org/about/new_to_cwe.html

One of the strongest use cases for CWE, aside from categorizing vulnerabilities into standardized classifications, is the ability to try to eliminate mistakes earlier in the software development life cycle (SDLC) by educating those designing and developing systems regarding common mistakes and weaknesses that can mature into vulnerabilities, which can then be potentially exploited by malicious actors.

Much like the push to "shift security left" and implement activities such as threat modeling, which we'll discuss elsewhere in this book, having a list of common mistakes and weaknesses can let software and system producers evaluate whether their system falls victim to any of the most prevalent weaknesses prior to it being deployed to a production environment, or subsequently, categorizing vulnerabilities in production systems based on the CWE category of identified vulnerabilities.

In addition to the CWE list that is open for public use as an industry resource, there are other efforts, such as the Top 25 CWEs we previously discussed, the Common Weakness Scoring System (CWSS), the Common Weakness Risk Analysis Framework (CWRAF), and CWE Coverage Claims Representation (CCR), each of which provides additional capability to the community in various forms. You can find out more about each of them in the CWE FAQ (https://cwe.mitre.org/about/faq.html).

Summary

As we have discussed in this chapter, there are a variety of vulnerability scoring methodologies and systems in use today. Some have evolved over a long period of time and arguably are on the cusp of being replaced or at a minimum augmented with more modern and practical models that can aid in activities such as vulnerability prioritization.

6

Vulnerability and Exploit Database Management

Vulnerability and exploit databases play a fundamental role in the conversation surrounding vulnerability management. At a high level, a *vulnerability database* can be described as an effort to collect information about known security flaws in software and products, and then make that information available either publicly or to some community of users. Some vulnerability databases have been around for many years, while others are new and starting to gain increased use in the technology and cybersecurity community. Exploit databases are collections of public exploits, used for research and to aid practitioners and defenders. In this chapter, we discuss some of the most notable examples, as well as their challenges and strengths and how they can be used by both vulnerability management vendors and end-user organizations.

National Vulnerability Database (NVD)

Vulnerabilities help inform activities to drive down risk, both for organizations creating and producing software as well as those using and consuming it and providing broad industry knowledge of the vulnerabilities present in the ecosystem.

While there are several vulnerability databases in the industry, one of the most notable examples is the National Institute of Standards and Technology's National Vulnerability Database (NVD). NVD is a comprehensive cybersecurity vulnerability database that integrates all publicly available U.S. government vulnerability resources and provides references to industry resources.

NVD was formed in 2005, and reports on the Common Vulnerabilities and Exposures (CVEs) within the industry. The origins of the NVD trace all the way back to 1999, with NVD's predecessor, Internet – Categorization of Attacks Toolkit (I-CAT), which originally was an access database of attack scripts. The I-CAT name can be traced to one of the largest defense contractors, Booz Allen Hamilton. I-CAT originally involved students from the SANS Technology Institute who worked as analysts involved with the project. I-CAT faced some funding challenges, but it was kept alive through efforts by SANS as well as employees of NIST, going on to reach over 10,000 vulnerabilities before receiving some additional funding from the Department of Homeland Security (DHS) to create a vulnerability database rebranded as NVD, as it is known today. As the project evolved, NVD went on to adopt popular vulnerability data and scoring that's still in use today, such as the Common Vulnerability Scoring System (CVSS) and Common Platform Enumeration (CPE).

As of September 2023, NVD contains over 200,000 vulnerabilities that continue to grow as new vulnerabilities emerge. NVD is utilized worldwide by professionals interested in vulnerability data, as well as vendors looking to correlate vulnerability findings and their associated details.

NVD facilitates this process by analyzing CVEs that have been published in the CVE dictionary. By referencing the CVE dictionary and performing additional analysis, the NVD staff produce important metadata about vulnerabilities, including CVSS scores, Common Weakness Enumeration (CWE) types, and associated applicability statements in the form of CPEs.

It's worth noting that the NVD staff does not perform the vulnerability testing and uses insights and information from vendors and third-party security researchers to aid in the creation of the attributes previously discussed in the chapter on vulnerability scoring systems, such as CVSS. As current information emerges, the NVD revises the metadata, such as CVSS scores and CWE information.

The NVD integrates information from the CVE program, which is a dictionary of vulnerabilities that we'll discuss elsewhere. The NVD assesses newly published CVEs after they are integrated into the NVD with a rigorous analysis process. This includes reviewing reference material for the CVE, including publicly available information located on the Internet. CVEs are assigned one or more CWE identifiers to help categorize the vulnerability, and the vulnerability is also assigned exploitability and impact metrics through the CVSS. Applicability statements are given through CPEs to ensure that specific versions of software, hardware, or systems are identified through these applicability statements. This helps organizations take the appropriate action, depending on whether the vulnerability impacts the specific hardware and software they're using. Once this initial analysis and assessment is performed, any assigned metadata such as the CWEs, CVSS, and CPEs are reviewed as a quality assurance method by a senior analyst before a CPE is published on the NVD website and associated data feeds.

The NVD offers a rich set of data feeds and application programming interfaces (APIs) for organizations and individuals to consume published vulnerability data. APIs allow interested parties to programmatically consume the vulnerability information in a much more automated and scalable manner than manually reviewing the data feeds. The NVD APIs also include other benefits such as being frequently updated, searchable, and able to perform data matching, and more, and they are often used by security product vendors to provide vulnerability data as part of their product offering.

Despite its broad adoption and use by nearly all reputable vulnerability management platforms and firms, the NVD isn't without its critics. Popular bloggers such as Tom Alrich, who is part of groups such as the Software Bill of Materials (SBOM) Forum and has been involved in activities around software supply chain security, met with the NVD team in 2023 and noted that the team discussed funding challenges and the nearly 20 percent decrease in headcount as well. This is discussed in a blog regarding the call for a global vulnerability database beyond the U.S.-centric NVD (check out `http://tomalrichblog.blogspot .com/2023/08/a-global-vulnerability-database.html`).

Others have raised concerns about the NVD's process for ingesting vulnerabilities through what the NVD calls CVE Numbering Authorities (CNAs). CNAs are qualified organizations that volunteer to research vulnerabilities and contribute them for the NVD's consideration and inclusion. Some have raised concerns about how cumbersome and inefficient the process is. Others have noted that the NVD is a "broken" system, allowing for vulnerability submissions and entries without the proper coordination with the party responsible for the software and without validation that the issue is genuinely a vulnerability, which can contribute noise to vulnerability management issues across the industry.

Lastly, organizations such as the Open Worldwide Application Security Project (OWASP) and the SBOM Forum have raised concerns regarding the accuracy and effectiveness of the NVD when it comes to open source software (OSS) package identification for vulnerability management purposes. They have called for the NVD to begin to support additional software identifiers such as Package URL (PURL), which is key for identifying specific OSS packages and their associated vulnerabilities as part of the broader package manager ecosystem.

Sonatype Open Source Software Index

Some vulnerability databases take the approach of focusing on specific aspects of the software ecosystem. That is the case with Sonatype's Open Source Software (OSS) Index, which is a free catalog of open source components aimed at helping organizations identify vulnerabilities and the associated risks of specific OSS components.

These insights are even more pertinent due to factors that we've discussed in other chapters, such as the exponential growth and adoption of OSS by organizations and the increased targeting of OSS components as part of the broader increase in software supply chain attacks. As we will discuss in Chapter 10, "Vulnerability Chaining Blindness," OSS components are pervasive in modern applications, making up nearly 80 percent of modern codebases and presenting a large and enticing attack surface for malicious actors.

Sonatype's OSS Index lets you search millions of components, seeking any known or publicly disclosed vulnerabilities from the various package manager ecosystems that exist like Maven, npm, and the Python Package Index (PyPI), among others. Unlike proprietary databases, the OSS Index uses public sources and doesn't rely on human-curated insights or expert guidance. As a security vendor, Sonatype makes use of these insights to provide a variety of capabilities such as informing development teams early in their software development life cycle (SDLC) of the risks of components, curating internal repositories of trusted/approved components, and aiding in activities such as vulnerability remediation.

The OSS Index also offers a public Representational State Transfer (REST) API, which is used by a variety of vulnerability scanning tools to identify OSS vulnerabilities.

Open Source Vulnerabilities

The Open Source Vulnerabilities (OSV) schema was launched by the team at Google in 2021. It is intended to help developers and consumers of OSS triage vulnerabilities by providing precise data on where vulnerabilities are introduced and when they are fixed, empowering OSS consumers to accurately assess the impact on their environments due to vulnerable OSS components. Building on this, Google also announced the OSV Scanner, which can help identify vulnerabilities in OSS dependencies and serves as the frontend for the OSV database.

OSV was born of the 2021 Google Security and OSS effort dubbed the "Know, Prevent, Fix" framework, which aimed to frame the discussion around OSS and its associated vulnerabilities (`https://security .googleblog.com/2021/02/know-prevent-fix-framework-for- shifting.html`). This effort centers on empowering organizations to identify vulnerabilities in their OSS, to prevent the addition of new vulnerabilities, and to fix or remove vulnerabilities from their environments. To conduct these activities, organizations must have precise vulnerability data from rich data sources as well as accurate tracking of their dependencies, so they know what their OSS inventory looks like. Furthermore, there's a push to have a standard schema for vulnerability databases to allow for interoperability and easier vulnerability sharing and coordination.

Building on the need for interoperability and schema standardization, the OSV database uses the Open Source Security Foundation (OpenSSF) OSV format, which was developed by the OSS community. It is a human- and machine-readable format that describes vulnerabilities mapping to their specific package versions or commit hashes, which is a more efficient method than the traditional format used by sources such as CVD and the NIST NVD.

OSV uses a robust set of data sources that support the OSV format, which include the GitHub Advisory Database, OSS-Fuzz, and various language-specific databases such as PyPI, Go, and Rust, among others.

Figure 6.1 is an example of how vulnerability data is aggregated from various vulnerability data sources and fed into OSV.dev, which is the database of vulnerabilities allowing open source users to query for known vulnerabilities by version numbers and commit hashes. It also allows for interaction with upstream package repositories for data on versioning and more.

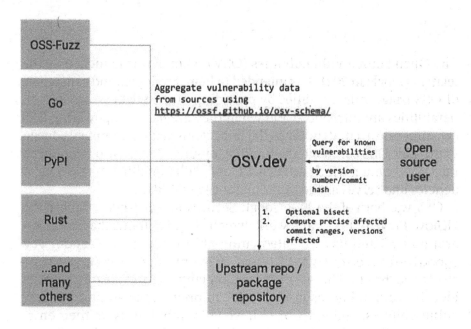

Figure 6.1: OSV data aggregation

Source: https://google.github.io/osv.dev \\Open Source Vulnerabilities(OSV)

OSV.dev provides a publicly available API that can be used by organizations and third parties, such as vulnerability management vendors and other vulnerability database providers, and can even be downloaded in its entirety as well.

The OSV's schema is JavaScript Object Notation (JSON)-based. If you're interested in learning more, visit the OSV schema overview page at https://github.com/ossf/osv-schema.

GitHub Advisory Database

While organizations have increased their efforts in using technology to drive business outcomes, they have increasingly begun to employ software developers, whether it's those writing software natively for the organization or those working to integrate software products into their business workflows and operations. There is no commercial organization used more worldwide to facilitate software development activities than GitHub, which boasts over 100 million users worldwide.

As the use of GitHub has grown, the organization has expanded its offerings to include what is known as the GitHub Advisory Database, a list of known security vulnerabilities and malware. These advisories are grouped into two categories: reviewed and unreviewed.

The GitHub Advisory Database sources vulnerabilities from sources such as the NVD, which we discussed earlier, as well as many others such as popular language and package databases from npm, Go, Python, and Ruby, among others. It also accepts community contributions, allowing users to submit vulnerabilities information that might be beneficial to the broader community.

The GitHub Advisory Database (https://github.com/ossf/osv-schema) makes use of the Open Source Vulnerability (OSV) format, which aims to provide a standard interchange format for vulnerability databases to facilitate an easier exchange of vulnerability data. This format is supported by other databases that we've discussed such as OSV.

In the context of the GitHub security advisories (GHSAs), the database makes use of a GitHub security advisories identification (GHSA ID), which is a unique identifier that every security advisory in the GHSA database is assigned. The GHSA provides a robust REST API that the community can interact with for doing activities such as creating security advisories or consuming advisory data.

With the continued growth of software developers and organizations performing software development activities and adopting development security operations (DevSecOps) methodologies and practices, we anticipate that the GitHub Advisory Database will continue to experience growth and adoption rather than developers going to original sources such as the NIST NVD.

Exploit Databases

Much like vulnerability databases are used to inventory and describe vulnerabilities, *exploit databases* are used to inventory and describe exploits. *Vulnerabilities* are often defined as qualities or characteristics of a given system, software, or environment that might allow a threat to be realized. *Exploits*, on the other hand, are often pieces of software code or techniques that allow a security flaw or vulnerability to be taken advantage of.

Exploit-DB

Exploit-DB, the Exploit Database, is one of the most popular databases of publicly available exploits on the Internet. It offers functionality such as `searchsploit`, a command-line search tool that allows users to search for specific exploits. In addition, it is integrated with some very popular security and hacking tools. Users can download and locally store Exploit-DB locally and use the tools to conduct research as well as identify malicious activities targeted at specific vulnerabilities, products, and software. Users can search for specific software, versions, titles, and use cases. Exploit-DB also boasts a robust set of additional resources, such as the Google Hacking Database, Exploit Database Security Papers, specific shell codes, and online training.

Metasploit

While not necessarily an exploit database, Metasploit is a widely popular tool that is used by not only security professionals but also hackers and malicious actors due to its ease of use and open source availability. Metasploit is open source and actively developed and maintained. It helps facilitate large penetration tests via automation but can also be used for nefarious purposes, such as allowing malicious actors to easily pivot between payloads during testing and exploitation activities. It can also allow for malicious actors to minimize the potential that their activities are noticed or identified, challenging activities such as investigation and response.

GitHub

As we discussed earlier, GitHub is a fundamental platform in the modern software ecosystem, with over 100 million users worldwide. It also plays a part in exploitation, most notably in exploit code. This is because there are repositories—some public and some private—that host proofs-of-concept and exploit code associated with vulnerabilities. These exploits can be useful not only for security researchers and vendors but also for malicious actors looking for quick ways to exploit known vulnerabilities.

Summary

This coverage of vulnerability and exploit databases is far from exhaustive. You can search the Internet for discussions and details about vulnerabilities, and their associated exploits can exist in nearly infinite locations as reported on by its diverse and expansive community. That said, the items discussed in this chapter represent some of the most popular vulnerabilities and exploit databases often used in security and hacking communities alike. It is also worth noting, as we have discussed in other chapters, that the presence of a vulnerability or even the existence of exploit code does not guarantee a system or software can be exploited or compromised. Organizations must take into account a myriad of factors such as configurations, architectures, compensating controls, and reachability to determine whether a specific vulnerability can be exploited. However, by using some of the resources we've discussed, organizations can gain a strong understanding of the vulnerability landscape as well as the existing exploits associated with popular vulnerabilities, products, and software.

7

Vulnerability Chaining

Vulnerability chaining is defined as the usage of multiple vulnerabilities to create critical cyberattacks in the FIRST CVSS User Guide (www.first.org/cvss/v3.0/user-guide). The use of multiple vulnerabilities in combination is a common tactic used by hackers and red teamers to compromise systems. Vulnerability chaining, however, isn't typically defined in Vulnerability Management Programs (VMPs), or used as a technique for prioritization and remediation.

This chapter will explore the use of vulnerability chains within a cybersecurity program, specifically in the remediation aspect of VMPs. Examples of chained vulnerabilities will be provided, including possible remediation paths for each situation. Each organization will have its own unique vulnerability considerations, but each scenario will provide a path forward to implementing chained vulnerabilities into their cybersecurity programs.

Vulnerability Chaining Attacks

Vulnerability chaining attacks have only recently become part of the mainstream conversation of vulnerability management, but they have been leveraged by advanced persistent threat (APT) groups for many years. Some documentation links vulnerability chaining directly to APT-type attacks, including a 2020 article by the Cybersecurity and Infrastructure Security Agency (CISA) on how APT groups leverage vulnerability chains against critical infrastructure and election organizations (read the article at www.cisa.gov/news-events/cybersecurity-advisories/aa20-283a).

A 2023 article by Walter Haydock outlines both direct and indirect chaining, because vulnerability chaining is more complex than simply adding multiple vulnerabilities in a row to conduct an attack (see `https://blog.stackaware.com/p/vulnerability-chaining-part-1-a-logical`). He's one of the few writers and cybersecurity experts who writes about vulnerability chaining. His background includes everything from product management to founding a company for managing AI-related cyber and compliance risk.

Direct chaining allows an attacker to gain access to a second or third vulnerability simply by exploiting the first vulnerability. However, *indirect chaining* is when an attacker can gain access to a second vulnerability by using the initial vulnerability to learn details of the next vulnerability.

An example of direct chaining provided by Haydock would be the combination of using CVE-2017-5638, which would lead an attacker to leverage CVE-2012-2122. CVE-2017-5638 is a vulnerability in Apache Struts that allows an initial attack vector, using arbitrary command execution into the system (`https://nvd.nist.gov/vuln/detail/cve-2017-5638`). From there, using CVE-2012-2122 (`https://nvd.nist.gov/vuln/detail/CVE-2012-2122`) provides access for a remote attacker to bypass authentication and gain access to a MySQL database and potentially sensitive information.

An example of indirect chaining from the same article by Haydock is the use of CVE-2014-0160 to steal a hashed password, and subsequently use a *pass-the-hash vulnerability* to compromise a system. A pass-the-hash vulnerability is commonly used to conduct attacks against Windows systems; a hacker could look for password hashes on the system for a user and ideally use the hash (or password) for the account to elevate privileges to an administrator account (refer to `www.bleepingcomputer.com/news/security/pass-the-hash-attacks-and-how-to-prevent-them-in-windows-domains`). CVE-2014-0160 is relatively "famous" in the vulnerability management world and dubbed the *Heartbleed bug* (`https://nvd.nist.gov/vuln/detail/cve-2014-0160`). This CVE allows an adversary to gain access to sensitive information (including private keys). Then that same attacker can use a pass-the-hash vulnerability in any number of other devices to gain access to more systems or attempt to elevate privileges further.

While it might seem unwise to use these older vulnerabilities in newer infrastructure or technical environments, many organizations are still holding on to legacy and outdated software. Research by Finnish cybersecurity enterprise F-Secure suggests that around 60 percent of vulnerabilities in corporate environments are from 2016 or earlier (see https://blog-assets.f-secure.com/wp-content/ uploads/2021/03/30120359/attack-landscape-update-h1-2021 .pdf). Based on that data, it's absolutely possible for attackers to leverage older vulnerabilities to conduct critical vulnerability chaining attacks.

Each example shows how starting with one vulnerability can lead to another and then another, until full-system compromise is conducted. With any vulnerability chain, a number of options become available to attackers. They can move from application to application, exploiting flaws along the way, either gaining access to data or dropping malware and ransomware. See Figure 7.1.

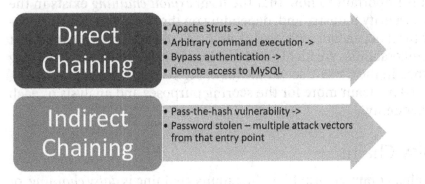

Figure 7.1: Direct vs. indirect chaining

This chapter explores the technical aspects of vulnerability chaining as well as the concerns with the language and terminology used in this space. We provide examples of vulnerability chaining, along with vendor-identified vulnerability chains and how organizations can integrate these concepts into their own vulnerability management programs (VMPs).

Exploit Chains

The concept of exploit chaining is like vulnerability chaining, and depending on the literature, it's possible that each term is interchangeable. According to Michael Hill (www.csoonline.com/ article/571799/exploit-chains-explained-how-and-why- attackers-target-multiple-vulnerabilities.html), exploit chains are specifically intended to conduct full-system compromise by gaining access to root or system credentials. Hill, the UK editor of CSO Online, has spent eight years researching and writing about information security topics. He's also one of the few writers in the industry who addresses exploit chaining (or vulnerability chaining) in a technical article. But with both terms (exploit chaining and vulnerability chaining), there are limitations to the scope of possible vulnerability chains.

Vulnerability or exploit chaining definitions don't currently define how vulnerability chains may be used once the system is compromised. Nor do the current definitions outline the other components outside of the Common Vulnerabilities and Exposures identifications (CVE IDs) and identified vulnerabilities for how chaining attacks may occur.

It is important to note that the term *exploit chaining* exists in the cybersecurity industry and, depending on the definition, it could confuse the independent aspects of chaining. Exploit chaining assumes that all vulnerabilities are highly exploitable, whereas *vulnerability chaining* defined in the CVSS User Guide (www.first.org/cvss/v3.0/user-guide) is meant more for the scoring purposes and analysis of each vulnerability.

Daisy Chains

Another common term for vulnerability chaining is *daisy chaining*, or linking vulnerabilities (see www.tenable.com/blog/daisy-chaining-how-vulnerabilities-can-be-greater-than-the-sum-of-their-parts). You can find some vendor-related documents from Tenable on daisy chaining, in addition to some documentation from Wiz.io (www.wiz.io/crying-out-cloud/4-customer-data-exposed-for-10-years) on how daisy chaining can be used in software supply chain attacks.

The confusion lies in talking about vulnerability chaining using multiple terms and different definitions. Ideally, vulnerability chains should be identified using the same language to provide consistency for security practitioners to identify and remediate effectively.

Using consistent language will also help vendors and organizations to identify where vulnerability chains may exist in their own products. Another benefit of using consistent terminology is when analysts and engineers submit new vulnerabilities for the Common Vulnerability Scoring System (CVSS).

Vendor-Released Chains

In our discussion of vulnerability chains, we will provide specific vendor examples. Our intention of selecting specific vulnerabilities is to show that vulnerability chaining can be used across multiple types of software. The specific vendors aren't relevant—only that the types of services and software are showing an industry trend for vendors to discuss and categorize vulnerability chains.

The CVSS has offered the possibility of scoring multiple vulnerabilities together using their formula, but it wasn't until 2021 that vendors started to release multiple vulnerabilities in combination as identified chains. As this is relatively new in the vulnerability management space, VMPs may not account for resolving or prioritizing remediation for vulnerability chains.

However, numerous vendors and suppliers have started releasing chained vulnerabilities with multiple CVE IDs and providing remediation guidance based on those chains. This positive and growing industry trend helps practitioners and organizations understand what chained vulnerabilities are and how to resolve them.

Microsoft Active Directory

One of the first mainstream vulnerability chaining disclosures was about two CVEs: CVE-2021-42287 and CVE-2021-42278, each used in combination to conduct an Active Directory (AD) domain takeover (`www.fortinet.com/blog/threat-research/cve-2021-42278-cve-2021-42287-from-user-to-domain-admin-60-seconds`). Using both vulnerabilities allowed an attacker to obtain a Kerberos ticket to a domain controller (DC). By gaining access to the DC, the attacker could then elevate privileges to become a domain administrator.

From there, an attacker could drop malware, reset passwords, gain access to any other Windows or domain-joined system, and many other activities. The CVE-2021-42287 (`https://nvd.nist.gov/vuln/detail/CVE-2021-42287`) is an elevation of privilege vulnerability on AD DCs, and CVE-2021-42278 (`https://nvd.nist.gov/vuln/detail/CVE-2021-42278`) is a bypass escalation of privilege vulnerability, allowing an attacker to impersonate a DC using spoofing techniques.

Using these vulnerabilities in combination provided a direct path for attackers to gain domain administration access on any unpatched AD DC. These vulnerabilities were added to the CISA Known Exploited Vulnerabilities (KEV) Catalog and part of the Binding Operational Directive (BOD) 22-01 (www.cisa.gov/news-events/directives/bod-22-01-reducing-significant-risk-known-exploited-vulnerabilities).

VMware vRealize Products

In 2022, three vulnerabilities were identified in VMware vRealize products that were initially identified as individual vulnerabilities. The first vulnerability, CVE-2022-31706, is a directory traversal vulnerability, and the second, CVE-2022-31704, is a broken access control vulnerability. According to an article by Tara Seals, the vRealize Log Insight platform provides log retention and management for infrastructure and other components in a technical environment (see www.darkreading.com/application-security/critical-vmware-rce-vulnerabilities-targeted-public-exploit-code). Seals is the Managing Editor for news at Dark Reading, an important platform for articles on applications security, vulnerability management, and many other cybersecurity-related topics.

Because this is a comprehensive logging tool, vRealize Log Insight stores data from sensitive systems and potentially important corporate data. The third flaw, which was identified as CVE-2022-31710, could allow unauthenticated access to an adversary by triggering the deserialization of untrusted information.

Researchers at Horizon3.ai were able to exploit code using these three vulnerabilities in combination, and they provided the information publicly (www.horizon3.ai/vmware-vrealize-cve-2022-31706-iocs). This vulnerability chain would have to be conducted internally on a network but it is possible for exploitation to occur by an insider or once an external party has internal access.

iPhone Exploit Chain

In late September 2023, researchers at Google's Threat Analysis Group (TAG) found an exploit chain in iOS devices (https://blog.google/threat-analysis-group/0-days-exploited-by-commercial-surveillance-vendor-in-egypt). Bugs were found and patched by

Apple, and they were identified as CVE-2023-41991, CVE-2023-41992, and CVE-2023-41993. The attack was conducted using an *on-path* method and created a 0-click vulnerability chain.

The attackers were able to redirect users to a website and redirect a targeted user to their exploit server. Both the vulnerabilities and the on-path delivery method didn't require any user interaction to open documents or answer phone calls. CVE-2023-41993 was a remote code execution (RCE) in the Safari browser, CVE-2023-41991 was a bypass vulnerability, and CVE-2023-41992 was a local privilege escalation (LPE) in the kernel.

This exploit or vulnerability chain was leveraged by attackers to install their version of spyware to look at all the applications, usernames and passwords, and any other personal data on their mobile devices. TAG also noted that this vulnerability chain was used in an attempt to attack Android devices as well. This highlights another example of modern vulnerability chaining and how this attack method can be used to gain access to devices and conduct full-system compromise.

Vulnerability Chaining and Scoring

We covered vulnerability scoring in depth in Chapter 5, "Vulnerability Scoring and Software Identification," but to zoom in on chained vulnerabilities, we will briefly explore the associated CVSS and EPSS scoring systems. Each scoring system is used for different purposes, but they are both important in understanding how chained attacks can be leveraged against an organization. The majority of the information and guidance on scoring chained vulnerabilities is in industry whitepapers and blogs, but solid scoring guidance is available from organizations like the Forum of Incident Response and Security Teams (FIRST).

There's still work to do to mature and grow the language, scoring, and ultimately the guidance around vulnerability chaining. But both scoring systems can aid in that endeavor by leveraging the CVSS as a starting point for possible vulnerability chains, and then focusing on prioritization activities further, using EPSS or CISA KEV. The following sections examine where vulnerability chaining scoring and analysis is addressed in cybersecurity guidance.

Common Vulnerability Scoring System

The FIRST organization had the first vulnerability chaining guidance available in the Common Vulnerability Scoring System (CVSS) User Guide (www.first.org/cvss/user-guide), related to scoring and submitting vulnerabilities as part of a chained attack. This user guide provides the most comprehensive and standardized format for scoring and understanding vulnerability chains. The CVSS states that it's up to the analyst who submits the vulnerabilities to list each distinct vulnerability and their score, along with the chained vulnerability score.

In the CVSS User Guide, analysts are also encouraged to include other types of vulnerabilities that can create a vulnerability chain within their own submission. An example provided in the guide includes how a Structured Query Language (SQL) injection could be the initial vector to then conduct a cross-site scripting (XSS) attack. This scoring method has been used for multiple vulnerabilities since then, as discussed in the Microsoft AD and VMware vulnerability chains presented previously.

Based on the CVSS User Guide, chained vulnerabilities are scored using their analysts calculation between Vulnerability A and Vulnerability B. The guidance only accounts for a combination of two vulnerabilities, which become Chain C in the formula for scoring. But this is a great start; it provides analysts with the ability to score and detail vulnerability chains as well as vulnerabilities within their own products.

EPSS

As of this writing, the FIRST EPSS model (www.first.org/epss/model) is still relatively new in the industry, but it shows promise to help organizations prioritize vulnerabilities and provide another opportunity to understand risk. The EPSS noted that there are far too many vulnerabilities for an organization to remediate them all as soon as they are released. Based on prior research, the EPSS also stated that organizations are only able to remediate up to 20 percent of vulnerabilities per month. As discussed more in depth in Chapter 5, the EPSS uses multiple sources to determine how exploitable a vulnerability can be.

But currently the EPSS is still growing and evolving, and it is limited in the amount of information available on vulnerability chaining. In the EPSS User Guide, the team noted that future research would be needed to determine whether specific vulnerabilities could be used in a chained attack. As the EPSS continues to mature, there might be more specific data and solutions discovered on vulnerability chaining and scoring.

The EPSS User Guide also defines the term *co-exploitation*, which is when multiple vulnerabilities can be exploited at the same time. The definition includes a note about the possibility of vulnerability chaining, or using multiple exploits in combination to compromise a system. Although there's no official guidance as of this writing for how EPSS aligns with vulnerability chaining, there's enough to show that chained vulnerabilities are possible based on their findings.

Gaps in the Industry

One of the first challenges of vulnerability chaining is the lack of updated and consistent guidance on vulnerability chaining remediation. Some technical blogs, academic research papers, and guidance from the CVSS exist, but limited information can be found at an industry level (see Figure 7.2). Thus, it's very important to explore this topic in depth, regarding building a mature and comprehensive VMP.

Another gap identified in the industry is the missing requirement for vendors and suppliers to identify vulnerability chains and score them when submitting for CVE IDs. Without this requirement, vulnerability chains are still incredibly difficult to identify and considered unknown risks. In general, there's a lack of knowledge and education about vulnerability chaining in current industry certifications and training on vulnerability management. The SANS Institute has a course on vulnerability management (www.sans.org/cyber-security-courses/building-leading-vulnerability-management-programs), and several vendor certifications are offered in products like Tenable and Qualys, but limited material is available for organizations and practitioners using general concepts.

Specifically, no training or certifications are available to network defenders on vulnerability chaining. While these concepts are taught to red teamers and used in certifications like Offensive Security Certified Professional (OSCP), many network defenders only have options to receive training from vendors that may (or may not) include vulnerability chaining information.

Without specific guidance or training on vulnerability chaining, organizations will continue to struggle to identify and remediate chains. There will also still be limited information from vendors on chains, without the requirements to annotate and score those chains in their CVE analysis. With more vendors and security researchers discussing vulnerability chaining, it's simply a matter of time before more guidance becomes available in the forms of industry scoring, research, and widespread industry recognition.

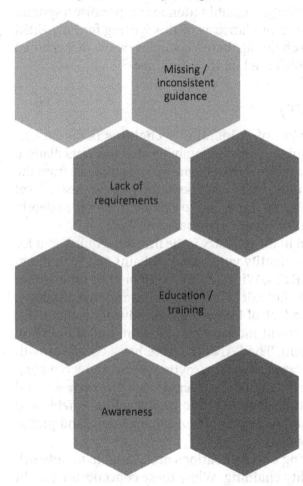

Missing / inconsistent guidance

Lack of requirements

Education / training

Awareness

Figure 7.2: Diagram of gaps

Vulnerability Chaining Blindness

Vulnerability chaining blindness (VCB) is a term coined by one of the authors, Dr. Nikki Robinson. This language was developed based on academic and technical research using established language from law enforcement and combining the concept of vulnerability chaining. This term was created to help define the phenomenon of how vulnerabilities are chained together and the difficulty in addressing multiple vulnerabilities in remediation activities.

Terminology

This new terminology was developed by initially using the term *linkage blindness*, coined by S. A. Egger in the early 1980s (www.ojp.gov/ncjrs/virtual-library/abstracts/working-definition-serial-murder-and-reduction-linkage-blindness). Egger was the original creator and publisher of the term linkage blindness, which helped to change the way that law enforcement agencies work together and share information. This term was invented to describe the inability of different agencies or departments to share information that might lead to an arrest or finding a specific criminal. For research purposes, the term was used specifically based on the inability to link or share information with different agencies that led to the inability to solve crimes and ultimately resolve cases.

The reason this term was used as the basis for VCB was the inability to link disparate information. Without the combination or sharing of this information (see Figure 7.3), it would be difficult to find the root cause or to identify possible crimes. As with vulnerability management, without the proper understanding of how vulnerabilities can be used in combination, it could lead organizations to try to remediate every single vulnerability.

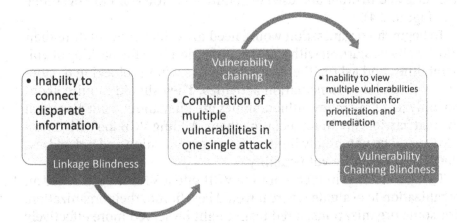

Figure 7.3: Combination of terms to create VCB

As stated previously, it's impossible to remediate every vulnerability across an enterprise. Some cannot be fixed because of functionality or operability concerns, whereas others might be left unresolved due to the lack of dedicated time and resources to remediate them. To help with the decision-making on how vulnerabilities should be prioritized, understanding vulnerability chaining can be a major factor in reducing risk and the time spent on remediation.

The combination of vulnerability chaining and linkage blindness to create the term VCB is the inability to link multiple vulnerabilities in combination, which could lead to difficulties in prioritizing and remediating vulnerabilities. To solve this, organizations can use this language and definition within their VMPs to help identify, define, and ultimately create a process to remediate chained vulnerabilities.

VCB has major implications for organizations as well as the cybersecurity industry. This terminology defines a new phenomenon and allows practitioners to become more aware of this topic. Once more network defenders, IT professionals, and developers are aware of VCB, it can start to become part of the vulnerability remediation methodology and processes.

Usage in Vulnerability Management Programs

How can VMPs leverage the use of VCB and, to a larger extent, vulnerability chaining concepts in their VMPs? There are several ways that teams and organizations can build chaining into their security policies, processes, and even tooling. Each recommendation should be taken and reviewed in order and used to mature and grow the VMP over time (see Figure 7.4).

To begin, an organization would need to evaluate how mature their VMP really is, starting with a real examination into the backlog of vulnerabilities and asking their team members what is blocking or stopping vulnerability remediation activities. They should inquire about not only just how many vulnerabilities are outstanding, but also what the real barriers are in remediating them. Adding VCB too early into a VMP could be potentially limiting for an organization and not address the root cause of the vulnerability.

The second step in incorporating VCB into a VMP would be for an organization to evaluate where it would best fit into their organization. For some organizations, a red team might be served more effectively with incorporating VCB into their feedback on penetration test reports, providing any data back to their blue teams (or network defense teams). Penetration test reports are typically written by the red team after a penetration test has been conducted. These tests include attempting to infiltrate the network by exploiting vulnerabilities, compromising credentials, or otherwise trying to gain unauthorized access to systems. The final report is essential in helping an organization to understand what risks may exist in their networks and then work on a remediation plan.

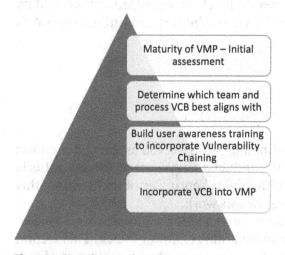

Figure 7.4: Solutions for VCB

However, other groups might elect to incorporate VCB into their blue teams to help streamline and organize remediation. Finally, some organizations with smaller cybersecurity teams might choose to incorporate this concept into their DevSecOps processes to identify and prioritize vulnerability chaining in their development environments.

A third step organizations can take to build vulnerability chaining is in their user awareness training. Typically, user awareness training covers using multifactor authentication (MFA), phishing examples, and the organization's security policies.

However, even users can benefit from understanding what attackers do and how they leverage multiple vulnerabilities in combination when conducting attacks. Not every user must understand chaining, but as with phishing tests, the more knowledge that is available to the user population, the more you can spread knowledge and lower risk.

A final component to incorporating VCB into any organization would be the inclusion of vulnerability chaining concepts into the organization's security policy. Each security policy will be unique to the organization; for example, smaller organizations may not be ready to leverage these concepts as they build their infrastructure. But larger organizations with a more mature VMP will want to build vulnerability chaining identification and remediation into their security policies and processes. Without understanding vulnerability chaining, organizations will be stuck with massive backlogs of vulnerabilities and limited resources to prioritize remediation.

The Human Aspect of Vulnerability Chaining

Vulnerability chaining is defined by FIRST CVSS as the combination of multiple vulnerabilities to conduct a single attack. Because this is the industry standard for vulnerability scoring as of this writing, this definition is used as the basis for this work.

However, this definition does not include how humans are a component as an initial vector to a vulnerability chaining attack. This section includes different examples of how users can be a component of vulnerability chaining, including phishing, business email compromise (BEC), and other social engineering tactics.

> **NOTE** We do not intend to pass blame to users, but simply highlight the limitations of the current definitions of vulnerability chaining. Understanding where vulnerability chaining starts (i.e., outside of CVE IDs and technical vulnerabilities) will allow security teams and organizations to begin considering the entire path of possible exploitation.

Phishing

Phishing, a common attack technique of sending emails to users to ask them to click a link or provide sensitive data over email, is an easy example of how vulnerability chaining can be conducted with a single click. Whether it is via email phishing, targeted spear-phishing, or vishing via a phone call, phishing is still the number one way that attackers gain access to systems. According to CISA's Stop Ransomware campaign, over 90 percent of attacks start with a phishing attack (see www.cisa.gov/stopransomware/general-information).

Each phishing method can be used to convince a user to click a link to malicious software or a server, to reset their password and allow the attacker access to systems, or to download malware. In any of these cases, the user is the initial link in the chain that can lead to exploiting vulnerabilities.

One example would be where a user is sent a phishing email, asking them to reset their password for their bank or favorite shopping site. This website captures the credentials they enter, allowing the malicious actor to steal the user's credentials and log in to their personal or business accounts. Once a malicious actor can leverage those credentials in an attack, they can then conduct a privilege escalation or use lateral movement by gaining access to other systems.

Once the malicious actor can gain entrance to these systems, the possibilities for vulnerability exploitation from there are endless. They could leverage any vulnerabilities left open either on the system itself or from web applications that the user has access to in order to gain access to databases or directory services. The initial attack vector would be the user's interaction with a malicious website, leading potentially to a full-system compromise.

Business Email Compromise

A more targeted and sophisticated type of attack, the business email compromise (BEC), begins in a similar manner, but the vulnerability chains are exploited quite differently (see www.fbi.gov/how-we-can-help-you/safety-resources/scams-and-safety/common-scams-and-crimes/business-email-compromise). BEC attacks are typically conducted by spoofing (i.e., when an actor sends an email with a fake sender address to an executive's email address) or by compromising their account. Once the bad actor has access to the email account, they can sit and wait for three to six months, watching how the individual sends emails.

During that time, they'll study their language, the frequency of emails sent, and ultimately how they conduct wire transfers or send money within the organization. Their intention is to encourage a financial executive or officer to approve a wire transfer to a foreign bank account. The bad actor who compromised the email account simply sits idly by, monitoring email traffic to understand the executive's behavior.

Then a different type of vulnerability chaining attack occurs, assuming that the email account is already compromised versus a spoofed account. Once the email account is compromised, a fake email is then sent requesting a wire transfer to a foreign or offshore bank account outside of the organization. The email is sent with some urgency and mimics the language and cadence of the executive's emails.

If successful, the bad actor might stop there. But if unsuccessful, they still have gained access to an executive's email account and might conduct privilege escalation or exploit other vulnerabilities to gain access to sensitive information. However, in the event of a spoofed account requesting wire transfers, an account or system may never be compromised. The actor may simply be hoping that they will be able to catch someone off guard.

Social Engineering

There are many other forms of social engineering that could be leveraged to begin a chained vulnerability attack. *Vishing* is when a bad actor calls an individual, trying to gain access to data. *Smishing* is when a bad actor uses texting to get a user to click a link or send data back to them. (See www.cisecurity.org/insights/newsletter/vishing-and-smishing-what-you-need-to-know). In either scenario, the intention is to compromise systems, to gain access to a user's account, or to encourage a user to download malware or connect them back to their own servers.

An example of vishing is the MGM breach (www.nbcnews.com/tech/security/mgm-las-vegas-hackers-scattered-spider-rcna105238), in which an actor claimed to call a helpdesk technician and ask for a password reset. This cyberattack is still relatively new and more information continues to come out about possible entry points for attackers. But this example highlights how attackers may leverage phone calls to access user accounts and gain access to systems, which would be the beginning of a chained vulnerability attack.

Both the Federal Communications Commission (FCC) and Internal Revenue Service (IRS) noted in 2022 that smishing and vishing attacks were trending upward (see `www.bleepingcomputer.com/news/security/us-govt-warns-americans-of-escalating-sms-phishing-attacks` and `www.bleepingcomputer.com/news/security/irs-warns-americans-of-massive-rise-in-sms-phishing-attacks`). Whether it's phishing, vishing, or smishing, users are an initial attack vector for bad actors to conduct several types of chained vulnerability exploits.

Integration into VMPs

Now that the foundation has been laid for vulnerability chaining, including existing guidance and research, examples of exploits, and usage in the industry, we will provide several options for how organizations can build this information into their own cybersecurity programs. Vulnerability chaining concepts and remediation can be built into organizations from the leadership level down to practitioners and users (see Figure 7.5).

Leadership	Security Practitioners	IT and Developers
• Approval of language and VCB use in policy • Reinforcement of prioritization of efforts • How vulnerability chaining is used by APT groups	• IR – integrate techniques into forensics • Prioritize remediation on VCB and externally facing vulnerabilities • Assessors identify possible missing VCB controls	• Understand risk of exploitable / EOL software • SAST/DAST integration • Security stage gate reviews

Figure 7.5: Integration into a VMP diagram

As mentioned earlier, incorporating vulnerability chaining into security awareness programs can help users understand their own role in these attack types. And because vulnerability chaining attacks continue to be used by APT groups (`www.cisa.gov/news-events/cybersecurity-advisories/aa20-283a`), the more awareness and prevention is built into VMPs, the better, as organizations will be prepared to protect themselves against highly sophisticated attacks.

Leadership Principles

At the executive leadership level, a basic understanding of vulnerability chaining is required. Because executive leadership would be the determining factor in adding language to an organization's cybersecurity policies, it is essential that they understand the impact of these attack types. Vulnerability chaining attacks can be used to compromise all systems, drop ransomware, or steal corporate data to sell on the dark web.

From the mid- to senior-level leadership perspective, vulnerability chaining is a concept to understand and in which to provide training for technical professionals. If executives did approve some language to incorporate into the company's cybersecurity policy, it would mean a reinforcement of these policies throughout the organization. It could also mean some additional training in basic chained attacks and exploitation for their incident response (IR) leadership if they aren't already aware.

Leaders across the organization need a basic understanding of how exploitation can occur with chained attacks. Our recommendation is to have separate cybersecurity awareness training for executive leadership (versus practitioners) and management. This training ensures that there's awareness, but there isn't necessarily action required on their part unless they're handling an incident or preparing budgets for security programs and tools.

Security Practitioner Integration

Many security practitioners may already be aware of the vulnerability chaining attacks leveraged against users and systems. However, this concept might be more prevalent within red teams, penetration testers, or ethical hacker circles. It is important for each organization to gauge their practitioners' general awareness of vulnerability chaining before determining the best course of action or where it best fits in their cybersecurity policies and processes.

From the IR team's perspective, it's important to understand how chained vulnerabilities work in combination to help lead forensics investigations. While many IR specialists may already be aware, they may not use the same terminology or have processes for handling these chained attacks. Building these concepts into an IR method and process encourages the analysts and responders to identify possible chains or how each exploit was leveraged to gain access to multiple systems.

From a vulnerability analyst perspective, anyone who works in remediation should be aware of vulnerability chaining and how these chains can be broken. This knowledge will help teams collaborate with their IT and developer partners to resolve their highest-priority vulnerabilities. It's also essential for anyone responsible and accountable for vulnerability remediation to be skilled in and understand the technical components of vulnerability chains.

For security assessors and auditors, this may not be a concept built into their training or certification programs or a part of their daily routines. Incorporating vulnerability chaining as a potential security control, or something to evaluate, could be beneficial for all parties. While not an official security control as part of the NIST 800-53 series, it is another area for assessors to review and determine if there are any concerns.

IT and Development Usage

For system owners—who could be IT professionals owning a cloud infrastructure or running operations for development environments—vulnerability chaining doesn't need to be understood in depth. The most crucial detail is that vulnerability chains can be broken through remediation activities. Leaving older or end-of-life (EOL) software in an environment increases the risk of chained vulnerability attacks. Through collaboration with their own security engineering teams, system owners could identify and potentially break those vulnerability chains.

For developers, it's essential that they understand how leaving a SQL injection, cleartext passwords, or XSS vulnerability could be the entry point for a chained vulnerability attack. Developers should be learning about vulnerability chaining as part of a DevSecOps program, and it should be built into their dynamic application security testing (DAST) and static application security testing (SAST) processes.

For any other technical practitioners who manage web applications or any network or platform engineers, vulnerability chaining should be built into the security review and vulnerability remediation activities, just as with any other team. Each group should be aware of and understand the technical implications for leaving highly exploitable vulnerabilities unremediated.

Summary

Vulnerability chaining continues to be a popular attack type for threat actors, but it's not as prevalent from the vulnerability management or remediation side. From a blue team perspective, there's still more to be done to integrate these concepts into daily routines and to assist in the prioritization of vulnerability remediation activities. This chapter introduced examples of vulnerability chains, guidance, and usage in the industry as well as recommendations for leadership and practitioners to incorporate into their own VMPs.

8

Vulnerability Threat Intelligence

Threat intelligence is a domain within cybersecurity where teams leverage open source information to determine and prioritize threats to an organization. While commonly a separate practice in larger cybersecurity teams, smaller teams may leverage the same tactics to determine if there are known bad domains, IP addresses, types of files and file hashes, or specific vulnerabilities that are being exploited in the wild. All this technical information can be used to create alerts, detect possible ongoing attacks, or block unwanted network scanning from bad actors. Threat intelligence is also known as cyber threat intelligence (CTI) and is used by multiple organizations, one example being the Cybersecurity and Infrastructure Security Agency (CISA) (www.cisa .gov/resources-tools/services/cyber-threat-intelligence).

Why Is Threat Intel Important to VMPs?

Using this intelligence, organizations can create alerts or focus remediation activities on the given information. For example, if a threat actor is found to be using a specific type of ransomware or a list of file types and specific hashes, techniques will be found and distributed among proper threat intelligence communication channels to combat them. A threat intel team will learn that this specific threat actor is using this attack type and may choose to increase detection and tailor alerting for specific IP addresses or domains. The SANS Whitepaper on Threat Intelligence is an excellent resource to use to get started when building a threat intelligence practice or team. (https://nsfocusglobal.com/ wp-content/uploads/2017/01/SANS_Whitepaper_Threat_Intel ligence__What_It_Is__and_How_to_Use_It_Effectively.pdf).

There might be a separate threat intelligence team, or the same tactics used within the cybersecurity teams (potentially the Security Operations Center [SOC] or CSIRT). These tactics can also be leveraged within vulnerability management programs (VMPs). Information from current targeted cyberattacks can be another tool to help teams hone in on the most critical vulnerabilities to mitigate or remediate.

Without leveraging threat intelligence, vulnerability teams will be solely leveraging Common Vulnerability Scoring System (CVSS) Base scores and possibly some system context (i.e., web applications or external-facing assets). With the known backlogs of vulnerabilities, any tools and techniques that focus remediation and apply mitigating controls will help reduce overhead on vulnerability management teams.

As with the other chapters in this book, adding threat intelligence might not be the first step in building a comprehensive VMP. However, threat intelligence techniques can be added once a solid asset management and vulnerability scoring and prioritization program is already in place.

Where to Start

First, it's important to understand the various types of threat intelligence that are applicable to a VMP: technical, tactical, strategic, and operational. Each type of threat intelligence can be used at different places within the VMP.

Technical Threat Intelligence

Technical threat intelligence is the specific indicators of compromise (IOCs) that teams can use to identify threat actors (https://socradar.io/what-is-technical-cyber-threat-intelligence-and-how-to-use-it). An IOC is information gained from an attack that has already occurred—for instance, learning that a specific list of domains and IPs are related to an advanced persistent threat (APT) group. The IOC may have been discovered either internally from an attack or from an attack that occurred at another organization and was shared through threat intelligence communication channels. This type of threat intelligence focuses on the tooling and techniques around gathering intelligence and technical resources. Resources and technical components include attack vectors, exploitable vulnerabilities, log sources, and domain information.

These technical data and resources may be available from internal vulnerability scanners, endpoint detection and response (EDR) monitoring, and network mapping tools. The biggest benefit of the technical threat intel components is that this data type is common between teams and is easy to share and utilize quickly. Chances are, this data is already available in the environment, and when combined with outside intel, it will be the beginning of leveraging tactical, strategic, and operational intel techniques.

Tactical Threat Intelligence

Tactical threat intelligence may be the most widely used and consistent form of threat intel that would be relevant to a VMP. This threat intel method gives organizations a peek into the type of potential attack vectors or methods of compromise that a bad actor might use. This intelligence type is most beneficial for SOCs, IT managers and leadership, as well as network engineering teams. This article from CrowdStrike provides a good source on tactical threat intelligence (www.crowdstrike .com/cybersecurity-101/threat-intelligence).

A few examples of the types of tactical threat intelligence that might be used in an organization are:

- Known bad IP addresses, domains, and URLs
- Trending signatures and types of malware and/or ransomware
- Types of network scanning patterns or techniques
- Phishing, vishing, or smishing attacks and trends

There are several methods that threat intel teams and vulnerability management analysts can use to gather this information. For example, if they have a separate network, they could access the dark web to monitor and track related signatures or patterns, as well as reports for associated known APTs and other groups. Teams could also leverage malware samples and human intelligence, or the gathering of information from individuals based on their experience. Organizations will commonly leverage a variety of data sources, including using their internal tooling, as well as industry groups, commercial products and vendors, as well as other third-party vendors and consultants.

But tactical threat intelligence can also be integrated into vulnerability management groups by using this information to test their own tooling and processes. This would align more with bringing red and blue teams together to create a purple team or a purple team process. They could also leverage this intel to fine-tune security tooling and alerts and find unknown gaps in their security processes and procedures. Tactical threat intelligence is the true alignment of people, process, and technology.

Strategic Threat Intelligence

In comparison to tactical, *strategic threat intelligence* is more about high-level information for senior leaders versus the technical details of specific Common Vulnerabilities and Exposures (CVEs) or exploited vulnerabilities. This information is available to help make decisions and may not be used as a main source of intelligence. The leaders from the threat intel and VMP teams should work closely together to identify strategic intel and bring it forward to other senior and executive leadership in the organization. The same article from CrowdStrike, mentioned that, provides an overview of threat intelligence types, including tactical and strategic.

Examples of strategic threat intelligence include:

- Policies and regulations (national and international)
- Media from regional, national, and international sources
- Information and data collected from social media (verified and unverified sources)

This information can be integrated within VMPs by helping to validate a specific remediation path for vulnerabilities. For example, suppose a hospital received word that an APT group was leveraging a specific type of malware to disrupt healthcare organizations. The senior hospital leaders might be aware of campaigns across the country to disrupt services and would encourage the VMP to identify any relevant vulnerabilities and report on any vulnerable systems. The VMP team could work closely with the threat intelligence team to determine the techniques, tactics, and procedures (TTPs) and any evolving information around vulnerabilities used by the APT group.

Operational Threat Intelligence

Operational threat intelligence focuses on the information that security teams use around a threat actor's motives, methods, and techniques, and how they perform attacks. Most of this data is not open source and may be difficult to find, and would require the skillset and capabilities of threat intelligence analysts. To gain more insight into operational threat intelligence, the article from CrowdStrike provides a high level overview of all threat intelligence types.

A few sources of operational threat intelligence are listed below:

- Social media or profiles on bad actors or APT groups
- Forums and chat sites (either that are open source or located on the dark web)

This type of information is best used by the threat intelligence team and parsed for the vulnerability management teams. The vulnerability management analysts and engineers may not need deep information on the specific motivations and behaviors of an APT group or individual, but they would benefit from understanding how they may conduct an attack. This information helps the analysts and engineers because they might be able to detect attacks simply by the patterns of behavior versus looking for specific files or intellectual properties. An example would be if it's known that a bad actor uses a specific email campaign to entice a user to enter their credentials into a website for credential theft. They would be able to look for specific email subject lines or types based on that behavior type.

For example, if an APT group prefers contacting users through social media to gather business information or attempt credential theft, the threat intel team could help the detection engineering team to create rules and alerts for that behavior type. This intel type would also benefit the SOC and incident response teams by helping them understand how a bad actor accessed systems and hopefully prevent future attacks using those methods. This intel would also benefit the VMP by offering prioritization for favorite methods by different groups, including specific vulnerability remediation or attack methods.

Threat Hunting

Using any of the discussed threat intelligence methods (technical, tactical, strategic, or operational), the threat intel and vulnerability management teams can conduct threat hunting activities together or through a cyclical process (www.splunk.com/en_us/blog/learn/threat-hunting.html).

Threat hunting can be broken down into a methodical approach:

1. Develop and test hypotheses based on intelligence and attackers' TTPs.
2. Investigate threats or alerts based on known IOCs or indicators of attacks (IOAs). IOCs focus on identifying incidents and evidence after a compromise, whereas IOAs focus on detecting suspicious or anomalous behavior during an ongoing attack.
3. Leverage analytics and data science techniques to sift through mountains of data.
4. Fine-tune alerts and security tooling to detect novel attack methods and techniques.

A threat hunting team would then use this information to conduct a hunt:

1. **Trigger:** Find a system or location within the environment that might be associated with anomalous behavior.
2. **Investigation:** Leverage tooling available to the team to determine if there are additional alerts or components to investigate.
3. **Resolution:** After finalizing the investigation, gather the information, eliminate any missing security controls, and remediate vulnerabilities.
4. **Incident Response:** Based on the findings, incidents may be reported and investigated, information would be disseminated to the proper teams for resolution, and alerts would be tuned.

Threat hunting is a great way to use threat intelligence information and support the activities of a VMP. With actionable information, vulnerability management teams can use threat hunting reports and findings to focus remediation efforts. It cannot be stated enough—the more intel and data that teams are able to utilize will focus remediation efforts, save on administrative overhead, reduce the burden of manual patching, and ultimately improve the vulnerability management process over time.

Integrating Threat Intel into VMPs

Each of the various threat intelligence categories we've covered can be used to create a more mature and effective VMP. Solely using vulnerability scoring might create a backlog of vulnerabilities that could be difficult to completely remediate. Using the methods discussed, organizations can systematically focus on the vulnerabilities and configurations that are most important.

First, it is important to define the scope of what threat intelligence will mean to each individual group and organization. Each organization must have its own method and data that's important to collect—but not everything will be actionable. There's an important balance to strike around what data is important and what isn't. Not all data is consumable or even relevant to a business, sector, or organization. Spend the time up front to determine which sets of intelligence will help you hone your vulnerability remediation efforts.

Second, determine what skillset and training the teams currently have. Evaluate if the skill training can be held in-house, or if your teams will need additional training, consulting, or the hiring of outside personnel. There are a variety of open source, inexpensive, and expensive options available in the threat intelligence space. For example, Martin Lee's book *Cyber Threat Intelligence* (Wiley, 2023) is a great resource for teams to use to get started on basic threat intel processes and techniques.

Finally, integrate the technology and processes with people on both the threat intelligence and vulnerability management teams. Whether an organization ultimately decides to keep those teams separate, or leverage threat intel techniques within their vulnerability management team, the processes and technology are going to be just as important to define. Each team will most likely use a combination of open source and paid-for tools (depending on their budget), and those processes will be unique per organization, industry, and ultimately, team dynamics.

People

The first task within the *people* portion of leveraging threat intelligence is to ensure that the proper team members are in place, and that they have the proper training and understanding of how these separate tasks will align within the VMP. For example, if there are larger threat intelligence and VMP teams running independently, a plan needs to be coordinated for how frequently data is shared, what format is used, and ultimately who is responsible for actioning on the intel.

Your people will help to define the scope of what information types are important, how that information will be used, and ultimately who will be responsible for integrating this information into the VMP. For example, if there are separate teams for threat intelligence and vulnerability management priorities, then it would be essential to determine who owns which process, and from there, who will act on the intelligence.

Determine which teams should be involved and how communication will flow between those teams. In larger teams, data flow will potentially be confusing without a proper communication process, and each group might miss critical data points.

The best format is to integrate these teams and create a cohesive information flow diagram, as shown in the next section. The information should move fluidly through the teams, and each data type should be handled separately. For example, any intel for vulnerabilities that are being exploited in the wild should be communicated as quickly as possible, whereas other less critical intel may be shared during a daily or weekly digest (depending on severity and relevance to the organization).

Once the team and data flows have been organized and structured, the processes and documentation should follow.

Process

The threat intel and vulnerability management teams should collaborate to build *process* documentation for how the data flows will work, what types of data structures are important to the business, and even timelines for actions on the intel.

For example, if there's information about a known exploited vulnerability in a different sector (e.g., healthcare versus technology), this intelligence might be put into a daily or weekly briefing. Because the intelligence received is from a different sector, it may not indicate a direct threat to the organization. However, that information about the exploitation might be relevant to their systems if they have the same vulnerabilities on external-facing systems. It would still be beneficial to evaluate those vulnerability details and remediation information, but it should be prioritized around other vulnerabilities or exploits that are more pertinent to their business.

Processes and associated workflows like the following would be built based off the scenario previously discussed:

1. Take an inventory of, and define, your specific usage of intel and vulnerability management tooling.
2. Create your architecture diagrams for tooling integration.
3. Designate a timeline for your intelligence gathering and reporting requirements.
4. Document an understanding between teams covering their areas of responsibility.
5. Write your organization's standard operating procedures (SOPs) for how intelligence is gathered and from what sources.

A final recommendation would be to process or document a workflow to indicate how these processes align and your teams' associated roles and responsibilities within each process. Documentation, especially when integrating teams or different processes, should be updated as appropriate and follow organizational guidelines. As stated in previous chapters, it's crucial that this documentation be improved over time. Threat intelligence is incredibly dynamic and evolving all the time—these documents and processes should be evaluated quarterly to keep your organization up-to-date.

Technology

There are an incredible number of open source and paid-for solutions in the threat intelligence space. Tools include Bitdefender, Recorded Future, and CrowdStrike, and open source options include AlienVault Open Threat Exchange (OTX), GreyNoise, and OpenCTI, to name a few. Numerous options are available that provide strategic intel, workflows, and taxonomies for classification of data as well as data sharing and notifications.

The most important components of selecting tooling will be budget and ultimately how mature the VMP is. For example, smaller organizations or startups might only need open source tooling to start. As the business grows and matures, they may want to create a more robust tooling solution and separate threat intel and vulnerability management teams. That way, the teams can integrate, like a purple team, to share information and iterate over time.

But the tooling must align with the people and processes defined in previous sections. The recommendation is to start small and build up tooling over time. Giving teams too much information, tooling, or alerts can overwhelm them and reduce teams' effectiveness. Select your tools with purpose, and continuously evaluate if they still aid the teams, reduce their stress, and improve their effectiveness.

Summary

Incorporating threat intelligence into regular vulnerability management practices has so many incredible benefits. By reducing the noise and constant barrage of vulnerabilities to sift through, organizations can focus remediation efforts from technical, tactical, strategic, and operational intelligence practices.

Including threat intelligence would not be a first step to creating a vulnerability management program, but it would enhance and mature the program over time. Whether an organization chooses to leverage open source threat intelligence tools or hire a full-time team, this information will help provide prioritization for vulnerability remediation activities.

Cloud, DevSecOps, and Software Supply Chain Security

While vulnerability management has been a long-standing practice and comes with its own challenges in traditional on-premises environments, the era of widespread cloud adoption has added new complexities to the challenges, while also ushering in opportunities for innovative technologies and approaches to addressing those challenges. We will spend this chapter discussing some of those unique considerations and aspects as they relate to vulnerability management in the cloud.

Although the definition is a bit dated, for the purpose of the book we will be leveraging guidance from National Institute of Standards and Technology (NIST) as it relates to defining the cloud and its various service models. NIST's Special Publication (SP) 800-145 defines cloud computing as follows:

> *Cloud computing is a model for enabling ubiquitous, convenient, on-demand network access to a shared pool of configurable computing resources (e.g., networks, servers, storage, applications, and services) that can be rapidly provisioned and released with minimal management effort or service provider interaction. This cloud model is composed of five essential characteristics, three service models, and four deployment models.*

Throughout this chapter, we will discuss each of the service models as well as aspects of the various deployment models that organizations may need to take into consideration as they build their vulnerability management programs.

Cloud Service Models and Shared Responsibility

As previously discussed, the cloud operates with three service models:

- Infrastructure-as-a-service (IaaS)
- Platform-as-a-service (PaaS)
- Software-as-a-service (SaaS)

Starting with the first service model, IaaS is where fundamental computing resources and activities are managed by the cloud service provider (CSP). This means things such as compute, storage, networking, and the underlying physical materials that make them possible are handled by the CSP. The CSP either owns or works with data center providers to host the physical materials that provide these services to consumers and handles activities such as the physical security of the facilities, which would traditionally be done by individual organizations or managed service providers with whom they work.

Cloud computing operates in a multi-tenant model, with CSPs providing core infrastructure services to consumers similar to a utility model with consumption-based billing. Depending on the deployment model and risk tolerance of consumers, CSPs utilize logical and sometimes physical isolation to ensure proper segmentation among tenants, their resources, and their data.

As you'll see later in this section, there is potential for vulnerabilities that can impact multiple tenants, or allow malicious actors to compromise the isolation between tenants and their environments and data, which can present systemic risks.

Traditionally, organizations had to do things such as order physical equipment, wait for it to arrive, rack it, run cabling, and ensure connectivity and sufficient power, all of which is now handled by the CSP. On one hand, it minimizes the risk and vulnerabilities that consumers need to be responsible for regarding physical infrastructure, security, and basic functions such as computing and networking. However, on the other hand, the explosion of cloud adoption and use, application programming interfaces (APIs), and SaaS has rapidly expanded the attack surface of most modern organizations as well.

A good depiction of the shared responsibility model (SRM) can be found in Figure 9.1 from Microsoft Azure, one of the largest IaaS providers.

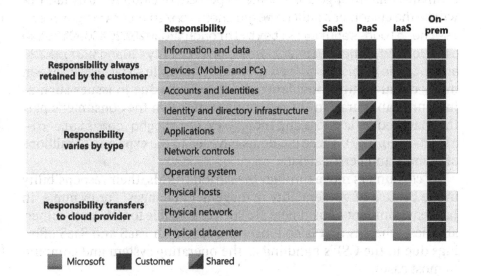

Figure 9.1: The shared responsibility model

As shown in Figure 9.1, what the customer or consumer needs to be concerned with in terms of responsibilities and vulnerabilities is dictated by the service model in which they're operating. That said, most modern organizations live in complex hybrid-cloud environments with a combination of on-premises infrastructure and systems, applications, and workloads residing in the cloud, and consuming applications via SaaS from cloud providers. This means the modern vulnerability management program needs to account for this complex reality.

One thing that we want to emphasize is that while you might be able to outsource responsibility via the shared responsibility model, you *cannot* outsource accountability. It is ultimately still your organization's data and reputation on the line in the event of a vulnerability's exploitation, whether the vulnerability belonged to you as the consumer or was actually on the CSP's side of the SRM. This is why it's critical for organizations adopting the cloud to understand this paradigm and base their decisions on their respective risk tolerance.

Historically (and still), the majority of cloud security incidents have occurred on the customer's side of the SRM, and are most often due to customer misconfigurations. In fact, industry analyst organization Gartner estimates that through 2025, some 99 percent of cloud security failures will be the customer's fault (www.gartner.com/smarterwithgartner/ is-the-cloud-secure#:~:text=Through%202025%2C%2099%25%20 of%20cloud,ownership%2C%20responsibility%20and%20risk%20 acceptance). This has proven to be fairly accurate so far, as we've seen many cloud security incidents and data leaks due to issues such as insecure configurations or misconfigurations on the consumer's part that have led to data loss and more (www.datadoghq.com/state-of-cloud-security). These incidents have led to the exposure of millions of records and personal data.

As consumers move through the various SRMs, their responsibility in the context of vulnerability management changes. For example, in IaaS environments, customers are still responsible for OS-level vulnerabilities, whereas that is no longer the case with PaaS and SaaS offerings due to the CSP's handling of the operating system and compute in most cases.

In the following sections, we will discuss some cloud aspects that have allowed innovative modern approaches to vulnerability management, in addition to some unique considerations for cloud-native technologies that should be accounted for in vulnerability management programs.

Hybrid and Multicloud Environments

While cloud adoption has undeniably increased (except for entirely cloud-native greenfield organizations that were "born" in the cloud), most organizations still have legacy or on-premises infrastructure and systems that must be accounted for. This means that organizations need to include these complex hybrid cloud (e.g., on-premises and cloud) environments as part of their broader vulnerability management programs.

This approach can be complex, due to disparate and diverse technological stacks and tooling that may only work in one environment or another. This often can lead to organizations needing to implement multiple tools to ensure they are covering the systems on-premises and in the cloud with regard to activities such as asset management, inventory, configuration management, and vulnerability management.

Malicious actors often look to pivot laterally between systems in the on-premises and cloud environments due to their ubiquitous connectivity. Due to this reality, leading vulnerability management vendors have been expanding their platforms and capabilities to account for hybrid cloud environments to ensure that organizations can see all their assets and exposures, enrich findings with business-specific context, and mitigate the various hybrid attack paths that may exist.

Multicloud environments, which are scenarios where organizations are using multiple CSPs, is another challenging aspect of vulnerability management in modern digital environments. Some often discuss multicloud environments in the context of IaaS—for instance, with organizations using a combination of the largest IaaS providers like Microsoft Azure, Google Cloud, and Amazon Web Services (AWS)—but the reality is that SaaS is also part of the cloud, and therefore nearly every organization is already considered "multicloud" by definition. That said, SaaS has some unique considerations that we will discuss in a separate section to follow.

Remember, as we have discussed, the majority of cloud security incidents are due to customer misconfigurations. In addition, the potential of such incidents increases when you're dealing with multicloud environments because of their increased complexity. Organizations often struggle with configuration and vulnerability management in cloud environments due to the myriad of potential configurations, services, and implementations, and the complexity is exponential across the clouds. From a vulnerability management perspective, organizations need to aggregate vulnerabilities from their multicloud environments to avoid needing to have disparate vulnerability details for each unique cloud provider and environment, and instead understand a holistic picture of their vulnerability posture across clouds.

Containers

With the growth and evolution of cloud computing, we've also seen the growth and adoption of modernized forms of computing, including containers. Cloud-native surveys by organizations such as the Cloud Native Computing Foundation (CNCF) found that 96 percent of organizations are either currently using containers or evaluating them for use (www.cncf.io/reports/cncf-annual-survey-2021). In the world of the cloud-native ecosystem, containers fit into what is called the "four Cs" of cloud security: cloud, clusters, containers, and code (https:// kubernetes.io/docs/concepts/security/overview). Each layer builds upon the next, and vulnerabilities at any layer can impact the layers that follow, such as applications deployed using insecure or vulnerable containers (see Figure 9.2).

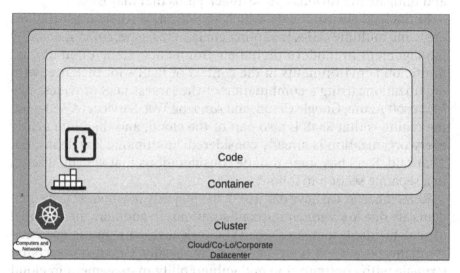

Figure 9.2: The four Cs of cloud security

Source: https://kubernetes.io/docs/concepts/security/overview / The Kubernetes Authors/CC-BY 4.0

In the context of computing, industry leader Docker defines a container as "a standard unit of software that packages up code and all of its dependencies, so the application runs quickly and reliably from one environment to another (www.docker.com/resources/what-container)." Worth emphasizing in that definition is the concept of *portability*—being able to move from one environment to another—as well as characteristics such as the packaging of dependencies, which has ramifications for vulnerability management. Containers represent an evolution of compute abstractions built on the world of virtual machines (VMs).

Both VMs and containers are compute abstractions to host applications and virtualized workloads but with some key differences. Virtual machines turn one server into many; many VMs can run on a single piece of hardware, each with its own guest operating system and applications. Containers, on the other hand, package the code and dependencies together; multiple containers can run on the same machine, sharing the same OS kernel with other containers, running as isolated processes in their respective spaces. Containers tend to be more compact and less sizable than VMs, making them more efficient in terms of size and cost. In Figure 9.3, you can view a depiction of some of the key differences between the two abstractions.

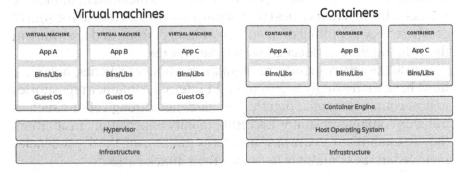

Figure 9.3: Containers vs. virtual machines

Containerized applications are lightweight and enable needed capabilities in cloud-native workloads, such as immutability, scalability, and portability. They're often managed by what is called a *container orchestrator*, with the most popular one being Kubernetes, which we will discuss in the next section. It is these unique aspects of containers that provide not only benefits but also challenges when it comes to vulnerability management.

Container images are stored in what is referred to as a *container registry*. Some of these registries are open to the public Internet, while others are privately hosted with access controls in place. In 2021, security vendor Palo Alto Network's Unit 42 Threat Research group analyzed over 1,500 distinct images in popular public registries such as Docker Hub, Quay, and Google Container Registry (GCR) (www.paloaltonetworks.com/prisma/unit42-cloud-threat-research-2h21). They found that 96 percent of the images had vulnerabilities and 91 percent of them had critical vulnerabilities. Their research also highlighted that the higher the number of dependencies a container has, the higher the number of vulnerabilities it tends to have as well. This is why you will often see best practices advocated for such as limiting the container's attack surface by only including dependencies and libraries that are absolutely required for the application to function.

On one hand, while there are tremendous benefits of containers, such as their declarative nature and ability to be portable across environments and distributed much like traditional code, they also enable the widespread distribution of vulnerable container images, which can then be consumed by organizations and have applications built on top of them, inherently including the vulnerabilities included in those base images. This makes it critical that organizations understand the source of where they're pulling their container images from, and are aware of the vulnerabilities associated with those images.

Due to the security concerns of public container registries, organizations have increasingly begun to build internal container repositories to host container images that they've hardened through efforts such as utilizing container scanning and vulnerability remediation. In addition, they've established secure base images by minimizing the dependencies included in the containers to reduce their attack surface.

Some examples include the Department of Defense (DoD) United States Air Force (USAF), which has established the "Iron Bank," a secure container image repository that allows DoD mission/system owners to utilize these hardened container images for running their applications. Commercial industry efforts are also underway, specifically by software supply chain vendor Chainguard and their Chainguard images offering, which includes maintaining updated and hardened container images for some of the most widely popular container images in the ecosystem. This minimizes the toil on enterprises by offering them something to consume, rather than the respective organizations needing to do the container hardening activities themselves.

To demonstrate the importance of secure base images, Chainguard produced a paper titled "All About That Base Image," which looked at popular base images and the associated security technical debt (e.g., vulnerabilities and vulnerable dependencies or components) associated with them by using various popular open source software (OSS) vulnerability scanners (https://uploads-ssl.webflow.com/6228fd bc6c97145dad2a9c2b/624e2337f70386ed568d7e7e_chainguard-all-about-that-base-image.pdf). It demonstrated that some of the most popular base images come with tens or even hundreds of inherent vulnerabilities that organizations then build their applications on top of, creating a situation where applications are vulnerable from their inception due to building on insecure base images.

In addition to highlighting the nature of vulnerable base images, the report demonstrates the wide range of findings across different vulnerability scanners, making the case for potentially using more than one scanner, or at least ensuring standardized tooling across an organization to not have disparate findings between teams within the organization. It is worth emphasizing that no single tool is infallible, and that multiple tools can help compensate for weaknesses or gaps from any single tool. Figure 9.4 provides an analysis of base images.

Container security, much like other areas of security, exists in a life cycle and warrants securing container use throughout that life cycle. This includes initial container hardening, securing the repository where the images are stored from malicious access and tampering, in addition to ensuring that the containers are monitored for vulnerabilities in runtime environments because new vulnerabilities are constantly emerging, even after a container image may have initially been scanned.

As a result of their ephemeral and declarative nature, many organizations opt for a "cattle vs. pets" approach to managing container workloads. This approach means that, rather than patching systems in place, they simply update the container image in the repository and then rip and replace the existing containers in the runtime environment, while taking advantage of capabilities from the container orchestrator to ensure that service disruption is minimized. This approach has additional security benefits such as potentially disrupting malicious actors' dwell times, as containers are cycled and have a shorter life cycle than long-lived persistent systems where malicious actors can establish a foothold and maintain a presence over an extended time period.

Organizations like NIST have published detailed guidance on container security, such as their 800-190 Application Container Security Guide (`https://nvlpubs.nist.gov/nistpubs/SpecialPublications/NIST.SP.800-190.pdf`), which discusses container security best practices and recommendations. The guidance also discusses how container images include all components used to run an application, and that any of the components may be missing critical security updates, be outdated, or have associated vulnerabilities that can be a pathway for malicious actors.

node:17

scanner	# Critical	# High	# Medium	$ Low	# Unknown
trivy	33	122	183	503	16
grype	33	112	163	485	68
Docker Scan/Snyk	13	26	38	138	0

debian:11.2

scanner	# Critical	# High	# Medium	$ Low	# Unknown
trivy	6	4	5	56	0
grype	6	2	2	55	6
Docker Scan/Snyk	3	2	1	37	0

redhat/ubi8:8.5

scanner	# Critical	# High	# Medium	$ Low	# Unknown
trivy	0	0	59	39	0
grype	0	2	65	40	4
Docker Scan/Snyk	0	0	57	46	0

ubuntu:20.04

scanner	# Critical	# High	# Medium	$ Low	# Unknown
trivy	0	0	27	31	0
grype	0	0	25	31	0
Docker Scan/Snyk	0	0	5	23	0

alpine:3.15.0

scanner	# Critical	# High	# Medium	$ Low	# Unknown
trivy	0	0	0	0	0
grype	0	0	0	0	0
Docker Scan/Snyk	0	0	0	0	0

Figure 9.4: Chainguard analysis of base images

Source: https://uploads-ssl.webflow.com/6228fdbc6c97145dad2a9c2b/624e2
337f70386ed568d7e7e_chainguard-all-about-that-base-image.pdf /
Chainguard

It also points out that just because best practices, such as container vulnerability scanning, were conducted in places such as a repository or continuous integration/continuous delivery (CI/CD) pipeline, new vulnerabilities may emerge and impact containers operating in runtime environments. This is why organizations must implement container vulnerability scanning throughout the container's life cycle, from repository to build and pipelines, and in runtime environments to identify vulnerabilities that might put the workloads and organization at risk.

There are, of course, additional security controls and steps to take to secure the use of containers for running virtualized workloads that extend beyond vulnerability management, such as limiting privileges, implementing access controls, segmenting network environments, and monitoring for malicious activity. All that said, starting with a secure base image, minimizing unnecessary and potentially vulnerable dependencies, and regularly conducting vulnerability scanning of containers throughout their life cycle as discussed previously is critical.

For an incredibly detailed deep dive on container security, we recommend resources such as industry leader Liz Rice's *Container Security* (O'Reilly, 2020). Rice dives into the basics of containers, their potential risks and vulnerabilities, and details of securely adopting containers at scale in large enterprise environments.

Kubernetes

Moving on from the containers themselves, next up in the cloud-native paradigm are container orchestrators. A *container orchestration platform* helps automate the deployment, management, scaling, and networking of containers running on top of a cluster. While there are several potential container orchestration options to discuss, *Kubernetes* is the most widely popular container orchestration tool of choice, so we'll focus our discussion on it.

As we discussed in the previous section, containers are portable, immutable, and ephemeral, using their declarative nature, coupled with the dynamic and elastic nature of cloud computing, to allow organizations to scale services up or down due to factors like customer demand and network traffic. Container orchestration tools such as Kubernetes aid this activity by facilitating the scaling demands of the applications and services they orchestrate and host.

Kubernetes itself has a variety of components that make up its architecture, including the control plane, data plane, API server, controller manager, and so on, in addition to kubelet, nodes, and scheduler, just to name a subset (https://kubernetes.io/docs/concepts/overview/components). These components function as part of either the control plane or data plane within its architecture. Organizations choose to either do what is referred to as "roll your own" Kubernetes, which is taking on responsibility for the control plane of the Kubernetes clusters and environments as well as the data plane, or to alternatively consume a Kubernetes-managed service from entities such as CSPs, with examples including AWS Elastic Kubernetes Service (EKS) or Microsoft Azure Kubernetes Service (AKS). Figure 9.5 from the Kubernetes documentation helps demonstrate the complexity and number of moving parts associated with a Kubernetes cluster.

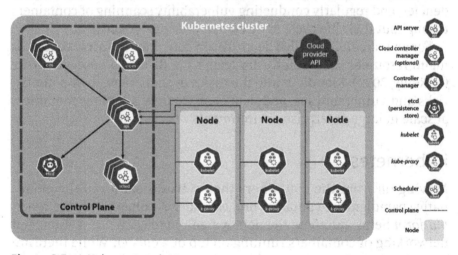

Figure 9.5: A Kubernetes cluster

Source: https://kubernetes.io/docs/concepts/overview/components / The Linux Foundation/CC-BY 4.0

While organizations may opt for the do-it-yourself (DIY) approach, security practitioners generally recommend against it due to the complexity and administrative burden associated with managing the Kubernetes control plane, unless the organization has the internal expertise and resources to do so. Instead, many security and technology professionals recommend consuming managed Kubernetes offerings to offload the administrative toil, let organizations focus on their core competencies, and minimize the potential for misconfigurations and vulnerabilities, both of which can be exploited by malicious actors.

Much like containers, research from groups such as Palo Alto Network's Unit 42 Threat Research Group (www.paloaltonetworks.com/prisma/unit42-cloud-threat-research-2h21) found that publicly available Kubernetes manifests and configuration documents often include inherently insecure configurations and vulnerabilities that, if not reconciled, can present risk to downstream organizations deploying these systems.

A variety of tools organizations can be used to assess the security and posture of their Kubernetes environments, such as kube-hunter (https://github.com/aquasecurity/kube-hunter) and kube-bench (https://github.com/aquasecurity/kube-bench). These open source tools can help organizations assess the configuration and security posture of their Kubernetes environments, and identify vulnerabilities that malicious actors might exploit. They can even assess the deployment of Kubernetes clusters in alignment with industry references such as the CIS Kubernetes Benchmark. Increasingly, cloud-native security vendors have also included security capabilities and functionality in their platforms to let organizations securely deploy and manage Kubernetes clusters and their associated workloads.

OWASP has published a Kubernetes Security Top Ten on site project, which aims to help organizations address the most common misconfigurations, vulnerabilities, and threats associated with deploying and managing Kubernetes workloads (https://owasp.org/www-project-kubernetes-top-ten). Among those risks are items like workload misconfigurations, supply chain vulnerabilities, and poor secrets management, all of which can be exploited by malicious actors to compromise Kubernetes deployments.

It hasn't taken researchers long to identify concerning trends occurring as part of broader Kubernetes adoption. For example, in 2022, the Shadowserver Foundation identified 380,000 open Kubernetes API servers exposed to the Internet using HTTP GET requests, and stated the figures represented 84 percent of *all* global Kubernetes API instances observable online (www.darkreading.com/application-security/more-than-eight-in-10-kubernetes-api-servers-exposed-to-the-internet). However, they did emphasize that it doesn't mean they are fully open or vulnerable to an attack, but they do represent an unnecessarily exposed attack surface for many organizations and environments.

Additionally, in 2023, it was reported that more than 350 organizations, OSS projects, and individuals had Kubernetes clusters that were detected as openly accessible and unprotected (www.csoonline.com/article/648756/kubernetes-clusters-under-attack-in-hundreds-of-organizations.html). More concerning, more than half of those clusters had been breached or had an active campaign underway to deploy malware or backdoors, as reported by the Nautilus research team at cloud-native security vendor Aqua Security (www.aquasec.com/news/kubernetes-clusters-under-attack).

In efforts to mitigate insecure adoption and implementation of Kubernetes in the ecosystem, various organizations both public and private have produced a variety of guidance to facilitate secure Kubernetes use. Examples include the NSA's Kubernetes Hardening Guide (https://media.defense.gov/2022/Aug/29/2003066362/-1/-1/0/CTR_KUBERNETES_HARDENING_GUIDANCE_1.2_20220829.PDF), CIS's Kubernetes Benchmark (www.cisecurity.org/benchmark/Kubernetes), and the DoD's Information Security Agency's Kubernetes STIG (www.stigviewer.com/stig/kubernetes/2021-04-14). A common collection of recommendations in these guides includes items such as scanning containers and Pods for vulnerabilities and misconfigurations, utilizing network segmentation and running containers and pods with least privileges, as well as implementing proper monitoring and logging to ensure malicious activity can be observed and responded to.

In addition to publications and secure configuration guidance, organizations such as the Linux Foundation have begun to publish a variety of Kubernetes certifications to upskill the broader workforce and enable organizations to securely adopt Kubernetes (https://training.linuxfoundation.org/certification/certified-kubernetes-administrator-cka). These credentials are important, given it is often misconfigurations by users/administrators or a lack of implementing best practices that lead to organizations using these technologies in a vulnerable way.

Cloud-native security vendors have begun to provide and integrate capabilities to enable Kubernetes security efforts, such as scanning Kubernetes manifest files for vulnerable configurations, as well as monitoring runtime Kubernetes environments to identify vulnerabilities and potentially malicious activities in production. A collection of these security concerns includes networking, configurations, CVEs in running images, role-based access control of the cluster and pods, and runtime monitoring and alerting.

All said, Kubernetes is an incredibly powerful cloud-native technology that allows organizations to provide dynamic, scalable, and self-healing workloads in modern environments, all through a declarative approach of defining Kubernetes manifests to detail how the clusters should operate. It is also, however, an incredibly complex technology that requires decisions around self-hosting or utilizing managed services, as well as a comprehensive understanding of deploying, configuring, and managing Kubernetes-orchestrated workloads to ensure that organizations don't fall victim to vulnerabilities and misconfigurations that can introduce risk.

Serverless

While many organizations have embraced cloud-native options such as Kubernetes and containers, many have also embraced technologies such as functions-as-a-service (FaaS) or serverless services. We've discussed the cloud-shared responsibility model, where cloud consumers increasingly trade off responsibility for underlying activities like physical infrastructure, networking, computing, and more to CSPs in exchange for ease of use, potential cost savings, and a decrease in administrative overhead. These trade-offs allow consumers to focus on their application's core competencies and deliver value to their customers and stakeholders, which, of course, come with a level of implicit trust in the CSPs to ensure they are properly securing their share of the responsibility model.

The next compute abstraction that goes beyond containers is serverless, with popular examples including AWS Lambda and Microsoft Azure Functions. In the serverless paradigm, consumers no longer need to worry about the underlying infrastructure as in IaaS, but also shed the responsibility for managing hosting things such as a virtualized infrastructure, and performing activities like patching, updates, and maintenance. Instead, consumers can simply take their code and run it on serverless functions, letting the CSP retain full responsibility for the underlying infrastructure and only paying for the period in which they're consuming the dynamic computing that CSPs provide.

While there may be a less traditional attack surface due to factors such as there being no managed server for the customer to maintain, serverless applications often functioning on HTTPS by default, and other aspects of the CSP handling security activities, concerns still exist.

As pointed out in this excellent blog on hacking AWS Lambda functions titled "Hacking AWS Lambda for security, fun and profit" (https://blog.appsecco.com/hacking-aws-lambda-for-security-fun-and-profit-c140426b6167), malicious actors can still abuse poor security practices around identity and access management (IAM) roles assigned to functions, exposed secrets, API authorizations, poor virtual private cloud segmentation, and a lack of access control.

In this model, organizations still need to perform security activities for the software or code they run in serverless environments. Just because the underlying infrastructure and computation may be handled by the CSP doesn't mean the code that organizations, which run on top of the serverless functions, will be insulated from vulnerabilities that can lead to exploitation. There are also considerations such as the underlying configurations in the cloud environments, and how these functions communicate, access, and interact within the environment and beyond, which must be accounted for from the vulnerability management perspective.

DevSecOps

With the increased adoption of cloud computing and cloud-native services and technologies, we've seen a parallel industry push to adopt DevOps, or what is now referred to as DevSecOps methodologies. With origins dating back nearly two decades ago (www.atlassian.com/devops/what-is-devops/history-of-devops), DevOps spawned out of the IT industry through efforts to break down silos between development and operations, to utilize tools and methodologies to release better software faster. Organizations have strived to move away from legacy approaches of software development, such as waterfall methodologies, instead to agile software development and models of integrating development and operations teams, and increasingly, security as well, all forming the phrase DevSecOps. While there can be, and are, entire books dedicated to the concept of DevOps and DevSecOps, we won't spend too much time defining it here. That said, we do recommend books such as *The Phoenix Project, The DevOps Handbook (2013) by Gene Kim, George Spafford and Kevin Behr*, and *Agile Application Security (2017)* by Laura Bell, Michael Brunton-Spall, Rich Smith, and Jim Bird as great references on the topic.

DevSecOps is defined by NIST as "helping to ensure that security is addressed as part of all DevOps practices by integrating security practices and automatically generating security and compliance artifacts throughout the process" (https://csrc.nist.gov/Projects/devsecops).

While not specifically tied to any tools or technologies, the adoption of DevSecOps practices and methodologies does include technology and tools such as source code management (SCM) repositories to store software/code, as well as the use of tools such as CI/CD. While there are nuances to CI/CD that we won't define here, the goal is to automate much of the traditional manual human toil associated with getting code from the commit through the various build, test, and deployment phases and infrastructure provisioning to runtime production environments.

DevSecOps often includes attempts to "shift security left" by integrating security tooling and activities earlier in the software development life cycle (SDLC) to catch vulnerabilities earlier in the life cycle, lead to potential cost savings, decrease business disruption from needing to fix vulnerabilities once they're in production systems, and mitigate the window of exposure that malicious actors have to exploit vulnerabilities in runtime environments.

This often includes using tools such as static and dynamic application security testing, software composition analysis, container and infrastructure as code (IaC) scanning, and increasingly producing artifacts such as software bills of materials (SBOMs), to understand any licensing violations or concerns, find vulnerabilities associated with software components, and also provide visibility to stakeholders internal to or external to the organization as part of a broader push for software transparency and software supply chain security. For those unfamiliar with these myriads of tools, we'll take a moment to briefly define each of them here:

- Static application security testing (SAST) is a form of testing that analyzes source code to identify security vulnerabilities that may present risk in applications.
- Dynamic application security testing (DAST) examines running applications to detect potential security vulnerabilities.
- Software composition analysis (SCA) is like SAST, but is primarily focused on tracking and analyzing open source components

and dependencies for vulnerabilities that may pose risk to the applications.

■ Interactive application security testing (IAST) utilizes a combination of aspects of both SAST and DAST. IAST executes application code and monitors behavior in real time to provide findings for vulnerabilities, flaws, and inefficiencies that can be remediated. It is often executed in quality assurance (QA) / testing environments prior to production.

■ As modern infrastructure increasingly is written in a declarative format such as CloudFormation templates or the vendor-agnostic Terraform, these IaC templates/manifests can be scanned to identify vulnerabilities or misconfigurations that may present risks to running environments.

■ Container vulnerability scanning helps identify vulnerabilities in containers, whether in a registry, as part of the build process, or even at runtime. There are several popular open source container vulnerability scanning tools, as well as support from leading proprietary vulnerability scanning vendors to cover containers.

While these tools enable "shifting security left," they also pose challenges of shifting work onto development and engineering teams due to the potential for false positives that can lead to developers spending significant time to justify findings to security teams or validate their accuracy.

As the industry push for DevSecOps has continued to mature, many practitioners, including one of the authors of this text, have begun to advocate an approach of "shifting smart" rather than shifting left, and have begun to dive into the topic on a podcast with the founder of Contrast Security and longtime AppSec leader Jeff Williams (https://podcasts.apple.com/us/podcast/shift-smart-its-not-about-shoving-security-into-devops/id1652615217?i=1000622279084). DevSecOps strives to break down silos between teams such as security and development, but the noisy scanners, which produce false positives or don't facilitate high-fidelity testing with sufficient context, can undermine this objective and cause frustration from developers toward security teams who are throwing findings and vulnerabilities over the fence with minimal context. Such actions are causing developers to spend significant time justifying their findings or remediating findings that didn't pose significant risks.

All of the security tools we've mentioned have their place, but it's also true that specific vulnerability types are best tested for at specific phases of the SDLC. This is why it makes sense to take a strategic approach to vulnerability tooling and testing. This approach is also necessary to ensure that vulnerability scan results and findings are enriched to provide context around known exploitations (e.g., the Cybersecurity and Infrastructure Security Agency Known Exploited Vulnerabilities [CISA KEV]), exploitation probability (e.g., Exploit Prediction Scoring Systems [EPSS]), and also validation around reachability to help minimize work and delays to development velocity, as well as help developers focus on the high-risk vulnerabilities posed to the organization.

Organizations conducting studies on the maturity of software development teams have found that teams with the highest performance in metrics such as DevOps research and assessment (DORA) have improved security outcomes and capabilities as well. DORA metrics include the following:

- Deployment frequency
- Lead time for changes
- Mean time to recover
- Change failure rate
- Reliability

Studies have shown that organizations with mature DORA metrics can address security vulnerabilities and concerns more proficiently. This was communicated in reports such as the "2022 Accelerate State of DevOps Report: A deep dive into security" (https://cloud.google.com/blog/products/devops-sre/dora-2022-accelerate-state-of-devops-report-now-out). This report found that high-trust, low-blame cultures are significantly more likely to adopt emerging security practices than low-trust, high-blame cultures. Another interesting finding is that the adoption of emerging security practices led to reduced developer burnout, showing that modernizing security practices can have improved outcomes on software development culture and delivery.

That said, we do want to highlight that blind adherence to any mantras in security is never a recommended practice. While the industry has pushed headfirst into efforts to "shift security left," merely putting security tooling in a CI/CD pipeline, producing scan reports of findings, and throwing those scan reports over the fence to developers is *not* a recommended practice. Doing so actually has an inverse effect of drawing resentment from development peers, further emboldening silos between development and security. It also runs counterproductively to another push in security, which is "being a business enabler."

This is because most vulnerabilities that scanners identify are never actually exploited in the wild, which leads to development teams needing to justify the vulnerabilities' existence in their software or system, and to potentially remediate vulnerabilities that actually pose little to no risk to the business. Developers are incentivized, and have their performance evaluated against, factors like the velocity of feature delivery to production, speed to market, and software development output, none of which make security a top priority for them, despite it being a top priority for security practitioners.

For this reason, it's critical that we recommend taking an approach of shifting "smart" over blindly shifting "left," and ensuring that security is testing for the appropriate vulnerability type at the appropriate point in the SDLC, as well as enriching vulnerability scans and data with additional context like the CISA KEV catalog, EPSS metrics, and environmental context such as mitigating controls or the system/data sensitivity to the business, all of which should be used to make mature vulnerability prioritization decisions.

We've also seen vendors begin to provide security scanning and capabilities that can be embedded into developer workflows without being disruptive, to try to empower those writing the code (i.e., developers) to resolve issues locally before they are committed to the codebase and promoted to runtime environments.

Open Source Software

While open source software (OSS) is far from being specifically tied to cloud computing, there has been an undeniable growth in the use of OSS over the past few decades. As we discussed in Chapter 5, "Vulnerability Scoring and Identification," research from organizations like Synopsys has shown that up to 78 percent of modern codebases are composed of OSS, along with several potential security concerns that we will discuss soon.

We want to start off by emphasizing that any arguments of whether proprietary code or OSS is more secure are foolish and lack the context to have a sufficient debate. The reality is that most modern codebases, even for proprietary software and services, are composed of large portions of OSS. Furthermore, there are a myriad of factors that go into determining the level of security of software or systems.

For example, there are significant differences in terms of resources, expertise, priorities, and capabilities between some of the leading software suppliers in the industry. Some have thousands of security staff and significant financial resources and bandwidth to address security concerns, while others may be a bootstrapped startup just striving to obtain initial market penetration and have little to no security staff on hand quite yet. On the contrary, there are also significant differences between OSS projects, with some boasting thousands of contributors and participants worldwide, while others may have a small group or even a single maintainer contributing code to the codebase and addressing vulnerabilities.

Furthermore, there are extrinsic factors at play that contribute to how "secure" a product, service, software, or organization is. For example, when looking at reports like CISA's 2022 Top Routinely Exploited Vulnerabilities report (www.cisa.gov/news-events/cybersecurity-advisories/aa23-215a), we know that malicious actors tend to prioritize their focus on widely used pervasive software and technologies, as opposed to software with a limited market footprint. The same goes for OSS, with projects such as Linux or Log4j serving as examples with widespread adoption and use, and therefore outsized interest from entities such as malicious actors and security researchers.

Factors like this contribute to facts such as Microsoft's long-standing position at the top of the CISA KEV catalog, for having the most-known exploited vulnerabilities, and frequently being in the news for being targeted by malicious actors including nation-state entities. These widely pervasive vendors/suppliers and software are obviously more enticing to malicious actors because they represent a richer target, with wider use and a larger attack surface when it comes to industry reach and presence across digital infrastructures.

Now that we've dispelled the false dichotomy of pitting OSS versus proprietary software against each other, let's look at some of the unique aspects of OSS that must be accounted for from a vulnerability management perspective.

As we have previously discussed, organizations are increasingly making use of the robust and diverse OSS ecosystem for obvious reasons.

It is financially appealing to be able to minimize the extent of native software development an organization must do, and instead leverage existing software components and libraries to expedite their product and software development. Much like malicious actors, developers will often opt for the path of least resistance and use an OSS component, rather than writing all functions and capabilities themselves, especially when their performance is evaluated based on how fast they can develop products and services. The incentives simply don't often exist to prioritize security over other competing metrics such as velocity, feature delivery, and so on.

This has led to widespread OSS adoption, which until recently hasn't been accompanied with widespread rigor and governance from a security perspective with the use of OSS. This has begun to change, however, with the exploitation of Log4j among many other OSS components. Malicious actors have realized how pervasive OSS use is, and that by exploiting an OSS component, they can potentially compromise an exponential number of OSS-consumer victims downstream, often without a good inventory of where the OSS exists within their environments. For example, the Cyber Safety Review Board (CSRB; www.cisa.gov/resources-tools/groups/cyber-safety-review-board-csrb), which was created after the release of President Biden's Executive Order (EO) 14028 to review major cyber events, reported in their review of the Log4j incident that some federal agencies were spending tens of thousands of hours just identifying where this vulnerable and compromised component existed within their environments. Similar challenges exist in the commercial sector, due to many organizations having a poor software asset inventory as it relates to OSS components in their software and applications.

Further complicating the matter is that studies such as Endor Labs' State of Dependency Management report found that six out of seven vulnerabilities are related to transitive dependencies of applications, rather than direct dependencies (www.endorlabs.com/state-of-dependency-management). These are dependencies that your direct dependencies use and this often clouds their impact in terms of both application operation and vulnerability. The report highlighted that 95 percent of vulnerable dependencies are transitive, not direct. This makes it difficult for developers and security teams to understand the vulnerability posture of their applications and software without modernized capabilities that can determine reachability and exploitability of a given OSS component. Many organizations don't have good visibility of the inventory of their direct dependencies, let alone transitive dependencies, especially the further you go along in a dependency graph.

OSS also has its own inherent risks, such as documented in the Endor Labs Top 10 Open Source Software (OSS) Risks report (www.endorlabs.com/blog/introducing-the-top-10-open-source-software-oss-risks). Those risks include items shown in Figure 9.6.

As Figure 9.6 shows, known vulnerabilities rank at the top of the chart for risks; however, they aren't the only risks with which organizations using OSS need to be concerned. Other factors, such as malicious actors looking to target the software supply chain, may look to compromise a legitimate package through methods like hijacking a maintainer account, or implementing name confusion attacks such as typosquatting, where malicious actors create malicious packages closely named to legitimate ones. Additionally, as discussed earlier in this section, concerns also center around unmaintained software as well. For example, researcher Chinmayi Sharma published a comprehensive paper titled "Tragedy of the Digital Commons" that demonstrated that almost 25 percent of *all* OSS projects have only *one developer* contributing code, and 94 percent of *all* projects are maintained by 10 or fewer developers (https://papers.ssrn.com/sol3/papers.cfm?abstract_id=4245266). This is often referred to as being a *bus factor*, due to the hypothetical question of what the impact would be if a maintainer got hit by a bus, or in other words, quit maintaining the software.

As pointed out by vendor Synopsys in their 2022 Open Source Security Risks report, 88 percent of codebases included components that have had no new development in *two years*, whereas 85 percent contained OSS that was more than *four years* out of date. See Figure 9.7.

However, despite the extensive use of OSS in modern codebases, it is worth noting the nuance associated with that OSS use as it relates to vulnerabilities. While some studies show that 78 percent of modern codebases are comprised of OSS components, some have pointed out that much of that OSS footprint isn't "active" code, meaning it isn't actually invoked by the application or reachable from a vulnerability exploitation perspective. For example, application security vendor Contrast Security, which focuses on runtime security, found in their State of Open Source (OSS) Security Report in 2021 that 62 percent of libraries are completely inactive with no active code, and that the average application or API, based on their assessment of over 100,000 real-world applications and APIs, had 71 percent of inactive library code, which was never loaded nor invoked by the application.

Risk	Description	Category
OSS-RISK-1 Known Vulnerabilities	A component version may contain vulnerable code, accidentally introduced by its developers. Vulnerability details are publicly disclosed, e.g., through a CVE. Exploits and patches may or may not be available.	Security
OSS-RISK-2 Compromise of Legitimate Package	Attackers may compromise resources that are part of an existing legitimate project or of the distribution infrastructure in order to inject malicious code into a component, e.g., through hijacking the accounts of legitimate project maintainers or exploiting vulnerabilities in package repositories.	Security
OSS-RISK-3 Name Confusion Attacks	Attackers may create components whose names resemble names of legitimate open-source or system components (typo-squatting), suggest trustworthy authors (brand-jacking) or play with common naming patterns in different languages or ecosystems (combo-squatting).	Security
OSS-RISK-4 Unmaintained Software	A component or component version may not be actively developed any more, thus, patches for functional and non-functional bugs may not be provided in a timely fashion (or not at all) by the original open source project	Ops
OSS-RISK-5 Outdated Software	A project may use an old, outdated version of the component (though newer versions exist).	Ops
OSS-RISK-6 Untracked Dependencies	Project developers may not be aware of a dependency on a component at all, e.g., because it is not part of an upstream component's SBOM, because SCA tools are not run or do not detect it, or because the dependency is not established using a package manager.	Security, Ops
OSS-RISK-7 License Risk	A component or project may not have a license at all, or one that is incompatible with the intended use or whose requirements are not or cannot be met.	Ops
OSS-RISK-8 Immature Software	An open source project may not apply development best-practices, e.g., not use a standard versioning scheme, have no regression test suite, review guidelines or documentation. As a result, a component may not work reliably or securely.	Ops
OSS-RISK-9 Unapproved Change (Mutable)	A component may change without developers being able to notice, review or approve such changes, e.g., because the download link points to an unversioned resource, because a versioned resource has been modified or tampered with or due to an insecure data transfer.	Security, Ops
OSS-RISK-10 Under/over-sized Dependency	A component may provide very little functionality (e.g., npm micro packages) or a lot of functionality (of which only a fraction may be used).	Security, Ops

Figure 9.6: Inherent OSS risks

Source: www.endorlabs.com/blog/introducing-the-top-10-open-source-software-oss-risks / 2024 / Endor Labs

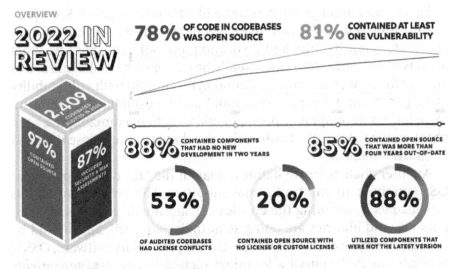

Figure 9.7: 2022 OSS security risks

This is demonstrated in Figure 9.8, shared by Contrast Security founder, Jeff Williams (www.linkedin.com/posts/planet level_what-about-transitive-dependencies-i-hear-activity-7090447433146515456-n4GW?utm_source=share&utm_medium=member_desktop). The intent is to point out that only 9 percent of OSS on average is active, so proprietary code at runtime may be the most concerning for organizations from an AppSec perspective.

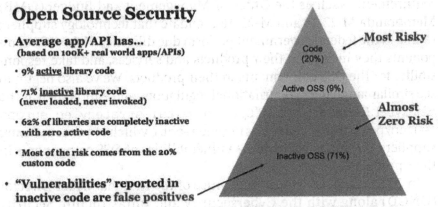

Figure 9.8: OSS in 2021

Source: www.linkedin.com/posts/planetlevel_what-about-transitive-dependencies-i-hear-activity-7090447433146515456-n4GW?utm_source=share&utm_medium=member_desktop/Jeff Williams/INKEDIN.

Figures and findings, such as those illustrated in Figure 9.8, emphasize the importance of innovative capabilities that can add critical context such as reachability and invocation, providing insight into what aspects of an application can actually be exploited by malicious actors and are functional at runtime. Coupling this insight with vulnerability intelligence around exploitability and known exploitation can minimize toil on development peers, in addition to maximizing the time spent on the most critical vulnerabilities that genuinely pose the most organizational risk.

Another challenging dynamic at play in the OSS discussion is that OSS suppliers are *not* traditional suppliers. The majority of OSS is provided as is, meaning the entities consuming these projects, components, and libraries are doing so at their own peril, and should be taking full responsibility for its use. Unlike proprietary software, OSS is generally *not* in the purview for things such as service level agreements (SLAs) or contractual language that requires them to update or patch software within a defined time period, nor address vulnerabilities in a timely manner, if at all. Many organizations have begun widespread adoption and use of OSS in their applications and systems without accounting for this reality. This isn't to say that OSS maintainers won't address vulnerabilities or risks for the community, but they are typically not required to do so.

This reality is starting to be addressed by emerging requirements in some sectors, such as in the U.S. federal ecosystem, where emerging requirements such as the Office of Management and Budget (OMB) Memoranda M-22-18 and M-23-16 mandate that technology suppliers selling to the federal government perform due diligence of the OSS components they include in their products and services, and take responsibility for the OSS components in their products. We've also begun to see similar language in international regulations and efforts such as the EU Cyber Resilience Act (https://digital-strategy.ec.europa.eu/en/policies/cyber-resilience-act), which requires software suppliers to remain aware of the vulnerabilities of OSS components in their products.

In 2023, the White House and Office of the National Cyber Director (ONCD) along with the Cybersecurity and Infrastructure Security Agency (CISA) and others released a request for information (RFI) on open source software security. The RFI's intent is to help federal leadership develop a strategy and action plan to strengthen the security of the OSS ecosystem. Following the Log4j incident, the White House also established an interagency working group named the Open-Source Software Security Initiative (OS3I) to use policies and government resources to bolster OSS security.

Luckily, guidance has begun to emerge about secure OSS use and governance. NIST, for example, has provided a dedicated page stemming from the cybersecurity EO titled "Software Security in Supply Chains: Open Source Software Controls" (www.nist.gov/itl/executive-order-14028-improving-nations-cybersecurity/software-security-supply-chains-open). It focuses on software supply chain security, providing guidance to organizations on securely using OSS. Although these guidance sources aren't exhaustive, they can move organizations in a positive direction with regard to consuming, securing, and governing their use of OSS, as well as gaining a baseline level of understanding of the potential security implications of OSS usage. The guidance lays out recommendations across a maturity spectrum from foundational, sustaining, and enhancing capabilities. It includes activities such as identifying publicly known vulnerabilities in OSS, acquiring OSS via secure channels and from trustworthy sources, as well as utilizing tooling such as software composition analysis (SCA) and internal repositories of known and trusted OSS components.

However, as many practitioners will note, some of these activities can be difficult in large complex environments with many development teams, systems, and processes. To address these challenges and others associated with OSS consumption and integration, innovative vendors have begun providing capabilities to help developers make risk-informed decisions around OSS use, including not just known vulnerabilities that are trailing risk indicators, but also metrics that serve as leading risk indicators such as maintenance, provenance, and others that can inform secure OSS usage.

We're supporters of a diverse, vibrant, and thriving OSS ecosystem, but we also understand that it comes with its own unique risks and considerations, and that organizations must account for these issues as part of their broader vulnerability management program. While OSS adoption and use has grown significantly over the last several decades, organizations' governance and rigor around secure OSS usage hasn't followed the same trajectory.

We're hopeful with the increased dialogue in the industry and the growth of software supply chain attacks, that organizations will begin to implement security practices to mitigate the risk of insecure OSS usage, while still allowing OSS to serve as a critical part of the modern digital landscape.

Software-as-a-Service

While it may seem odd to specifically call out software-as-a-service (SaaS) from the broader cloud discussion, there is good reason for doing so. Studies show that while organizations may be using two to three IaaS providers, they're often using several *hundreds* of SaaS providers. This means that an increasingly large portion of software is being consumed over the IaaS.

Anyone who has been around cybersecurity for some time is inevitably familiar with the concept of *shadow IT*, which is IT that's being used within an organization unbeknownst to the IT/security team(s). This IT, or software, can (and often does) have security implications for the organizations, because it may have misconfigurations, vulnerable implementations, or outright vulnerabilities that are not on the radar of the organization's security staff and, therefore, go unaddressed.

This challenge is further exacerbated by SaaS, where organizations often struggle to have good visibility into the extent of the SaaS that an organization is consuming, especially when business units can simply use a credit card and email address to begin consuming SaaS and begin placing potentially sensitive organizational data into the SaaS environment without any sort of governance or oversight. When we discuss the fundamental need for software asset inventory, as long advocated for by sources such as the CIS Critical Security Controls, SaaS is included in that equation, as it's still part of the organization's software asset inventory, albeit consumed over the Internet rather than hosted in their own environments.

Many organizations rely on compliance frameworks to gain a level of assurance around their SaaS consumption. While frameworks such as SOC-2 and the Federal Risk and Authorization Management Program (FedRAMP) do have their place, compliance doesn't equal security. Just because a SaaS provider has a compliance certification doesn't mean there won't be any vulnerabilities or risk associated with that SaaS application. Furthermore, going back to the SRM, the CSP is responsible for their side of the model, such as the underlying compute, infrastructure, and hosting environment. In the case of SaaS, this, of course, includes the application and software itself, but it doesn't mean SaaS providers are infallible, nor that consumers can't misuse the SaaS offering by implementing vulnerable configurations, or by not properly safeguarding sensitive data or doing fundamentals such as proper access control.

This is where tooling such as SaaS Security Posture Management (SSPM) comes into play. Much like the broader Cloud Security Posture Management (CSPM) tooling category, SSPM tools help organizations conduct scans of their SaaS environments for vulnerabilities and misconfigurations that may be placing them at risk and exposing them to malicious actors' nefarious activities. As we've discussed, malicious actors have continued to realize the concentrated rich targets that entities such as CSPs, including SaaS providers, represent, and have begun targeting them. For example, in 2022, a malicious campaign targeted popular SaaS providers such as Twilio and 130 other organizations, as part of a several months' long hacking spree using phishing techniques.

In addition to tooling, we've seen increased industry efforts to push for SaaS governance and security, including publications by organizations such as the Cloud Security Alliance (CSA) with their paper "SaaS Governance Best Practices for Cloud Customers" (https:// cloudsecurityalliance.org/artifacts/saas-governance-best-practices-for-cloud-customers). This paper advocates for not only tooling such as SSPM, but also for organizations to bolster their governance and security of SaaS usage, moving beyond compliance frameworks into SaaS-specific security practices and considerations.

Systemic Risks

While it's true that the majority of cloud security incidents are and have been due to customer misconfigurations, increased calls have been made by U.S. leaders such as CISA for "Secure-by-Default/Design" systems and software (www.cisa.gov/securebydesign). There's also an emphasis in the 2023 National Cybersecurity Strategy (NCS) that has called for shifting the burden of responsibility from downstream consumers to those best positioned to address insecure systems, software, and vulnerabilities, which often includes software suppliers like CSPs.

Other industry organizations such as the Atlantic Council have begun raising concerns around the ubiquity of cloud and adoption across critical infrastructure, and the need to ensure that the cloud is secure. In fact, the Atlantic Council's article titled "Critical Infrastructure and the Cloud: Policy for Emerging Risk" states that cloud security is directly tied to U.S. economic and national security (https://dfrlab.org/2023/07/10/critical-infrastructure-and-the-cloud-policy-for-emerging-risk). It points out how hyperscale CSP outages and incidents have had cascading impacts across some of the largest technology companies in the world, who often build on top of these IaaS CSPs. The article emphasizes how, depending on the functionality of a critical infrastructure sector, concerns such as data storage, scalability, and continuous availability requirements could have consequences that impact key services and safety. The potential concerns and systemic risks range across sectors such as healthcare, transportation, energy, and defense, among others.

We've also seen government leaders criticize some of the leading CSPs for not providing basic security functionality, such as logging and monitoring, without charging customers extra for these features. In 2023, this occurred to CSP Microsoft Azure due to malicious activity by Chinese hackers. It led to hackers accessing users' Exchange Online and Outlook.com environments and potentially more due to compromised keys, allowing the threat actors to forge access tokens for multiple types of Azure Active Directory applications such as SharePoint, Teams, and OneDrive. This particular situation left millions of Microsoft and customer applications vulnerable, and many customers lacking the sufficient logging to determine if they were impacted, leading to outcry from leaders such as U.S. Senator Ron Wyden, who called for the government to hold Microsoft accountable for "negligent cybersecurity practices" (www.reuters.com/technology/us-senator-wyden-asks-ftc-cisa-doj-take-action-against-microsoft-following-hack-2023-07-27).

Some CSPs such as Google Cloud have begun to call for a shift from the traditional SRM to one of "Shared Fate" (https://cloud.google.com/security/shared-fate). Google points out that a "trust issue in one cloud can impact the trust in all clouds," alluding to the fact that if one of the major CSPs experiences a security incident, or even a perceived lack of trust, it can undermine the trust in the entire cloud computing ecosystem.

Much like the CISA publications we discussed previously, there's an emphasis on shifting the responsibility to the CSP, who has the resources and expertise that customers often lack, to take an increased role in securing cloud environments. Some key configurations and services have experienced several notable security incidents, such as the inadvertent exposure of AWS S3 storage buckets where customers' sensitive data was publicly exposed to the world through a misconfiguration. AWS made the S3 default configurations private in late 2022 (www.securityweek.com/aws-s3-buckets-exposed-millions-facebook-records), but this was after a decade and several visible and damaging misconfigurations by AWS customers that exposed millions of sensitive records (https://aws.amazon.com/about-aws/whats-new/2023/04/amazon-s3-security-best-practices-buckets-default), including those found in industries such as defense and intelligence (www.bleepingcomputer.com/news/security/top-secret-us-army-and-nsa-files-left-exposed-online-on-amazon-s3-server).

Hyperscale CSPs represent rich targets for malicious actors looking to exploit organizations. And if they are able to compromise a CSP, it can have a cascading impact on the downstream consumers and customers using those platforms. As we discussed in the chapter's introduction, CSPs function on a multi-tenant model, and depending on the compromise's severity as well as the security control levels in place, some malicious activity can move laterally, impacting many customers utilizing cloud services. Security vendors have begun to advocate for best practices to enhance tenant isolation when operating in cloud environments such as PaaS and SaaS. For example, security vendor Wiz published their "PEACH" framework (www.datocms-assets.com/75231/1671033753-peach_whitepaper_ver1-1.pdf), which focuses on items such as external interfaces, security boundaries, hardening, and vendor transparency.

Security practitioners and researchers have begun to highlight *cross-tenant vulnerabilities*, which have the potential to impact multiple tenants via a single vulnerability exploitation, allowing malicious actors to impact multiple tenants of a CSP concurrently. For example, in late 2022, vendor Lightspin highlighted an AWS Elastic Container Registry Public (ECR Public) vulnerability that allowed external actors to delete, update, and create ECR Public images that belonged to other AWS accounts (www.bleepingcomputer.com/news/security/amazon-ecr-public-gallery-flaw-could-have-wiped-or-poisoned-any-image). Similarly, in early 2022, a security researcher identified a zero-day vulnerability in Microsoft Azure impacting the

Azure Cognitive Search (ACS) service that allowed malicious actors to access data located in private instances of the ACS service from any tenant and location (www.mnemonic.io/resources/blog/acsessed-cross-tenant-network-bypass-in-azure-cognitive-search). There was a six-month window from when the vulnerability was reported to when it was remediated by Microsoft Azure.

Although it stands true that the majority of cloud security breaches and incidents are due to activities on the customer's side of the traditional SRM, there are indeed systemic risks and concerns associated with cloud computing as industries increasingly move their infrastructure and operations to CSPs. Because of these realities, vulnerabilities or incidents impacting CSPs have the potential to impact thousands of organizations and millions of individuals as a result of the widespread societal dependence that now exists for CSPs.

This is an issue that not only individual organizations need to consider from a vulnerability management perspective, but also one that society must consider from a risk management and resilience perspective as well.

Summary

As it's easy to see, vulnerability management in the age of cloud and DevSecOps can be a complex subject. On one hand, the introduction of concepts such as shared responsibility models and shifting left, along with the massive growth of open source software, have presented several challenges for vulnerability management. That said, many innovations have also been introduced by sharing the responsibility for vulnerability management, offloading some activities to a provider, utilizing declarative languages to codify and version-control infrastructure, and being able to automate traditional security activities. The challenges are further exacerbated by the growth of software supply chain attacks, and malicious actors realizing how entities like CSPs, managed service providers, and widely used proprietary products and OSS components represent rich targets due to their potentially massive downstream dependencies. We hope that readers walk away from this chapter with an understanding of how to manage vulnerabilities in the era of cloud-native technologies and DevSecOps methodologies and tooling.

10 The Human Element in Vulnerability Management

It should be evident by this point in the book that vulnerability management is quite complex. Several tools, techniques, and processes can be used to reduce complexity and automate where possible. However, the same difficulties still exist, and organizations with a massive backlog of vulnerabilities must consider alternatives. In the cybersecurity space, the human element has come to the forefront as the way forward to enhance cyber programs and reduce risks in enterprise.

This chapter discusses the psychological components that should be incorporated into a modern vulnerability management program (VMP). This program includes the discipline of human factors, security engineering methods, as well as cognition and perception. Each piece of the human experience impacts how vulnerabilities are identified, prioritized, and ultimately resolved.

Many legacy vulnerability management documents and guidance, however, don't speak to the human aspect of vulnerability management programs. Each person, whether they are a system owner, an IT professional, systems engineer, security analyst, or technical manager, has a unique experience to bring to the table. Incorporating the human element in vulnerability management includes the way that individuals process information, make decisions, and ultimately are responsible for aspects of the VMP.

This chapter covers how organizations can build better VMPs by understanding how their users as well as their IT and security practitioners interact with systems. Modernizing vulnerability management can no longer solely focus on the technical aspects and specific common vulnerabilities and exposures identifications (CVE IDs) of vulnerabilities. To mature VMPs and reduce risk, organizations must consider the impact of the people behind the vulnerability management life cycle.

Figure 10.1 illustrates the entire vulnerability management life cycle. There are many variations of this life cycle, but for the purposes of creating a mature VMP, there are six overall steps to follow. The full life cycle starts with identification, then categorization, prioritization, mitigation, validation, and reporting. Each step as outlined in the figure is essential to create a mature and comprehensive VMP.

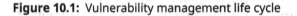

Figure 10.1: Vulnerability management life cycle

While neither author is a trained psychologist, the psychological concepts discussed in this chapter are meant to give management and practitioners the opportunity to evaluate vulnerability management outside the typical technology problem set. The human factors concepts presented next are meant to encourage individuals to pursue potential avenues for vulnerability remediation, instead of simply patching or applying configurations.

Consider each section of this chapter as an opportunity to enhance and grow your organization's vulnerability management practices using human factors engineering (HFE) and psychological concepts.

Human Factors Engineering

Human factors engineering (HFE) is defined by the Human Factors and Ergonomics Society (HFES) as "an applied science that takes research about human abilities, limitations, behaviors, and processes and uses this knowledge as a basis for the design of tools, products, and systems" (www.hfes.org/About-HFES/What-is-Human-Factors-and-Ergonomics).

While there are numerous different versions of this definition, we think the one from HFES covers the most important factors of HFE. The mission of HFE is to understand the psychological aspects of people in order to design systems that are efficient and tailored for our use.

HFE originated during World War II (www.hfes.org/about-hfes/hfes-history#:~:text=Human%20factors%20concerns%20emerged%20during,systems%20performance) as a reaction to building better manned systems on land, air, and sea. The initial HF studies focused on systems performance, information presentation, and recognition issues, as well as physical workspace areas and skills. Human factors have been integral in aviation maintenance and security, including studying human conditions like stress, complacency, and levels of fatigue. To learn more, see www.faasafety.gov/files/gslac/courses/content/258/1097/AMT_Handbook_Addendum_Human_Factors.pdf.

HF became so incredibly important to the aviation industry because of the need to avert accidents, reduce workplace injuries, and avoid wasting time on similar activities. Each HF component aims to improve the safety and efficiency of the humans performing a task. And while HFE began as a physical discipline—an example being the design of a hammer to suit a human hand—it has evolved over time to account for other areas of study.

As technology has evolved and we've ushered in the digital age, human factors have become a staple of people-centered design. This means that HFE no longer is designing hammers or physical objects, but improving products or designs where there is user interaction, as explained in the article "Human Factor Principles in UX Design" in *UX Magazine*: https://uxmag.com/articles/human-factor-principles-in-ux-design#:~:text=Human%20factors%20design%20(or%20people,tasks%20on%20your%20desktop%20computer. A simple example includes the shopping cart experience on a website.

HF's goal within the design and user interaction (UI) is to reduce mistakes by users and create an easier use of applications and software products. Human factors are the integration of many different disciplines like psychology, engineering, design, and sociology, not to be confused with user experience (UX), which is the entire user's experience, from browser interaction to authentication process. Figure 10.2 shows the various psychological, engineering, and design components that make up the human factors discipline.

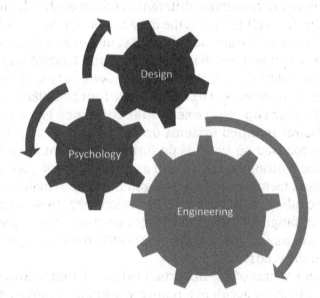

Figure 10.2: How human factors incorporate psychology, engineering, and design

Human factors are mostly focused on the interaction of the system and based on ergonomics, and they are incredibly important to human-computer interaction (HCI). The following article speaks in depth about how HCI is a multidisciplinary field that is hyper-focused on the interaction between users and their computers (www.interaction-design .org/literature/topics/human-computer-interaction). This evolution of human factors, HCI, and UI has become a separate field of study and expertise within the last several years.

As human factors become increasingly spread among areas of technology, their relevance to all areas of IT grows. And it's not just IT, but HFE has been used across information security and cybersecurity since the mid-2000s. HF research has grown in academic areas to insider threat, information security culture, and threats to critical infrastructure.

To delve into how HFE has impacted cybersecurity, this chapter covers various areas of psychology and design. From context switching to cognition, each piece of human factors security engineering will align into building a mature and comprehensive VMP.

Human Factors Security Engineering

Cyberattacks are only increasing and becoming more sophisticated. Unfortunately, they are also easier to conduct, and will continue to be, based on the major advances with artificial intelligence (AI) and ease of purchase, like ransomware-as-a-service (RaaS). See the Crowd-Strike article on RaaS at www.crowdstrike.com/cybersecurity-101/ransomware/ransomware-as-a-service-raas. To combat these growing threats, cybersecurity programs must consider finding the root cause of missing security controls or lack of maturity in their VMPs.

As Calvin Nobles identified in the paper titled "Human Factors in Cybersecurity: Academia's Missed Opportunity" (https://aisel.aisnet.org/mwais2023/8), the lack of human factors in cybersecurity education has limited the knowledge of human behavior in cyber programs. This paper focused on the lack of human factors in education, but there's also a missed opportunity in the technical space. From retention and recruitment of cybersecurity professionals, to understanding the burnout and stress levels of IT and cyber practitioners, human factors security engineering can help identify the human components affecting risk in an organization.

Context Switching

One of the overlaps between psychology and cybersecurity is the idea of multitasking and context switching. The American Psychological Association (APA) defines multitasking as doing more than one complex task at a time, which can reduce productivity. An example would be as simple as having six different email accounts, all for different purposes, and checking them all multiple times in a row. The same APA definition also notes that when people perform multiple tasks at once, they are more likely to experience mental overload, which can be disastrous depending on the type of work the individual is attempting to do (www.apa.org/topics/research/multitasking).

But multitasking can also have a few other meanings. It can also mean when someone tries to do two tasks at once, switches tasks, or performs multiple tasks back-to-back. Psychologists have been conducting studies on multitasking and switching costs for many years, and even more recently in the field of cybersecurity. Any cybersecurity professional is typically managing multiple products, dashboards, tools, systems, and applications all at the same time.

As an example, security analysts who work in a security operations center (SOC) might manage multiple vulnerability dashboards, use numerous security tools for investigations or analysis, and would need to review large data amounts for security incidents and monitoring. The Panaseer 2022 Security Leaders Peer Report study noted that large corporations may be using around 75 security tools within their organizations (https://online.sbu.edu/news/top-10-cyber-security-tools#:~:text=As%20cyberattacks%20increase%2C%20companies%20are,security%20tools%20for%20their%20companies). These tools include endpoint detection and response (EDR), network monitoring, vulnerability scanners, and security information and event management (SIEM) tools.

Figure 10.3 shows how complex SOC tooling can become, especially for larger organizations that may be managing hundreds or thousands of devices.

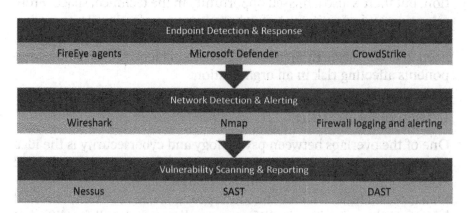

Figure 10.3: Example of SOC tools and complexity

Each of these dashboards, tools, or applications would be independent and require its own web apps, login pages, configurations, and different user experiences. An analyst needs to review each tool several times a day, while also monitoring emails and messaging systems, attending meetings, and responding to alerts. Typically, they will be monitoring all at one time or switching quickly between each application as they gather more information.

Another example: Security engineers may be working between development teams, management, and the security analysts when either developing new applications or responding to incidents. Depending on their specific job roles, they might have many responsibilities across teams, vulnerability management, and development activities to support their cybersecurity program. Security engineers would be experiencing the same types of context switching between different cloud environments, development projects, and even various standards and legislation that would affect different systems.

Vulnerability Dashboards

Ideally, an organization would have one vulnerability scanner and reporting tool within its environments. Usually, these tools come with configurable dashboards that display known vulnerabilities, exploits, vulnerable systems and applications, and much more. Because these dashboards are highly configurable, each organization will have a unique setup. The trouble comes when there are multiple dashboards for monitoring many vulnerabilities, environments, system types, and applications.

Even with just the vulnerability dashboard, security analysts and engineers might have to switch between multiple dashboards and areas within the tool to obtain the whole vulnerability management view. Figure 10.4 shows a typical vulnerability dashboard, including the total volume of vulnerabilities in the environment, recent scan data, and other relevant metrics. There are many customization options, from heat maps to pie charts or specific system information.

This example highlights one possible dashboard that an analyst or engineer would need to review. If there were multiple systems, types of vulnerabilities for tracking, or various systems owners, the dashboards would multiply. This does not include the various vulnerability reports that would be sent to the systems administrators to show vulnerabilities for tracking remediation and validating that configurations are still in place.

Each view of vulnerabilities, whether through the dashboards or reports, is another web page or spreadsheet to review. Again, this is only one example of context switching for information that individuals would have to review on a daily or weekly basis. This example alone highlights exactly why mature automated patch management strategies are the most effective at remediating vulnerabilities and cutting down on the cognitive loads that individuals experience daily.

Organizations should consider the way that vulnerabilities are visualized to users just as important as the data itself. Consider a 400-page vulnerability report in a Microsoft Excel file, versus a dashboard of the most important vulnerabilities. A 400-page report would require parsing, sorting, and filtering the data to find the most critical vulnerabilities to prioritize what is fixed first. That does not mean that a 400-page report should be excluded, but that it may be better as a secondary document. A large Excel spreadsheet or a dashboard with the top five exploitable vulnerabilities or top five most vulnerable systems limits the data volume that someone would need to ingest and then act upon.

Vulnerability Reports

As discussed, vulnerability reports are a common way to provide information to individuals who are responsible or accountable for vulnerability management. Figure 10.5 is an example of a typical spreadsheet or output from a vulnerability scan report. In this report, there are the names of vulnerabilities, CVE IDs, vulnerability severity scores, and associated details for remediation. Common reports also include hostnames, IPs, system tagging (association or type of system or application), and any other contextual information for the organization.

As seen in Figure 10.5, vulnerability reports can be complex and contain numerous data fields. These reports can consist of numerous pages and sent daily, weekly, or monthly to system owners.

Long gone are the days of using massive spreadsheet reports to track and resolve vulnerabilities. With any serious backlog of vulnerabilities, it is ineffective for anyone to review or act upon this amount of information. Making risk decisions based solely on large spreadsheets adds to confusion, frustration, and ultimately lost time. Trying to determine which items are most important in that manner can lead to missed potentially critical or exploitable vulnerabilities.

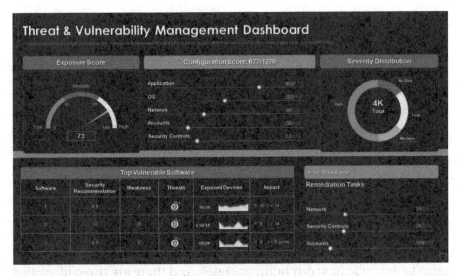

Figure 10.4: Example of vulnerability dashboard

Several other issues can arise from using a large vulnerability report, versus even a shorter document or dashboard. Consolidating those metrics shrinks the information window a user needs to consume by a large amount. This allows the individual to focus on the most critical vulnerabilities, most vulnerable systems, or maybe the most important assets to the specific organization.

CVE ID	CVSS Score	Severity	Hostname	IP	Remediation Details
CVE-2023-44487	7.5	High	Dev-01	10.0.2.3	Secure configuration
CVE-2023-22158	9.1	Critical	Dev-01	10.0.2.3	Patch to latest version
CVE-2022-22965	9.8	Critical	Dev-02	10.0.2.4	Patch to latest version
CVE-2022-3602	7.5	High	Dev-02	10.0.2.4	Replace certificate
CVE-2022-3786	7.5	High	Dev-02	10.0.2.4	Patch to latest version
CVE=2023-36730	7.8	High	Dev-03	10.0.2.5	Upgrade to latest version SQL
CVE-2023-36420	7.8	High	Dev-03	10.0.2.5	Upgrade to latest version SQL

Figure 10.5: Example of a vulnerability report

Cognition and Metacognition

Although the fields of human factors and psychology are large and cannot be covered in their entirety in this chapter, let's look at some of the most pertinent components of psychology as they relate to vulnerability management teams and remediation efforts. To start, the concepts of cognition and metacognition relate to VMPs and how system owners manage vulnerabilities.

Cognition, put very simply, is the way we think. The American Psychological Association (APA) (www.apa.org/topics/cognition-brain#:~:text=Cognition%20includes%20all%20forms%20of,the%20APA%20Dictionary%20of%20Psychology) explains that cognition includes knowing, awareness, perceiving, remembering, judging, problem-solving, and more. According to APA, this is a larger term to describe how our brain operates, and there are three identified components of the mind: cognition, affect, and conation. While this chapter's intention isn't to explore cognition in depth, it introduces the higher-level concept in psychology that will then be discussed as it specifically relates to cybersecurity and vulnerability management.

A paper titled "Metacognition" by the Massachusetts Institute of Technology (https://tll.mit.edu/teaching-resources/how-people-learn/metacognition) details metacognition, which is the process where humans use knowledge of a task, learning strategies, or their own thought process to monitor progress and evaluate outcomes of projects. In short, metacognition is evaluating the way that we think to improve our decision-making over time.

Metacognition is an important topic for vulnerability management because of our need to continue improving our thought process for identification and remediation over time. A VMP one year may not work the same way the next, and will require some additional thought as to what is working, what isn't, and what can be improved upon.

For example, if in prior years the VMP prioritized vulnerabilities based on Common Vulnerability Scoring System (CVSS) scores (not an uncommon practice), they may have access to the CISA KEV or have the bandwidth to implement more decision-making around emergency power supply systems (EPSS). This would change the VMP strategy for prioritizing vulnerability remediation activities. Each organization should have their own process for reviewing their VMP's decision-making techniques.

Vulnerability Cognition

The paper "Vulnerability Cognition and Communication" explores *vulnerability cognition* as the immense information that an individual would require to understand vulnerabilities in depth (www.softsideofcyber.com/vulnerability-cognition-and-communication). This terminology isn't to be confused with the psychological term *cognitive vulnerability*. Vulnerability cognition exists simply to describe the in-depth nature of vulnerability management, and how difficult it can be to be an expert in vulnerability management as well as a developer, infrastructure architect, or management and leadership. The point is, not everyone is required to be a vulnerability management expert, but they must loosely understand risk management and what vulnerabilities mean to the systems they own and manage.

The book *Emerging Cyber Threats and Cognitive Vulnerabilities* (Academic Press, Bensen & McAlany, 2019) dives deeper into the role that human behaviors have in the cybersecurity field. This book specifically delves into how psychology plays into the minds of hackers and the offensive side of cybersecurity, but not so much from the network defender's side.

Numerous textbooks, articles, and certification courses are aimed at including psychology in social engineering, decision-making implications for hackers to conduct attacks, and more from the red-teaming angle. But cognition, metacognition, and other psychological components are just as important to integrate into network-defense concepts, like vulnerability prioritization and remediation.

Decision-making and human behavior belong just as much within the creation of a VMP, including decisions around tooling, considerations for building proper processes, and helping the technical practitioners determine risk across the enterprise.

The Art of Decision-Making

Vulnerability management is primarily focused on how practitioners decide to remediate vulnerabilities, find and categorize systems, and prioritize vulnerabilities. In short, it's simply about decision-making.

Decision-making is the foundation to creating a successful VMP. The research article "Decision-making and biases in cybersecurity capability development: evidence from a simulation game experiment" centers around an experiment the authors conducted to determine how decisions are made within cybersecurity teams (see www.science direct.com/science/article/pii/S0963868717304353). This study wanted to understand how decision-makers would overcome two complex situations in a cybersecurity scenario.

Ultimately, the researchers found that decision-makers made errors when dealing with the uncertainty of incidents. They suggested that decision-makers in cybersecurity roles focus on systems thinking, but that additional research will be needed to determine the impact of decision-making on cybersecurity incidents.

While that research primarily covered cybersecurity incidents, this type of study highlights the need for proper decision-making techniques across cybersecurity programs. To investigate this further, the following sections cover decision fatigue, alert fatigue, and the sheer volume of vulnerabilities released that compound complexity on prioritization.

Decision Fatigue

Decision fatigue is a common phenomenon found across healthcare, technology, and other industries. The study "Decision Fatigue: A Conceptual Analysis" (www.ncbi.nlm.nih.gov/pmc/articles/PMC6119549) discusses this type of fatigue in healthcare. The researchers stated that decision fatigue was consistent across three separate themes in a healthcare setting: decisional, self-regulatory, and situational. However, the authors noted that, at the time, more research and investigation was required to fully understand the consequences of fatigue.

Decision fatigue is also seen in cybersecurity (and vulnerability management programs, specifically) across many areas. For the context of this book, the sheer volume of decisions that a VMP is required to make is based on vulnerability scoring, patches released, and the types of hardware and software in the environment, among other factors. These technical decisions must be balanced with business decisions and ongoing IT projects, audit and assessment findings, as well as any regulatory or legal considerations for determining which vulnerabilities to remediate first.

The possible risk implications of decision fatigue include potentially missing critical or highly exploitable vulnerabilities, limiting focus based on severity scores and missing other types of vulnerabilities, and potentially focusing resources on the wrong activity types. Each of these decisions can negatively impact the risk of the organization and lead to cyber incidents.

Alert Fatigue

Another type of fatigue, *alert fatigue*—discussed in the article "Combat Security Alert Fatigue with AI-Assisted Techniques" https://cset21 .isi.edu/papers/cset21-5.pdf)—is commonly noted in the security operations center (SOC) within a cybersecurity program. Alert fatigue is typically described as the inability to review and act upon the high volume of alerts noted in SIEM. It's also incredibly common for larger organizations to have multiple products that collect audit and security events into a location and alert on different requirements.

One example would be setting a threshold of alerting the SOC after five bad login attempts, followed by a successful one for an administrator account. This would trigger an investigation and the creation of tickets for the analysts to determine whether it is a true or a false positive.

Each event, alert, ticket, and investigation can lead to alert fatigue for SOC analysts. Regarding vulnerability management, the increased number of alerts around patches due, exploitable vulnerabilities, and even industry alerts based on the types of exploits can lead security engineers and system owners to be overwhelmed and ultimately frustrated by the constant onslaught of vulnerability information. Alert fatigue can lead to missed patches and late scheduled remediation activities, and ultimately increase the risk across the environment.

Volume of Vulnerabilities Released

Patrick Garrity, an industry expert on vulnerability statistics and visualization, has released several insightful graphics (https://nucleussec .com/insights-into-vulnerability-management-V1), including metrics for vulnerability statistics throughout the industry, with his goal being to help understand the problems behind large vulnerability backlogs. Of these articles and insights, he noted that there are 925 vulnerabilities in the CISA KEV catalog (as of this writing). There are also thousands of vulnerabilities catalogued annually within the National Vulnerability Database (NVD).

This incredible volume of vulnerability data could lead to cognitive overload, alert or decision fatigue, or overall stress and burnout for individuals managing vulnerabilities. Every year, there's an increase of vulnerabilities identified, analyzed, and updated within the NVD and CISA KEV. As the volume of vulnerabilities continues to grow, we will need to consider additional methods for understanding how the human in the loop handles this growing problem. Organizations should be aware that as vulnerability backlogs grow, their teams may feel overwhelmed and frustrated, and require more automation and augmentation to assist them in remediation activities.

Required Patches and Configurations

Patches are released constantly (as noted in the following article by Tenable)—a familiar day for any system owner is "Patch Tuesday" (www.tenable.com/blog/patch-tuesdays-impact-on-cybersecurity-over-the-years) where Microsoft releases bulk patches for products on every second Tuesday of the month. Anyone who manages Windows systems is familiar with the regular cadence for patches, as well as out-of-band patches for other products for zero-day or critical vulnerabilities. This is just one vendor. Given the wide variety of operating systems and applications available, patches are released daily.

Each vendor has their own patch cycle—some as long as quarterly, some as frequently as daily or weekly (like Google Chrome). So for any teams that manage multiple products and OS levels, managing patches can be complex and require multiple alerts, notifications, and monitoring for updates and patches on a consistent basis. Given this complexity, each organization and team needs to come up with their own patch management strategy.

But until teams reach some type of automated and easy-to-use patch management process, they will need to sign up for alerts, monitor vulnerability scan reports, and ultimately validate that those patches were installed properly. This includes reviewing multiple vendor websites, emails regarding patches, and the vulnerability dashboard, in addition to many more tools, simply to identify which patches need to be installed. This doesn't include the actual installation and monitoring of patching activities, however.

Figure 10.6 illustrates the sheer amount of data that an individual needs to ingest during patching and continuous monitoring. Whether an IT administrator, security analyst, engineer, or system owner, everyone has duties outside of patch management activities.

Anyone who manages patching will agree that this can be a cumbersome and lengthy task to juggle among their other responsibilities.

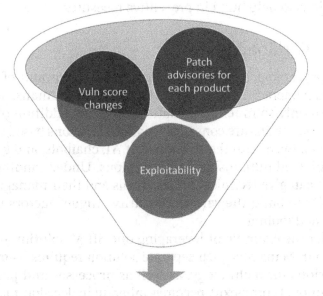

Patch Strategy

Figure 10.6: Funnel of data inputs for patching

Vulnerability Management Fatigue

Similar concepts, like alert fatigue, have been discussed previously in this chapter. However, *vulnerability management fatigue* specifically defines the burnout, stress, and frustration while completing vulnerability management tasks. Based on research by Ponemon and Rezilion (www.securityweek.com/vulnerability-management-fatigue-fueled-non-exploitable-bugs), it would take someone 430 days (working 12-hour days) to clear the backlog of vulnerabilities in larger organizations. With this statistic, they are focusing on just the known exploitable vulnerabilities, not the larger backlog of all vulnerabilities identified.

This fatigue can enter a VMP in a variety of ways, the main concern being the limited time, resources, and capability to remediate every vulnerability. Add the complexity with managing an operating environment in general, and vulnerability management becomes a mountainous task. Each VMP may handle this stress differently, but the awareness that this type of frustration and stress exists can allow organizations to help build in preventive measures.

Mental Workload

Another psychological concept that can be an aggravator of vulnerability management fatigue is *mental workload*. As humans, our brains can take in only so much information. With the addition of context switching, our brains are constantly making decisions based on mountains of data. Even with the assistance of AI, chatbots, and generative AI, we still need humans to make decisions. Understanding mental workloads can give technical professionals and their management an opportunity to build the various "security fatigue" factors into their processes and tooling.

Consider the example of leveraging one SIEM solution instead of three or four. Managing each separate solution requires its own security, decisions for technology, as well as processes and policies for each. Additional complexity becomes inherent in decision-making and mental workloads.

Specifically, within cybersecurity, a *Forbes* article in 2022 noted that cybersecurity professionals are at a much greater risk for increased mental workloads simply based on our changes in remote and in-office work environments, delayed IT projects and improvements, and alert fatigue from continuous and ongoing attacks in an environment (www .forbes.com/sites/forbeshumanresourcescouncil/2022/12/14/ tackling-mental-health-and-burnout-in-cybersecurity/?sh =e6e4c5036347). Add on the inherent complexity of modern infrastructure and multicloud environments, and it becomes a combination that makes it difficult to make proper decisions, increases turnover for technical professionals, and increases time for remediation.

Integration of Human Factors into a VMP

Building HFE into a modern VMP will not take a day or even a week. Organizations should thoroughly examine where their own problems lie within the organization, but they shouldn't focus simply on the technological or process challenges that exist. Leadership and practitioners could start with introspection, and then create a true problem statement for each of their concerns.

One initial consideration is how teams are organized. How large (or small) are the development, cybersecurity, and operations teams? Organizations must determine if their teams perform multiple actions across disciplines, or if everyone has their own responsibilities. For example, if there is a DevSecOps program, is there one individual who's responsible for each aspect, or are there teams dedicated to development, security, and operations missions?

A second step, specifically for cybersecurity professionals, is to share their own pain points within their role. Specifically, what technology, people, or process is making them less efficient and feeling frustrated with their daily tasks? For instance, if a security engineer determines that their largest inhibitor to efficiency is that they manage 10 different tools that all require separate logins, and it takes them too much time to log in to each tool independently, a simple solution could be integration of a single sign-on (SSO) tool to cut down on time for logins.

After the teams determine where their specific problems exist, then a roadmap can be created to consider the best course of action. Understanding that many organizations may not have the budget to build massive human factors security engineering programs, it is crucial to determine what is possible over time.

Start Small

With limited resources and budgets, organizations can consider the items that have a major impact without major costs. An initial recommendation is to do a simple survey within their cybersecurity programs and with neighboring departments like IT, cloud, development, and infrastructure. Even the following three-question survey could help get to the root of problems:

1. What technology problem is most inhibiting your productivity?
2. What process problem is most inhibiting your productivity?
3. Are there any individuals/teams who inhibit your productivity or completion of tasks? If so, how?

Leaving your survey questions open-ended and anonymous is crucial to allowing individuals to express themselves in the best way possible.

All surveys should ensure that participants feel comfortable being honest. Leadership can conduct these surveys to identify any patterns or challenges that are persistent across the teams. Once the surveys are completed, that roadmap for resolution can be created.

As shown in Figure 10.7, teams can come up with their own roadmap, depending on the types of problem statements that come from the initial survey. Of importance, these surveys can be done over time to determine the effectiveness of any solutions.

Add Human Factors into VMP
- Identify security fatigue
- Context switching concerns
- Develop roadmap for solutioning over time

Start Small
- Software inventory assessment
- Problem statement creation
- Evaluate team structure

Hire a Consultant
- Vulnerability Management expert
- Human factors security engineering
- Cyber Psychologist

Figure 10.7: Roadmap of solutions

Consider a Consultant

Another recommendation for building human factors into a cybersecurity program is to hire an HF consultant. This could be solely for leadership to understand HF factors in a working group, or a workshop for cybersecurity practitioners. Each team could develop new skills, understand how HF could be integrated into their daily tasks, and provide a new perspective when tackling tough technical problems.

A separate option would be to integrate HF specialists into technical teams. Start with one HF security engineering specialist, and see what benefits come to the teams. Allow this program to last 6 months to a year; behavioral change takes time, but the benefits could be long-lasting. Possible benefits of even an initial interaction between human factors and cybersecurity professionals could be repairing of relationships, improved processes and efficiencies, and overall risk reduction.

A final option for larger organizations, or even organizations that may be concerned with their overall backlog of vulnerabilities, would be to implement an HF security engineering team. This team would work between developers, infrastructure, operations, and other security teams, and they would be responsible for the reduction of overall organization risk, whether that's vulnerability remediation, implementing compensating controls, or improving the efficiency of communications to resolve incidents faster.

Summary

This chapter covered the major topics within human factors and their applicability to vulnerability management programs and teams. Each psychological component discussed is meant to encourage awareness and more discussion around each topic. Each component of cognition, metacognition, mental workloads, and so forth is documented widely in the psychological community.

The sole purpose of this chapter is to encourage new ideas and thought patterns within the vulnerability management space. If organizations continue to solely remediate vulnerabilities based on a severity score, the backlog of vulnerabilities (and inherent risk) will continue to grow. Consider human factors as an option available to grow and mature VMPs over time.

The first step to integrating these concepts is awareness within the organization and the cybersecurity teams. Then, problem statements can be created, an initial survey conducted, and a conclusion reached as to how HF engineers or practices could help create efficiencies and reduce tension or stress between teams.

A final note to those who may be skeptical about how human factors would be useful or impactful in their own teams or organizations: Try something new. If traditional vulnerability management principles worked, we wouldn't see the sheer volume of vulnerabilities in backlogs. So, consider starting small and see if there are any immediate benefits. This type of program may not be effective for every organization, so you should always carefully determine where time, resources, and personnel are best spent.

11 Secure-by-Design

While we've spent a significant amount of time discussing the vulnerability management landscape and its challenges, as well as how to go about addressing vulnerabilities and managing them in large complex environments, we would be remiss if we didn't take some time to discuss a fundamental shift that's needed—the shift to secure-by-design/default software and integrating security throughout the system and software development life cycle (SDLC) to stop the bleeding.

With modern organizations drowning in vulnerability backlogs in the hundreds of thousands to millions and consumers increasingly being faced with insecure products and software, no amount of innovation and efficiency in managing vulnerabilities will have the impact that addressing the root of the issue will. This is because most software and digital systems aren't made with security as a core part of the product development process.

We've begun to see an industry-wide shift and calls for secure-by-design software and products, with the message being championed by organizations such as the Cybersecurity and Infrastructure Security Agency (CISA) in the United States as well as key U.S. government technology and security leaders. The concept was even emphasized in the latest U.S. National Cybersecurity Strategy (NCS) (www.whitehouse .gov/wp-content/uploads/2023/03/National-Cybersecurity-Strategy-2023.pdf), which called for driving the adoption of secure-by-design principles and shifting the burden for addressing vulnerabilities and weaknesses onto upstream suppliers and vendors, rather than the current paradigm where downstream consumers and customers often bear this burden.

In 2023, while delivering a speech at Carnegie Mellon University (CMU), CISA Director Jen Easterly stated that "Consumer safety must be front and center in *all* phases of the technology product life cycle—with security designed in from the beginning." www.cisa.gov/cisa-director-easterly-remarks-carnegie-mel lon-university.

We've also begun to see organizations face legal and regulatory ramifications for not producing secure systems and software as well as failing to follow security best practices. For example, Progress Software, who produces the MOVEit product, faced class action lawsuits in 2023 as a result of the security incidents impacting their product and customers (www.darkreading.com/attacks-breaches/software-vendors-may-face-greater-liability-in-wake-of-moveit-lawsuit). In 2023, the SEC charged the Solar-Winds CISO for fraud and internal control failures relating to alleg-edly known cybersecurity risks and vulnerabilities (www.sec.gov/news/press-release/2023-227). These events and others point toward a trend of software vendors and suppliers facing increased liability, as well as similar trends impacting senior technology and security leaders at organizations tied to vulnerable systems and security incidents.

In this chapter, we look at the origins of secure-by-design systems and software, along with some of the leading publications as well as methods to facilitate securely designing software and systems.

Secure-by-Design/Default

In October 2023, CISA released an updated version of their publication "Shifting the Balance of Cybersecurity Risk: Principles and Approaches for Secure by Design Software," continuing their push to evangelize an ecosystem of secure-by-design software and systems and looking to shift the onus onto software suppliers, rather than the current par-adigm where the consequences of vulnerable systems and software overwhelmingly fall on customers and consumers.

As part of this push to shift the market dynamics and address the fact that many consider cybersecurity to be a market failure (see, for example, "Is There a Market Failure In Cybersecurity?" at www .mercatus.org/research/policy-briefs/there-market-failure-cybersecurity#:~:text=As%20a%20result%2C%20 proponents%20of,the%20right%20amount%20of%20cyber security), CISA is encouraging software suppliers to adopt the princi-ples laid out in their document and publicly document the actions they take, to demonstrate their commitment to secure design philosophies.

Many remain skeptical that suppliers will voluntarily make these investments. Given their primary motive is profit and security has a cost in terms of research, development, implementation, and maintenance, it could run counterintuitive to their primary motives, which are to maximize profit. That said, it's worth emphasizing that insecurity also has a cost in the forms of regulatory consequences, recovery costs, compensating controls, loss of customer trust, and ramifications for revenue.

For example, we've recently seen organizations such as the SEC passing rules driving publicly traded companies to report security incidents that are deemed "material." For insight into how big material cybersecurity incidents can be, Sounil Yu recently shared a resource from the FAIR Institute dubbed "How Material is That Hack?," which is a website covering recent incidents such as MGM Resorts International, Clorox, and Caesars Entertainment, with impacts ranging from tens to hundreds of millions of U.S. dollars.

Although it remains unlikely that suppliers will make the required security investments and efforts without associated demand, the CISA guidance emphasizes just that, stating:

> Just as we seek to create a pervasive Secure-by-Design philosophy within software manufacturers, we need to create a "Secure-by-Demand" culture with their customers.

In other words, they must help try to correct the market failure of cybersecurity, which won't voluntarily resolve itself on the supplier side. Increased demand for secure products and software from customers and consumers, however, *can* influence suppliers' behaviors, because then it's directly tied to customer demand and spending, which impacts revenue/profits, suppliers' primary concern.

Secure-by-Design

In our discussion of *secure-by-design*, we must start with a little primer on what secure-by-design means, at least from the perspective of CISA. In their publication (www.cisa.gov/sites/default/files/2023-10/SecureByDesign_1025_508c.pdf), they define it as follows:

> Secure-by-Design means that technology products are built in a way that reasonably protects against malicious cyber actors successfully gaining access to devices, data, and connected infrastructure.

Simple, right? Well, not quite.

The word *reasonable* means something different to the cyber practitioners industry as well as business peers and, of course, consumers, but it's a term that's used in other industry lexicons. In addition, it will likely have a precedent established, as litigation around insecure products and services continues to unfold, such as the class action lawsuits mentioned earlier being filed against Progress Software, which saw widespread impacts across hundreds of organizations and potentially millions of users due to exploitable vulnerabilities in their product and claims of negligence.

Nonetheless, CISA goes on to discuss how vendors should be performing risk assessments to identify and enumerate threats, including protections in their products to account for the threats, implementing best practices such as defense-in-depth, and using tailored threat models during product development and deployment. There are also calls for vendors to collaborate among their business and technical staff to ensure cybersecurity throughout the entire SDLC/product life cycle, including not just design and development but deployment and maintenance for customers as well.

Secure-by-Default

The CISA guidance also emphasizes another concept, which is *secure-by-default* (www.cisa.gov/sites/default/files/2023-06/principles_approaches_for_security-by-design-default_508c.pdf), and it is defined as follows:

> *Products are resilient against prevalent exploitation techniques out of the box, without added charge, without end users having to take additional steps to secure, and make customers acutely aware when they deviate from safe defaults.*

The primary point is that all products come with a baseline level of "security by default" and don't need significant effort by customers to "harden" the products and software against exploitation, which is typically the case now.

The guidance also states that "the complexity of security configuration should not be a customer problem," and that customers shouldn't be charged extra for implementing added security configurations like we saw with the debacle over Microsoft E5 licensing and incidents that limited victims' ability to use logs to understand the potential impacts to them (www.darkreading.com/remote-workforce/microsoft-logging-tax-hinders-incident-response).

Again, there is (and will be) a gray area where debates occur over what is a sufficient level of default security, in addition to what features and functionality are reasonable to charge for. Given the different incentives at play for suppliers and customers (i.e., profit and value), the two will have a different view of what should be done by default and what should be charged for.

Software Product Security Principles

The guidance lays out three primary software product security principles that it encourages suppliers to adopt and prioritize:

- Take ownership of customer security outcomes.
- Embrace radical transparency and accountability.
- Build organizational structure and leadership to achieve these goals.

Let's discuss each of them further.

Principle 1: Take Ownership of Customer Security Outcomes

This core principle focuses on ensuring that the burden of security doesn't fall solely on the customer, which is often the case in the modern paradigm of software and technology.

CISA also makes the case that by building security in throughout the SDLC rather than having cybersecurity be an afterthought or "bolted on," not only do they increase the customers' security, but they also increase their products' quality as product security and resiliency are subsets of overall product quality.

This principle emphasizes security efforts such as application hardening, application features, and application default settings. Application hardening can raise the cost for malicious actors and bolster products against attacks. Specific security-related features are called out such as supporting Transport Layer Security (TLS), multifactor authentication (MFA), role-based access control/attribute-based access control (RBAC/ABAC), and single sign-on (SSO), and for them to be configured securely out-of-the-box, rather than needing to be specifically configured and tinkered with by customers upon product deployment/provisioning.

There's an emphasis on placing the burden for security on suppliers/vendors rather than downstream customers—a theme that was prevalent in the recent NCS. The CISA publication states:

> *Manufacturers should take ownership of their customers'*
> *security outcomes rather than measuring themselves solely*
> *on their efforts and investments. The responsibility should be*
> *placed upstream, with the manufacturers, where it has the*
> *greatest likelihood of reducing the chances of compromise.*

It's pointed out that vendors commonly patch a single vulnerability only to see similar vulnerabilities continue to emerge for a specific product/software, because the symptom was addressed rather than its root cause.

Another key point made is the need for secure application default settings. Typically vendors focus on making applications as easy to use and as functional as possible by default for customers, but this can come at the expense of an increased attack surface or more vulnerable applications and software as well. CISA says that security controls shouldn't be toggled off by default, and vendors should use threat modeling to determine which features should be on by default or hardened upon delivery to customers to mitigate risks.

While maximizing functionality can be compelling from a product perspective, if the default configurations are insecure, exploitable, or make it easy for a customer to make a risky mistake, it also presents risk that is now distributed across all customers.

CISA calls out one of the long-standing aspects of the software industry, which is the release of hardening guides, either by the vendor directly or often by third parties (e.g., CIS Benchmarks, DISA STIGs, and so on). The challenges cited with the long-standing practice include hardening guides being difficult to find, not being well supported, complex to implement, or even requiring additional development effort. Challenges are also found on the customer/consumer side in regard to a lack of sufficient expertise in some cases to even go about implementing the hardening guides.

Source: www.cisa.gov/sites/default/files/2023-10/SecureByDesign_1025_508c.pdf

> *Millions of customers are taking on the responsibility to harden multiple instances of software or systems, often in resource-constrained environments.*
>
> *Relying on hardening guides simply doesn't scale.*

Parallels have been drawn to other industries, to bring risks and insecure configurations to the user's attention, such as vehicles notifying the driver that a door is open or a seatbelt isn't buckled. Examples provided include MFA not being configured for administrator accounts or insecure protocols being used.

CISA lays out the reality that as an industry we continue to see organizations needing to adopt more and more security tools to monitor their systems and software posture, all of which must be researched, funded, purchased, staffed, deployed, and monitored, often in resource- and expertise-constrained environments. This is far less scalable than software suppliers bolstering product security from the onset of development through customer delivery and maintenance. One key point below is made by CISA in their Secure-by-Design publication:

> *The software industry needs more secure products, not more security products. Software manufacturers should lead that transformation.*

There are obviously several challenges to this mantra, such as the fact we discussed that software manufacturers are incentivized to maximize profit, which security (and insecurity) can potentially impact, and that there is an entire thriving ecosystem of cybersecurity companies, including several with billion-dollar valuations incentivized to continue to treat the symptoms of insecure software and products. (We also must acknowledge that security vendors aren't in a position to force software manufacturers to properly address security in their own products.)

The CISA publication goes on to enumerate various steps that vendors should take to demonstrate a commitment to this initial principle of taking ownership for customer security outcomes. These steps are organized into three groups:

Secure-by-Default Practices:

1. Eliminate default passwords.
2. Conduct field tests.
3. Reduce hardening guide size.
4. Actively discourage use of unsafe legacy features.
5. Implement attention-grabbing alerts.

Secure Product Development Practices:

1. Document conformance to a secure SDLC framework (such as NIST SSDF, which CISA lists as an example).
2. Document cybersecurity performance goals (CPGs) or equivalent performance.
3. Perform vulnerability management.
4. Responsibly use open source software (OSS).
5. Provide secure defaults for developers.
6. Foster a software developer workforce that understands security.
7. Test security information and event management (SIEM) and security orchestration, automation, and response (SOAR) integration.
8. Align with a zero-trust architecture.

Pro-Security Business Practices:

1. Provide logging at no additional charge.
2. Eliminate hidden taxes.
3. Embrace open standards.
4. Provide upgrade tooling.

Principle 2: Embrace Radical Transparency and Accountability

The second principle that CISA recommends software suppliers embrace is one of radical transparency and accountability. CISA states vendors should associate themselves with pride when it comes to delivering safe and secure products, and use that as a competitive differentiator among their peers and with customers and consumers.

Refreshingly, CISA shoots down the tired trope of transparency providing a roadmap for attackers, or as it is often called "security through obscurity." The reality, as they point out, is that hackers are already achieving their objectives despite obscurity, and transparency aids defenders who are trailing adversaries and can use transparency to help bolster their defensive measures. It also helps the industry, as CISA states, establish what "good" looks like, so that vendors demonstrating security proficiency can be an example for others to emulate, and can foster trust among customers and consumers as well:

Transparency builds accountability into the product.

www.cisa.gov/sites/default/files/2023-10/Secure ByDesign_1025_508c.pdf

CISA makes the case that, while embracing radical transparency around product development and security may be uncomfortable for the current state of the industry, it will help propel us forward. Radical transparency will empower defenders more than adversaries, who already succeed wildly by most metrics.

This transparency can inform peers about practices and foster collaboration and upward use across the software ecosystem, while also informing both prospective customers and investors regarding the security posture of their purchases or investments.

CISA advocates for what we have seen some technology leaders embrace, which is radical transparency of security incidents, publicly detailing what occurred, what the impact was, and what improvements and lessons were learned that the vendor is integrating to mitigate similar future threats.

Much like the previous principle of ownership, CISA enumerates how suppliers can demonstrate a commitment to transparency:

Secure-by-Default Practices:

1. Publish aggregate security-relevant statistics and trends.
2. Publish patching statistics.
3. Publish data on unused privileges.

Secure Product Development Practices:

1. Establish internal security controls.
2. Publish high-level threat models.
3. Publish detailed secure SDLC self-attestations (e.g., SSDF).

4. Embrace vulnerability transparency.
5. Publish software bills of materials (SBOMs).
6. Publish a vulnerability disclosure policy.

Pro-Security Best Practices:

1. Publicly name a secure-by-design senior executive sponsor.
2. Publish a secure-by-design roadmap.
3. Publish a memory safety roadmap.
4. Publish results.

Principle 3: Lead from the Top

This principle emphasizes the reality that no matter the desire from folks on the ground, building products, the fostering of a security culture, driving the appropriate internal incentives, and ensuring the required resources to deliver secure products, all starts at the top:

> *Only when senior leaders make security a business priority, creating internal incentives, and fostering an across-the-board culture to make security a design requirement will they achieve the best results.*

www.cisa.gov/sites/default/files/2023-10/Secure
ByDesign_1025_508c.pdf

As the CISA publication points out, an organization's vision, mission, values, and culture all affect their products, and are derived at the top leadership level of an organization. They cite quality experts such as J. M. Juran, who are quoted as saying companies who demonstrated quality leadership all had the characteristic of upper managers personally guiding the initiatives. Given that security is a subset of product quality, the concept applies here as well.

Parallels are drawn to emerging corporate social responsibility programs. The CISA publication calls for corporate cyber responsibility (CCR) as an emerging idea. To demonstrate this principle, CISA lays out the following steps software suppliers should take:

1. Include details of a secure-by-design program in corporate financial reports.
2. Provide regular reports to your board of directors.
3. Empower the secure-by-design executive.

4. Create meaningful internal incentives.
5. Create a secure-by-design council.
6. Create and evolve customer councils.

Secure-by-Design Tactics

The next section of the CISA publication is one where they begin to specifically cite tactical actions and practices software suppliers can take to produce more secure software and aid in activities such as finding and removing vulnerabilities, mitigating potential impacts of the vulnerabilities' exploitation, and addressing root causes to prevent incidents from reoccurring in the future.

It should come as no surprise that CISA heavily leans on the NIST Secure Software Development Framework (SSDF) here, as the federal government is rallying around SSDF for secure software development and software supply chain requirements. This includes U.S. Office of Management and Budget (OMB) memos, such as 22-18 and 23-16, which require software suppliers selling to the federal government to self-attest to using SSDF practices to produce the products they sell to the government. One of the authors have done a deep dive into the memos 22-18, 23-16 and the CISA Self-Attestation Form and use this link https://resilientcyber.substack.com/p/sign-here-on-the-dotted-line.

CISA advocates for organizations developing a secure-by-design roadmap aligned with the practices discussed below, which they also cross-map to SSDF practice identifiers:

- Memory-safe programming languages (SSDF PW.6.1)
- Secure hardware foundation
- Secure software components (SSDF PW.4.1)
- Web template frameworks (SSDF PW.5.1)
- Parameterized queries (SSDF PW.5.1)
- Static and dynamic application security testing (SAST/DAST) (SSDF PW.7.2)
- Code review (SSDF PW.7.1, PW.7.2)
- SBOM (SSDF PS.3.2, PW.4.1)
- Vulnerability disclosure programs (SSDF RV.1.3)
- CVE completeness
- Defense-in-depth
- Satisfaction of cybersecurity performance goals (CPGs)

The CISA publication provides more information on each of these tactics/practices, and I strongly recommend reviewing the document if you need more details on what each mean.

CISA also recognizes that these changes will take time, resources, and effort, and recommends that organizations prioritize them based on tailored threat models as well as other factors such as criticality, complexity, and business impact. Organizations might initially target newly developed software and products before moving to implement these practices for legacy products and codebases as well.

Secure-by-Default Tactics

As has been discussed throughout this chapter, in addition to secure-by-design principles, CISA is recommending vendors begin to prioritize secure-by-default configurations in their software and products as well. The specific practices they cite follow:

- Eliminate default passwords.
- Mandate MFA for privileged users.
- Include single sign-on (SSO).
- Require secure logging.
- Maintain a software authorization profile.
- Require forward-looking security over backward compatibility.
- Track and reduce "hardening guide" size.
- Consider the user experience consequences of security settings.

I recommend diving deeper into the source publication if you need more details on each of the secure-by-default tactics and what they mean. CISA again also acknowledged the trade-off businesses must consider operational impacts and security considerations as well as concerns around customer experience. They also advocate for vendors to create incentives for customers to adopt secure configurations and settings, rather than leaving their implementation of the products in an insecure state.

Hardening vs. Loosening Guides

Another fundamental paradigm shift that CISA advocates for in their secure-by-design publication is the shift from vendors publishing

"Hardening Guides" to publishing "Loosening Guides." What this ultimately means is moving from delivering products that are insecure out-of-the-box by design/default based on configurations, and instead delivering products with secure defaults in place, and then empowering the customer/consumer to loosen the product configurations while clearly understanding the security ramifications and risks associated in doing so.

Delivering secure-by-default products can mitigate systemic risks and protect vulnerable customers not often familiar with the risks of insecure configurations or products and spread awareness.

Recommendations for Customers

Lastly, the CISA publication closes out with a brief section on recommendations for customers. While this may come as a surprise to some to be such a short section, it shouldn't, as we've said several times that the goal of CISA is to help drive an industry-wide shift of placing the burden of security more on the vendor/supplier than the customer, with the opposite being the current reality.

There's also the reality that there is a literal mountain of cybersecurity best practices, critical controls, hardening guides, and other relevant materials for customers, consumers, and enterprises using products and software. They have absolutely no shortage of materials. That said, let's take a look at the CISA-specific verbiage on recommendations for customers.

CISA recommends that customers/consumers hold their vendors and suppliers accountable for the security outcomes of their products. This means voting with your wallet and purchasing products and software that prioritizes secure-by-design/default products and software. It also means ensuring products are properly vetted by internal security staff *prior* to procurement, and utilizing angles such as contractual language and requests for information/requests for proposal (RFI/Ps), and so on, to help drive specific products and purchases.

CISA emphasizes that IT departments *must* have the organization's executive support when enforcing these purchasing decisions. If insecure/risky products are purchased, those decisions and inherent risks should be formally documented and approved by the senior business executives. This sort of activity ensures that the onus doesn't inherently fall on security when, in reality, the business is driving the purchasing activity and risk acceptance. In other words, the business owns the risk, and documenting risks and having them formally signed off on can help change behavior.

IT and security leaders are called upon to collaborate with industry peers to rally around services and products that value and prioritize the secure-by-design/default principles, and this collective consensus as well as spending decisions can help incentivize vendors to prioritize secure products associated with actual customer demand.

Many consider cybersecurity to be a market failure that will not voluntarily resolve itself until regulatory forces it to change or market incentives shift and change behaviors. Consumers rallying around vendors and products that prioritize secure-by-design/default products and services can function as that market signal, which can drive systemic changes across the software supplier ecosystem.

That said, not much is likely to change until/if market dynamics shift. As a society, we're at a crossroads where we must determine if we want to stick with the status quo of endless data breaches, security incidents, and increased safety concerns, especially with the continued convergence of cyber-physical systems and emergence of cyber as a domain of modern geopolitical tensions and warfare.

Which path will we take? Time will tell.

Threat Modeling

Another fundamental activity to ensuring secure system and software development is *threat modeling*. Threat modeling for IT systems can be summarized as identifying and enumerating potential threats to systems and software as well as potential countermeasures that can be implemented to mitigate said threats.

While the origins of threat modeling undoubtedly have military and warfare origins dating back centuries, the activity was adopted in cybersecurity as well. Early threat-modeling methodologies and activities were pioneered in the late 1980s and early 1990s by cybersecurity legends such as Edward Amoroso and Bruce Schneier, among others, as well as contributions from organizations such as the NSA and Defense Advanced Research Projects Agency (DARPA).

This work continued to evolve, being evangelized and matured by organizations such as Microsoft. In 1999, cybersecurity practitioners at Microsoft developed the now famous mnemonic STRIDE, which stands for Spoofing, Tampering, Repudiation, Information Disclosure, Denial of Service, and Elevation of Privilege. The use of this framework allows practitioners an opportunity to determine what impact identified threats have on a system, service, software, or other assets. There are other prevalent threat model methodologies, such as Octave, as well.

Many resources cover threat modeling. Trying to cover them all would produce a book of its own, and because several exist already, this section provides a high-level overview of some key threat modeling concepts, terms, and resources for the sake of brevity.

One basic but incredibly useful approach, as cited in the Threat Modeling Manifesto (www.threatmodelingmanifesto.org), is to ask the four following questions to consider security and privacy threats for a system:

- What are we working on?
- What can go wrong?
- What are we going to do about it?
- Did we do a good enough job?

While this might seem incredibly simplistic, this thought exercise can help not only security practitioners, but also peers such as engineers and developers consider the relevant threats to the systems that they're developing and potential mitigations that can be implemented, including from the earliest onset of the software development life cycle (SDLC). While threat modeling can (and should be) used throughout the SDLC, using it early in the process can help identify threats and weaknesses that can then be mitigated to avoid future issues in production environments, or after a product or application has been developed and distributed.

Threat-modeling IT systems has origins dating back decades, but it is experiencing what many would consider to be a resurgence, due to continued exploitation of widely distributed software and products, and the industry calling for adopting mantras such as shifting security left (i.e., earlier in the SDLC), and building systems and software securely by design and by default, rather than the burden falling onto customers and consumers.

Threat modeling has been specifically called out in resources such as CISA's 2023 secure-by-design publication. It has seen a growth in industry events, conference talks, and communities as well, as more practitioners and policymakers recognize its value to producing secure and resilient systems.

Secure Software Development

One historically overlooked aspect of the SDLC is security. While several software development frameworks have evolved to focus on security, we will focus on the SSDF from NIST.

While the original version of NIST's SSDF already existed, the 2021 Cybersecurity Executive Order (EO) in the United States directed NIST to issue guidance to identify practices that enhance the security of the software supply chain. NIST did exactly that when, in collaboration with industry, it published SSDF v.1.1, along with other software supply chain security guidance.

The SSDF points out that few SDLC models explicitly address software security. A common phrase many in the industry are familiar with is "bolted on, not baked in" when it comes to cybersecurity. This represents the fact that cybersecurity is often an afterthought in developing digital systems and is often addressed later in the SDLC, rather than earlier where security best practices and requirements can be integrated into software and systems from the onset.

It is worth noting that SSDF v.1.1 released in 2022 builds on an original SSDF version from April 2020. To facilitate the SSDF's update, NIST held a workshop with participants from the public and private sector and received over 150 position papers to be considered for the SSDF update.

The intended audience for the SSDF includes both software producers, such as product vendors, government software developers, and internal development teams, in addition to software acquirers or consumers.

While the SSDF was specifically created for use by federal agencies, the best practices and tasks it contains apply to software development teams across all industries and can be used by many diverse organizations. SSDF is not prescriptive but descriptive. This means that it does not specifically say how to implement each practice, and instead focuses on secure software outcomes and allows the organization to implement practices to facilitate those outcomes.

This is logical, given the infinite number of ways to secure software and the unique people, processes, and technologies that make up every organization producing and consuming software. The CISA guidance also clarifies that factors such as an organization's risk tolerance should be considered when determining which practices to use and which resources to invest in achieving said practices.

SSDF Details

The NIST SSDF is aimed at advocating for the use of fundamental and recognized secure software development best practices. One thing that makes the SSDF unique is that, rather than creating guidance from scratch entirely, it uses many known and implemented established sources of guidance, such as the Building Security In Maturity Model (BSIMM) (www.synopsys.com/software-integrity/software-security-services/bsimm-maturity-model.html) by Synopsys and the Software Assurance Maturity Model (SAMM) (https://owasp.org/www-project-samm) from OWASP, among several others.

SSDF's robust set of secure software development practices is broken into four distinct groups: Prepare the Organization (PO), Protect the Software (PS), Produce Well-Secured Software (PW), and Respond to Vulnerabilities (RV). Within those practices, you have elements that define the practice, such as practice, task, notional implementation example, and reference, which map the practice to tasks.

As previously mentioned, the latest SSDF version was created out of requirements from the Cybersecurity EO, so it also includes mapping to specific EO requirements, specifically in Section 4e. The desired goal of using the SSDF practices is to reduce the number of vulnerabilities included in the release of software, and reduce the impact of those vulnerabilities being exploited if they're undetected or unmitigated.

In the next section, we take a look at each of the groups of practices.

Prepare the Organization (PO)

Preparing the Organization (PO) for secure software development is a logical first step for any organization looking to develop secure software. Practices in this group include defining security requirements for software development, which incorporates requirements for the organization's software development infrastructure and security requirements that organization-developed software must meet.

Of course, these requirements need to be communicated to all third parties who provide commercial software components to an organization for reuse as well, which gets increasingly complicated when you consider third-party OSS components that comprise up to 80 percent of modern applications. Rather than those third parties being bound like a proprietary commercial vendor would be via contracts and other means, it falls on the software supplier to implement OSS governance and security practices to mitigate risks from the use of OSS components in their products.

Defining Roles and Responsibilities is another fundamental step that organizations must take, which includes roles for all parts of the SDLC, and provides appropriate training for the individuals in those roles. The guidance emphasizes the need for upper management commitment to secure development and ensure that individuals involved in the process are aware of that commitment. This is often referred to as getting *executive buy-in*.

Modern software delivery involves supporting toolchains that use automation to minimize the human toil associated with software development and lead to more consistent, accurate, and reproducible outcomes. Tasks in this area involve specifying the tools and tool types that must be used to mitigate risks and how they integrate with one another. Organizations should also define recommended security practices for using the toolchains and ensure that the tools are configured correctly to support secure software development practices.

Organizations should also outline and use criteria for software security checks. This includes implementing processes and tooling to safeguard information throughout the SDLC. Toolchains can be used to automatically inform security decision-making and produce metrics around vulnerability management.

Lastly, organizations should implement secure environments for software development. This typically manifests as creating different environments, such as development, testing, staging, and production. These environments are segmented to limit the blast radius of a compromise impacting other environments and allow for differing security requirements, depending on the environment.

These environments can be secured through methods such as MFA or conditional access control, least-permissive access control, and by ensuring that all activities are logged and monitored across the various development environments to enable better detection, response, and recovery.

Securing the environment also means that endpoints developers and users utilize to interact with the environments are hardened to ensure they do not introduce risk as well, or implementing contextual access control that takes device posture into consideration in dynamic access decisions. You will notice there are several parallels to these recommendations with the current guidance and best practices for zero trust as well.

Protect Software (PS)

Moving on from PO, we'll now cover Protecting the Software (PS) itself. Practices in this group involve protecting the code from unauthorized changes, verifying integrity, and protecting each software release.

Protecting all forms of code from unauthorized changes and tampering is critical to ensure the code is not modified either intentionally or unintentionally in a form that compromises its integrity. Code should be stored in methods that align with least-permissive access control based on its security requirements, which look different for OSS code or proprietary code. Organizations can take measures such as using code repositories that support version control, and commit signing and review by code owners and maintainers to prevent unauthorized changes and tampering. Code can also be signed to ensure its integrity with methods such as cryptographic hashes.

Code signing, of course, isn't infallible and can be compromised itself, leading to signed code that is malicious but appears trustworthy. Not only does the code's integrity need to be maintained, but there must be methods for software consumers to validate this integrity. This is where practices such as posting hashes on well-secured websites come into play. Code signing should be supported by trusted certificate authorities that software consumers can use as a measure of assurance or trust in the signature.

There are also emerging efforts, such as Sigstore that has been adopted by major OSS projects such as Kubernetes, which alleviate some of the administrative overhead traditionally associated with key management and signing.

Finally, each software release should be protected and preserved, which can be used to identify, analyze, and eliminate vulnerabilities tied to specific releases. This also facilitates the rollback ability in the case of compromised releases, enabling you to restore to "known good" states of software and applications. Protecting and preserving software releases allows consumers to understand the provenance of code and its associated integrity.

Produce Well-Secured Software (PW)

Now that requirements have been codified and development environments and the endpoints that access them have been addressed, the organization can focus on Producing Well-Secured Software (PW). This is not to say that each group doesn't occur concurrently throughout the life of an organization or program, but they do build upon one another while also warranting revisiting and revising as necessary.

You will note in the Prepare the Organization (PO) section of the SSDF that security requirements were defined and documented. Now software must be designed to meet those security requirements. This is where organizations can use methods of risk modeling such as threat modeling and attack surface mapping to assess the security risk of the software being developed. Organizations can train development teams in methods such as threat modeling to facilitate empowered development teams capable of understanding the threats to the systems and software they develop and measures to reduce those risks.

By using data classification methods, organizations can prioritize more rigorous assessments of high sensitivity and elevated risk areas for risk mitigation and remediation. Organizations should also review software design regularly to ensure that it meets security and compliance requirements the organization has defined.

This review includes not only internally developed software, but also software that is being procured or consumed from third parties as well. Depending on the nature of the software being consumed, organizations may be able to work with software designers to correct failures to meet security requirements, but this does not apply in situations such as OSS where there are no contracts or associated agreements like SLAs.

It is why organizations must have OSS governance and security measures in place, such as using software composition analysis (SCA) tooling, to understand known vulnerabilities in the OSS they consume, in addition to other methods like OpenSSF's Scorecard, which can look at leading indicators of risk such as contributor and maintainer activity, how frequently and quickly vulnerabilities are addressed, the posture of repositories, and much more.

Organizations are encouraged to reuse existing well-secured software, rather than duplicating functionality. This reuse has a myriad of benefits such as lowering the development costs, speeding up capability delivery, and reducing the potential of introducing new environmental vulnerabilities. It isn't uncommon for large enterprise organizations to experience code sprawl, particularly in the era of "as-code" where infrastructure and even security in cloud-native environments can be defined as code.

This "as-code" approach supports concepts such as modularity, reuse, configuration-as-code, and hardened code templates and manifests that can be safely used elsewhere in organizations or beyond. That said, if these manifests and code templates include vulnerabilities, they now become replicated at scale as well, so proper governance and security rigor is required.

Organizations, or even teams within organizations that make reuse of existing software and code, should ensure they review and evaluate code for security and misconfiguration concerns, as well as understand the provenance information associated with the code they are reusing. A similar recommendation SSDF makes is to create and maintain well-secured software components and repositories in-house for development reuse. This is similar to the recommendations made in NIST 800-161 Rev 1 for OSS governance and security.

Source code created by the organization should ensure it aligns with secure coding practices adopted by the organization as well as advocated by industry guidance. These include steps such as validating all inputs, avoiding unsafe functions and calls, and using tools to identify vulnerabilities in the code.

Respond to Vulnerabilities (RV)

While organizations may have defined security requirements, prepared their environments, and even strived to produce secure software, vulnerabilities will inevitably arise. This is due to the reality that identifying all possible known vulnerabilities during development is impossible, and as time goes on, vulnerabilities will be discovered. There is a common phrase that states "software ages like milk," due to the reality that the longer software has been around, the more likely it is that vulnerabilities will be discovered by researchers, malicious actors, or others.

Organizations should work to both identify and confirm vulnerabilities on an ongoing basis. This includes monitoring vulnerability databases, using threat intelligence feeds, and automating the review of all software components to identify any new vulnerabilities. This is key as new vulnerabilities will inevitably emerge from the initial time where code may have been scanned and examined. Organizations should also have policies for vulnerability disclosure and remediation, and as previously mentioned, define roles and responsibilities to address vulnerabilities as they emerge. Such processes help inform software consumers of the vulnerabilities associated with code and products from software suppliers, and allows these vulnerabilities to be mitigated before they can be identified and utilized by malicious actors. It typically materializes in the form of vulnerability disclosure policies and processes, as well as reports from product security incident response teams (PSIRTs).

Organizations will not only need methods to identify and confirm vulnerabilities, but they will also need to remediate vulnerabilities in a way that aligns with the risk that vulnerabilities pose. It means having a process to assess, prioritize, and remediate software vulnerabilities. Using tools and governance, organizations can then make risk-informed decisions such as remediating, accepting, and in some cases, transferring the risk if possible.

Traditionally, vulnerabilities are often largely prioritized based on metrics such as the Common Vulnerability Scoring System (CVSS), but we're now seeing innovative methods such as the Exploit Prediction Scoring System (EPSS) emerge to augment, or in some cases, take the place of CVSS. CISA has also advocated for the use of the Stakeholder-Specific Vulnerability Categorization (SSVC) system, along with their Known Exploited Vulnerabilities (KEV) Catalog, both of which offer opportunities to improve vulnerability management and prioritization. They do so by helping teams prioritize vulnerabilities known to be exploited or likely to be exploited in the next 30 days, for example.

Organizations producing software also need established methods to develop and release security advisories to software consumers that help them understand the vulnerabilities in the software and the potential impact to them as a consumer, and the steps to resolve the vulnerability if possible. While traditional advisories occurred in static formats such as websites, emails, and static documentation, the industry is increasingly shifting toward machine-readable advisories, such as the Common Security Advisory Format (CSAF) and Vulnerability Exploitability eXchange (VEX), the latter of which is supported by industry leader OWASP in their CycloneDX VEX BOM. This documentation allows organizations to shift to machine-readable formats for vulnerability disclosure and communication, which can be integrated into tooling via APIs and automation.

Lastly, organizations should take steps to identify the root causes of vulnerabilities through analysis. Doing so helps reduce their frequency in the future by addressing the root cause, rather than just an individual vulnerability. This can also help organizations to eliminate classes of vulnerabilities, which are often categorized as Common Weakness Enumeration (CWEs).

As evident from the vast array of secure software development tasks and practices discussed, no organization of significant size or scale will always perform all these practices perfectly or immediately, if ever. That said, organizations can take steps to codify their secure software development practices by using the SSDF as a guide and helping ensure proper steps are taken to secure software throughout the SDLC.

Security Chaos Engineering and Resilience

While organizations can continuously plan, no plans are infallible. It has long been said, "no plan survives contact with the enemy." Every organization will inevitably experience security incidents and should prepare accordingly. One methodology that is gaining traction is that of security chaos engineering (SCE), which is championed by industry leaders such as Kelly Shortridge, coauthor of the book *Security Chaos Engineering: Sustaining Resilience in Software and Systems* (O'Reilly Media, 2023), who defines security chaos engineering as "the organizational ability to respond to failure gracefully and adapt to evolving conditions."

Advocates of security chaos engineering argue that it can improve the security's return on investment (ROI) by minimizing attack impacts and generating valuable evidence that can be used to drive continued improvement of system and software design and operations. As pointed out by Shortridge in the article "From Lemons to Peaches: Improving Security ROI through Security Chaos Engineering" (https://arxiv.org/pdf/2307.03796.pdf), the potential to stop all attacks isn't practical or realistic, and it is only a matter of time until every organization has a security incident. Given this reality, organizations instead should be striving to create secure resilient digital systems and software that can minimize the impact of an incident when it does occur and to facilitate a culture of iterative improvement where deficiencies are addressed through continuous learning and improvement.

SCE involves conducting experiments to verify that a system operates the way we believe it will in the face of attacks, and using the results and lessons learned to bolster the system's resilience moving forward. Historically, security has used activities such as tabletops, which involve hypothetical scenarios and reactions whose value is suspect at best. Real incidents don't deal in hypotheticals, and the best role-playing is no substitute for real-world impacts and the need to respond accordingly.

SCE builds on earlier efforts under the broader chaos engineering domain, which were pioneered by leading technology companies such as Netflix who produced tools and conducted exercises that would randomly introduce failure and disruption to their production environment to ensure their systems were resilient and fault-tolerant. See `https://netflixtechblog.com/tagged/chaos-engineering` to learn more.

SCE strives to do something similar, but in the security context, helping systems become more resilient to attacks and minimizing friction that security typically imposes on development and engineering peers through burdensome processes that can stifle agility. This approach aligns with results from studies like the "Accelerate State of DevOps Report," (`https://cloud.google.com/blog/products/devops-sre/dora-2022-accelerate-state-of-devops-report-now-out`), which finds that systems and organizations that deploy software more frequently and integrate agile practices and methodologies are more resilient to security incidents and are able to respond faster and more effectively.

These results contradict long-standing security practices that seek to minimize and control change to the maximum extent possible. SCE practices have additional benefits as well, such as verifying that an organization's financial investment in security tools and resources has the desired impact against security incidents, as opposed to speculating or waiting until an actual real-world malicious attack occurs. This benefit is appealing because many organizations suffer from security tool fatigue while managing dozens of security tools, causing both cognitive overload on staff and exhausting financial resources in commonly fiscally constrained environments.

Ultimately, SCE leverages the concepts of continuous experimentation, feedback loops, iteration, learning, and continuous improvement, grounded in real-world practical exercises, rather than the traditional hypothesis and mental exercises used in cybersecurity. In striving to mitigate system vulnerabilities and weaknesses and produce more resilient systems, SCE is a promising methodology that more practitioners and organizations should leverage moving forward.

Summary

In this chapter we touched on the push for secure-by-design/default systems and software by organizations such as CISA, as well as historical context showing how long-standing this concept is. We also discussed key industry changes it would take to pivot to a secure-by-design model and some of the key challenges associated with it. We discussed key activities to secure systems from the onset of the SDLC, such as threat modeling and the latest NIST SSDF, which helps organizations cultivate the practices to produce secure software. We closed by covering emerging concepts such as security chaos engineering, which look to actually test the resilience of systems.

12 Vulnerability Management Maturity Model

This book has covered vulnerability management from asset and patch management to scoring and prioritization, all the way through threat intelligence and human factors. Each chapter of this book has laid the foundation for the development of a maturity model that organizations can implement for their vulnerability management program (VMP). All the previous information was meant to describe how to build these concepts and practices into your own VMP.

These strategies are not a one-size-fits-all solution, but merely a recommendation of steps to follow to either build a VMP from scratch or determine how mature the existing VMP is, and ultimately get to a state where vulnerability management is not a burden on a team or organization.

As you read through each step, ask yourself the following questions as you study Figure 12.1:

1. Is this step already implemented as described?
2. Do I consider our organization's VMP to be at full maturity with these steps?
3. Are there any areas where we need to improve upon our own VMP?
4. Who within my organization should I consult with about each step?
5. What step is my team/organization at, and can we create a plan to build to the next step?

We recommend that you read each step thoroughly and reference the prior chapters as you begin building upon your own practices and identifying gaps. VMPs are not built or matured in a day but over time. Take these steps and consider how best to reach a mature VMP within your own team. Much like other cybersecurity aspects such as zero trust, vulnerability management is an iterative process of continuous improvement, refinement, and learning.

Figure 12.1 A maturity model pyramid

Step 1: Asset Management

Without a proper asset management strategy and inventory, a VMP will not succeed. Let's begin with Step 1.

Begin with the tooling. First, meet with the appropriate stakeholders to determine what tools are already set in place and whether they meet the needs of your organization's environment. If you've recently moved to a multicloud environment, it might be time to reevaluate your inventory requirements. Similarly, if your organization is pursuing larger and more complex development projects, it means evaluating the continuous integration/continuous delivery (CI/CD) pipeline and determining which applications and libraries are currently being used.

Continue with your asset inventory—conduct a thorough analysis of the hardware and software throughout the environment. Don't stop at assets that are known—find and identify unknown assets.

Also, consider ongoing IT/development projects, as these projects will inevitably bring in new devices and applications. An inventory should also account for the extensive use of open source software (OSS) and the associated libraries and projects that the organization might be consuming.

In combination with building their asset inventory, each team should develop a responsible, accountable, consulted, and informed (RACI) matrix to annotate who's responsible and accountable for each asset. For example, if there is a mobile device management (MDM) team, they would be responsible and accountable for the inventory, as well as the patch management and continuous monitoring of those mobile devices.

Continuous monitoring processes should be developed around the asset management program. For example, that same MDM team should consider how often they scan for rogue devices and configurations for detection and containment. These processes should be documented and updated on a monthly or quarterly basis, and the configurations should be built into the MDM and asset inventory tools used for the group. Continuous monitoring should include both the process and technology components of people, process, and technology.

Once automation and some initial processes have been built, all associated documentation should be created and maintained in a central location. This documentation would be used in the event of an audit or assessment, as well as to set expectations for team members. Each document or process should be maintained and updated frequently as technology changes, regulations, or laws become applicable, or audit findings dictate changes. It's also common to refine processes after a security incident or other situation highlights gaps that might have been initially overlooked.

Here's a condensed version of these steps:

1. Select your enterprise application and configuration management tools.
2. Build a comprehensive asset inventory, including devices, hardware and software, software-as-a-service (SaaS), and application programming interfaces (APIs), including libraries and OSS components.
3. Develop a RACI matrix to note who's responsible for each area of the asset management program.

4. Prepare to develop a continuous and automated solution for finding and cataloguing new devices, applications, and components.
5. Develop the associated processes and documentation to support your asset inventory.

Step 2: Secure Configuration

The next major step, Step 2, is to build or improve upon the secure configuration throughout the organization. A comprehensive VMP has a mature and focused secure configuration strategy. Each step within this section builds upon the first and should be done sequentially.

First, identify relevant secure configuration guidance for your respective industry and technology stack. It might include sources that have been discussed in Chapter 3, "Secure Configuration," such as Center for Internet Security (CIS) benchmarks, as well as vendor-specific configuration guidance that often documents how to securely configure products and software to ensure that organizational risk is mitigated. Secure configuration guidance generally consists of industry-wide best practices, such as encryption-at-rest and least permission access control, as well as vendor- and product-specific guidance aligned with a particular product or application.

The team then should decide which controls are most appropriate for their own systems. This might include which data types are on these systems and which regulations are applicable to the business type. A system that manages credit card transactions would need to comply with Payment Card Industry Data Security Standard (PCI DSS) (www.pcisecuritystandards.org) regulations, and healthcare data would need to follow Health Insurance Portability and Accountability Act (HIPAA) guidance (www.hhs.gov/hipaa/index.html). These controls would be selected based on the type of data stored, the industry along with its associated regulations, and what security level is expected on the systems—for example, System and Organization Controls (SOC) 1 versus SOC 2 (www.itgovernanceusa.com/soc-reporting). Applicable-regulatory frameworks and controls often drive specific configurations, in addition to industry best practices and vendor-specific guidance.

Next, the team implements the controls on each system as determined in the previous step. Each control should be tested and validated before implementing it in the production environment. It is well known that security configuration changes can impact performance and usability. Each organization needs to align secure configurations with their risk tolerance and be willing to make trade-offs where required about performance and usability. Potential risks to consider include everything from safety and security of personnel to operations and uptime for systems.

That said, increasingly, product vendors are being encouraged to produce secure products by design, to mitigate vulnerabilities from the onset of production and ideally minimize performance impacts from needing to add security after the fact. The expected controls should be documented at this step, and as with previous steps, the team should decide on a monthly or quarterly review and update—even if it is a 15-minute meeting between system owners to review and validate that there are no changes.

Once the controls are implemented, teams can validate that the controls are in place as expected. This can be done with a vulnerability scanner or by using additional security tools to run scans and report those findings. During this initial review, the team can ensure the controls are as expected and document them in the initial assessment folder.

After the controls have been validated, the organization should have a comprehensive exemption program in place for any controls that cannot be implemented. Some systems will not be able to hit 100 percent compliance, so teams should account for any controls that will not be implemented or will require additional testing before being added in the future. Whether it is a 30-, 60-, or 90-day policy to add required configurations, this policy should be documented and updated over time, as with all previously mentioned documentation and processes. Organizations can, and should, also be prepared to implement compensating controls where a vulnerability or insecure configuration might not be able to be resolved directly, but compensating controls can be put in place to mitigate risk, aligning with the concept of defense in depth.

Finally, similar to the patch management step, configurations and expected controls should be implemented and monitored over time. Each configuration group should be documented at initial approval of the systems and monitored over time, and any anomalies or missing configurations should be investigated. Mature organizations can also explore innovative capabilities that help facilitate auto-remediation of configuration deviations or insecure configurations.

Here's a condensed version of these steps:

1. Identify your relevant secure configuration guidance, both from industry organizations as well as from specific vendors/products.
2. Determine which controls are applicable to each system identified.
3. Implement the controls using automation as appropriate for each system.
4. Validate that your controls are implemented as expected.
5. Develop an exemption policy for your controls that cannot be implemented.
6. Develop a continuous monitoring process for your expected controls and configurations.

Step 3: Continuous Monitoring

Continuous monitoring (ConMon) is integral to the success of a mature VMP. *ConMon* is the practice of reviewing vulnerabilities, alerts, incidents, and processes over time. It isn't limited to the technology used in a VMP, but also includes the people and processes within the group. For example, a RACI matrix for asset management should be reviewed monthly or quarterly to determine if the areas of responsibility still make sense or if they should be adjusted over time.

The first step to building a cohesive ConMon implementation is to determine which assets, processes, networks, systems, and environments will require continuous monitoring. It's essential to understand the scope of ConMon before implementing any kind of alerts or automation. If assets or systems are missing in the tooling and reporting, vulnerabilities could go unnoticed, secure configurations could be removed without notification, and documentation would go stale. All those assets, applications, or systems missing from the ConMon process increase the risk of the environment.

Determining the tooling and reporting mechanisms for the ConMon strategy is just as important and could be done in conjunction with the first step. The tools should be selected based on their ability to monitor appropriate assets, and they should include some automation for dynamic scanning and reporting. And of course, the tools selected (whether open source or proprietary, vulnerability scanning or asset management) should be evaluated over time to validate that they still work for the mission and business.

Once the tooling has been selected and a full inventory of all ConMon assets has been taken, it's time to develop a RACI matrix for who will be responsible for each program area. ConMon responsibilities include creating and managing vulnerability scans, adding assets to an inventory, or configuring dynamic asset discovery, all the way to implementing and monitoring configurations for systems. An example would be applying settings within a Group Policy Object (GPO) in Active Directory (AD), and then running a vulnerability scan to validate that those controls are in place. Another example is leveraging cloud-native services to automatically evaluate the configurations and vulnerabilities of assets such as virtual machines (VMs) and containers. That scan would run daily or weekly to continuously validate that the controls are still in place as expected and notify the system or application owner in case those settings change or are removed.

Once the RACI matrix has been developed and teams are aware of their own responsibilities within the ConMon program, they should focus on tailoring alerts for all the systems and applications that are being continuously validated.

Each application or tool that requires configuration and provides alerting or notifications to system owners will take additional time to reduce "noise" like false-positive data from their consoles. However, true-positive vulnerabilities that have already been through the exemption process will not be remediated for six months. Those vulnerabilities should be tuned out of vulnerability reports for four months; once the vulnerabilities appear on the report again, it allows the team one month to remediate based on initial timelines.

Beware of excluding vulnerabilities for any length of time. There will be very few vulnerabilities that should be tuned out completely. All vulnerabilities that require an exemption should be reviewed following the corporate guidelines on vulnerability remediation. For example, if a vulnerability is exempted for six months, that vulnerability should be reviewed at four months into that exemption to determine how to remediate risks. Tuning out vulnerabilities, especially true positives, should be reviewed on a regular basis as part of risk management activities.

Vulnerability reports should also be enhanced for additional context beyond base Common Vulnerability Scoring System (CVSS) scores— for example, to include enrichment of known exploitation, probability of exploitation, business criticality, and reachability. Modern scanners and vulnerability management tooling enable this via sources such as the Cybersecurity and Infrastructure Security Agency (CISA)'s Known Exploited Vulnerabilities (KEVs) and Exploit Prediction Scoring System (EPSS), and determine if components are called and reachable at runtime, as well as where assets reside in an enterprise architecture and the nature of the data the assets contain.

A final step to a mature ConMon practice is to automate and augment manual processes. An example is running manual scans to determine if new assets are online—this could be automatically run every hour or every day to find new assets that come online within specific intellectual property (IP) ranges. Another example is tailoring alerts based on updated threat intelligence information so that teams can focus on the alerts relevant to their organization. A final example would be to implement scripts for infrastructure as code (IaC) such as Terraform, which can be used to automate the installation of endpoint detection and response (EDR) tools and configuration files to limit manual processes on system setup.

Here's a condensed version of these steps:

1. Determine which assets, processes, and networks require continuous monitoring in place.
2. Identify the appropriate tools and reporting required for ConMon across your enterprise.
3. Develop a RACI matrix for who reviews alerts and develops ConMon plans and who is ultimately responsible for these activities.
4. Tailor your alerting for EDR, vulnerability scanning, and industry alerts.
5. Automate your detection and response capabilities with minimal manual intervention whenever possible.

Step 4: Automated Vulnerability Management

At this point in the process, a VMP should be well developed and in some form of steady state. Now is the time to mature and build upon the tools and processes already established. While this list is not all inclusive, each exercise should bring the VMP to a more automated approach and require less manual intervention.

The first step should be to annotate where in the organization manual tasks are performed within the VMP. This could be manual patching processes, manual review of configurations, or even intervention required within the asset discovery process. Once each manual process has been defined, be sure to document who's responsible and accountable for each of those tasks. This is an important exercise to determine what should be done next.

Second, the groups responsible for VMP practices should review their tools and technology as well as the configuration setup in each group. Then the system owners and managers can review what tools are working, which are not, and ultimately what needs to be improved upon or replaced. Each group may determine that they either need a new tool or require additional time to review configurations and tailor alerts and reporting further to improve the usage of the existing tools.

Once a tooling gap analysis is conducted, the individual groups can document their possible limitations or concerns by introducing automation. An example might be the automated reboots of servers that might impact production resources. Another concern might be that if patches are automatically installed on some systems without proper testing and validation, they could break functionality. All these concerns can be addressed by building in testing time and validation steps.

After concerns have been identified, the group can continue to determine how to build automated techniques into their VMP processes. It could be people, process, or technology that must be developed and matured. For example, the people managing the systems might require upskilling to create automated scripts or configurations within the environment. Another example would be if a specific tool didn't cover the new technologies (e.g., Red Hat OpenShift) as part of their automation strategy. This would require both upskilling and potentially new detection and configuration tools to manage and automate updates.

Once tooling is addressed and updated, automation can be tested in a sandboxed or test environment before applying it to production systems. Without a proper testing environment, it will be impossible to get patching, configuration, and other VMP concerns addressed. Once tested, there should be a process documenting where the patches are applied and how they are implemented in production with automated scripts or processes.

Finally, you must tune the automation over time. Automation is not a one-time project or implementation. Automation must be evaluated continuously, just like any other process or tool. The scripts might require additional configuration with new technology, or the automated tools might require updates over time as technology grows and evolves. Nothing about technology is stagnant or will be the same year after year. Develop a timeline that fits within your organization to evaluate the automation monthly or quarterly.

Here's a condensed version of these steps:

1. Define the manual processes that currently exist within your VMP.
2. Identify gaps in your VMP technology and review your application configuration.
3. Identify any possible limitations or concerns with your automation.
4. Determine which tooling/techniques are required to implement automation.
5. Test automation techniques in your development environment and validate their efficacy.
6. Integrate automated processes over time—develop a roadmap for your automation.

Step 5: Integrating Human Factors

As described in Chapter 10, "The Human Element in Vulnerability Management," about human factors (HFs), several considerations must be considered when implementing these concepts into a cybersecurity program. We don't recommend that you implement HFs into an immature VMP, but that you follow the steps, and when ready, determine where these concepts fit into your VMP.

Organizations should identify gaps or concerns within their VMPs, including unconscious bias, stress, or infighting between teams, or even risk associated with a lack of movement or progress. It's incredibly important to identify where HFs would be required before making program changes. For example, a team could find that there are communication issues between the development and cybersecurity teams. These communication issues could potentially impact risk, specifically the time to identify and remediate risks across the enterprise.

Once a team has identified gaps in their VMP, it should request to hire a consultant within the human factors or cognitive psychology space. Without industry and education knowledge, it will be difficult to implement psychological and human factor recommendations.

Hiring an expert to identify other gaps in technology or processes will be worth it in terms of overall cost or return on investment (ROI) for organizations.

Integrating these human factor recommendations won't happen overnight. Like this larger maturity model, you must consider which concerns are easiest to deal with. For example, say an HF consultant determines that there are far too many security tools in the environment, leading to a higher turnover rate within the cybersecurity department. The team should develop a plan to remove redundant tools, potentially replace tools that are too complicated or ineffective, and ultimately configure the remaining tools properly to reduce noise or false positives.

Another example of integrating recommendations over time would be if the HF consultant finds that there's an incredible backlog of vulnerabilities, leading to decision paralysis within the team. In this situation, the groups are overwhelmed and cannot find a place to start remediation. The HF expert may recommend meeting with each stakeholder to determine the highest risk and to develop a remediation plan. Then they might work with the overwhelmed individuals to help them understand the signs of decision paralysis and how to overcome them. It would be a win-win scenario for the organization, as team members would be given an opportunity to address concerns while also remediating vulnerabilities and reducing environmental risk.

And if the larger problems within the organization require more HF expertise, organizations should consider hiring a full-time HR security expert. If there are positive outcomes from consulting with an HF expert, it might be time to integrate an HF expert between cybersecurity and development or management teams to continuously identify problems and develop solutions. After some time, the organization can determine if this group should be expanded to other areas within the organization.

Here's a condensed version of these steps:

1. Identify areas of concern within your teams, tools, or processes that require intervention.
2. Hire an HR or cognitive psychologist consultant for an initial review and problem statement creation.
3. Based on your initial assessment, develop a plan to integrate HF into your VMP.
4. If applicable, hire an HR security engineer/subject matter expert (SME) to work between groups.

Step 6: Vulnerability Threat Intelligence

The final step in the maturity mode, Step 6, is the integration of threat intelligence techniques into vulnerability management practices and processes. This should only be done once a solid asset management process is in place, secure configuration activities are complete and actively monitored, automation has been implemented in tooling, and the human element has been considered across the organization (within the context of vulnerability management). Once all the prior steps are fully implemented, it is time to consider threat intelligence to continue to focus on the right remediation and prioritization.

Not every organization will require an in-depth analysis of threat intelligence data or a massive threat intel team. But what is necessary is integrating the techniques and tooling for open source intelligence (OSINT) gathering and using it to your advantage. As stated in Chapter 7, "What Is Vulnerability Chaining?" there are numerous methods for gathering intelligence, and each organization should determine which one most benefits them, based on their size, team structure, and budget.

For example, a VMP could start simply by leveraging the OSINT tools to gather information and determine what is relevant to their industry, business, and region/location. With that information, the VMP can then begin to determine what outstanding vulnerabilities and risks exist in their environment and prioritize those vulnerabilities. Teams should see an immediate benefit to focusing on the vulnerabilities that matter most, based on the context of their business.

Hopefully by incorporating this data, leadership can see the benefits of focusing remediation activities and reducing risk. Then teams can start to purchase tools as necessary and hire individuals to build a threat intelligence team. Again, not every business will require a full threat intelligence team, but it can be a great benefit to a VMP due to their unique skillset and technical abilities. With some time, integrating threat intelligence should help reduce their attack surface, save time on vulnerability remediation, and reduce stress and burnout with security and vulnerability management analysts.

Here's a condensed version of these steps:

1. Determine which teams or individuals should be involved.
2. Integrate threat intelligence and vulnerability management teams to determine which vulnerabilities are most critical.

3. Use OSINT tools to find intelligence about your business/organization and tailor your alerts and remediation activities.
4. Improve your vulnerability management processes and prioritization activities with intelligence and tooling.
5. Continuously monitor the integration of teams and tooling to create a cohesive and effective VMP.

Summary

We hope that this chapter provides a path forward for using all the concepts within this book. We have covered everything from asset and patch management to understanding the human element behind vulnerability management. Each chapter has laid the foundation for the maturity model.

Every organization will be at a different step in this maturity model within their own VMP. Review each step and consider which step your VMP is at, then decide where you want to begin. Don't be plagued by decision paralysis! Pick a step that makes the most sense, then start organizing and identifying gaps in your processes and technology.

As with any other VMP component, a maturity model should be evaluated over time. It is possible that as you arrive at Steps 4 and 5 that you might find additional gaps back at Step 1 or 2 that must be addressed before moving forward.

We hope you can use these steps to improve your VMP, develop skills and processes that align with your business, reduce risk, and build resiliency into your systems.

Acknowledgments

We would like to acknowledge and thank the broad vulnerability management and cybersecurity community who have contributed to the many resources, methodologies, and programs we cite throughout this text. Organizations and volunteers such as FIRST for their work on CVSS and EPSS to those individuals helping maintain major programs such as the NIST NVD, often unseen to the broad public leveraging their work. We also want to thank industry innovators, leading the charge with products and thought leadership around modernizing vulnerability management and the federal and commercial leaders calling publicly for a pivot to secure-by-design/default systems, software, and products. Without the broader community, we could never have produced such a work. We would also like to thank our Foreword author Ron Gula and our technical editor Karen Scarfone for their contributions to this publication.

About the Authors

Chris Hughes, M.S., MBA is the cofounder and president of Aquia, a cybersecurity consulting firm. Chris brings nearly 20 years of IT and cybersecurity experience to his role. Chris also serves as a cyber innovation fellow (CIF) at the Cybersecurity and Infrastructure Security Agency (CISA), focusing on software supply chain security. Additionally, Chris advises various tech startups, including serving as the chief security adviser at Endor Labs.

As a U.S. Air Force veteran and former civil servant in the U.S. Navy and the General Services Administration's FedRAMP program, Chris is passionate about making a lasting impact on his country and our global community at large.

In addition to his public service, Chris spent several years as a consultant within the private sector and currently serves as an adjunct professor for cybersecurity master's program at the University of Maryland Global Campus. Chris participates in industry working groups, such as the Cloud Security Alliance's Incident Response and SaaS Governance Working Groups, and serves as the membership chair for Cloud Security Alliance D.C. He is the co-host of the Resilient Cyber Podcast and runs the Resilient Cyber Substack, where he shares episodes as well as detailed articles on topics such as cloud security, vulnerability management, DevSecOps, and more.

Chris holds a BS in information systems, an MS in cybersecurity, and an MBA. He regularly consults with IT and cybersecurity leaders from various industries to assist their organizations with their digital transformation journeys, while keeping security a core component of that transformation.

Chris is coauthor of the book *Software Transparency: Supply Chain Security in an Era of a Software-Driven Society*" (Wiley, 2023). He has also contributed many other thought leadership pieces on software supply chain security and has presented on the topic at a variety of industry conferences.

Nikki Robinson, DSc, PhD has over 10 years of experience in the information technology space across multiple technologies, and over 5 years in the cybersecurity world, spanning vulnerability management, incident response, and architecture and design. She began her career working on a helpdesk for an IT company and most recently serves as a technical leader and security architect.

Nikki holds both a Doctorate of Science in cybersecurity and a PhD in human factors from Capitol Technology University. She began her academic career with a BS in IT and software engineering, moving into a master's of science in telecommunications and systems management. She has published academic research across vulnerability chaining, password security, malware, graphing malicious websites, and various other sectors within the cybersecurity space.

Nikki is also a professor of practice at Capitol Technology University and serves as the assistant director for the Center for Women in Cyber. She serves on multiple volunteer organizations mentoring young career professionals to gain certifications and choose an education path, and ultimately supporting them on their journeys. Nikki also serves as a fellow at the Institute for Critical Infrastructure Technology, where she speaks at conferences and publishes research.

Nikki has also written a book titled *Mind the Tech Gap* (CRC Press, 2022), in which she explores the conflicts between IT and cybersecurity teams.

But most importantly, Nikki is a mother of two girls and spends her time outside of cybersecurity with her family, doing everything from horseback riding to racing in triathlons.

About the Technical Editor

Karen Scarfone is the principal consultant for Scarfone Cybersecurity. She develops cybersecurity-related publications for federal agencies, media companies, and other organizations. She was formerly a senior computer scientist at the National Institute of Standards and Technology (NIST). Karen has coauthored over 100 NIST special publications and interagency reports on a wide variety of cybersecurity topics. In addition, she has coauthored or contributed to 17 books and published over 200 articles on cybersecurity topics. Karen holds master's degrees in computer science and technical writing, and she has worked in IT for more than 30 years, with over 20 years of that dedicated to cybersecurity. In recognition of her work for federal agencies, Karen has received a Federal 100 award and Department of Commerce Gold Medal and Bronze Medal Awards.

Index